THE
EVOLVING
SELF

THE EVOLVING SELF

A PSYCHOLOGY
FOR THE THIRD MILLENNIUM

MIHALY CSIKSZENTMIHALYI

HarperPerennial
A Division of HarperCollinsPublishers

The Library of Congress has catalogued the hardcover edition as follows:

Csikszentmihalyi, Mihaly.

   The evolving self : a psychology for the third millennium / Mihaly Csikszentmihalyi.
   — 1st ed.
     p.   cm.
   Includes bibliographical references and index.
   ISBN 0-06-016677-0
   1. Genetic psychology.   2. Behavior evolution.   3. Social evolution.   I. Title.
BF701.C676   1993
155.7—dc20   95-56220

ISBN 0-06-092192-7 (pbk.)
94 95 96 97 98 CC/RRD 10 9 8 7 6 5 4 3 2 1

CONTENTS

INTRODUCTION

What follows is a sequel to *Flow,* a book I wrote three years ago. *Flow* reported a quarter century of psychological research on happiness. It presented a summary of the principles that make living worthwhile. It dealt with questions such as these: Why do some people love their work, have a great time with their family, and relish the hours spent thinking in solitude while others hate their jobs, are bored at home, and dread being alone? How can the routines of everyday life be transformed so that they feel as exciting as skiing down a mountain slope, as fulfilling as singing the Hallelujah Chorus, as meaningful as taking part in a sacred ritual? The studies I and others had done suggested that such transformations were possible.

After many years of systematic research, the time came to take stock of what we had learned, and present it to a wider audience. *Flow* has been successful beyond expectation in reaching this aim; however, in order to complete its argument, many issues that could not be dealt with in that book still had to be explored. To do so is the aim of the present volume.

My interest in enjoyment began in 1963, when I was working on a doctoral dissertation in human development at the University of Chicago. The thesis revolved around a central issue in creativity: How do people go about thinking up new questions? How do they identify problems that no one else thought of before? To answer these questions, I resolved to observe artists at work. By taking notes and pictures of how paintings developed and then asking questions of the artists afterward as to what went on in their minds while they worked, I hoped to gain useful insights into the process of creativity.

Though my research into creativity proved successful, something even more important emerged from my observations of artists at work. What impressed me was how totally involved the artists became with what was transpiring on canvas. An almost hypnotic trance seemed to seize them as they struggled to give shape to their vision. When a painting was beginning to get interesting they could not tear themselves away from it; they forgot hunger, social obligations, time, and fatigue so that they could keep moving it along. But this fascination lasted only as long as a picture remained unfinished; once it stopped changing and growing, the artist usually leaned it against a wall and turned his or her attention to the next blank canvas.

It seemed clear that what was so enthralling about painting was not the anticipation of a beautiful picture, but the process of painting itself. At first this seemed strange, because psychological theories usually assume that we are motivated either by the need to eliminate an unpleasant condition like hunger or fear, or by the expectation of some future reward such as money, status, or prestige. The idea that a person could work around the clock for days on end, for no better reason than to keep on working, lacked credibility. But if one stops to reflect, this behavior is not as unusual as it may seem at first. Artists are not the only ones who spend time and effort on an activity that has few rewards outside itself. In fact, everyone devotes large chunks of time doing things that are inexplicable unless we assume that the doing is enjoyed for its own sake. Children spend much of their lives playing. Adults also play games like poker or chess, participate in sports, grow gardens, learn to play the guitar, read novels, go to parties, walk through woods—and do thousands of other things—for no good reason except that the activities are fun.

Of course, there is always the possibility that one will also get rich or famous by doing these things. The artist may get a lucky break and sell her canvas to a museum. The guitarist may learn to play so well that someone will offer him a recording contract. We may justify doing sports to stay healthy, and go to parties because of possible business contacts or sexual adventures. External goals are often present in the background, but they are seldom the main reason why we engage in such activities. The main reason for playing the guitar is that it is enjoyable, and so is talking with people at a party. Not everyone likes to play the guitar or go to parties, but those who spend time on them usually do so because the quality of experience while involved in these activities is intrinsically rewarding. In short, some things are just fun to do.

This conclusion, however, does not get us very far. The obvious question is, Why are these things fun? Strangely enough, when we try to answer that question, it turns out that contrary to what one would have expected, the enormous variety of enjoyable activities share some common characteristics. If a tennis player is asked how it feels when a game is going well, she will describe a state of mind that is very similar to the description a chess player will give of a good tournament. So will be a description of how it feels to be absorbed in painting, or playing a difficult piece of music. Watching a good play or reading a stimulating book also seems to produce the same mental state. I called it "flow," because this was a metaphor several respondents gave for how it felt when their experience was most enjoyable—it was like being carried away by a current, everything moving smoothly without effort.

Contrary to expectation, "flow" usually happens not during relaxing moments of leisure and entertainment, but rather when we are actively involved in a difficult enterprise, in a task that stretches our physical or mental abilities. Any activity can do it. Working on a challenging job, riding the crest of a tremendous wave, and teaching one's child the letters of the alphabet are the kinds of experiences that focus our whole being in a harmonious rush of energy, and lift us out of the anxieties and boredom that characterize so much of everyday life.

It turns out that when challenges are high and personal skills are used to the utmost, we experience this rare state of consciousness. The first symptom of flow is a narrowing of attention on a clearly defined goal. We feel involved, concentrated, absorbed. We know what must be done, and we get immediate feedback as to how well we are doing. The tennis player knows after each shot whether the ball actually went where she wanted it to go; the pianist knows after each stroke of the keyboard whether the notes sound like they should. Even a usually boring job, once the challenges are brought into balance with the person's skills and the goals are clarified, can begin to be exciting and involving.

The depth of concentration required by the fine balance of challenges and skills precludes worrying about temporarily irrelevant issues. We forget ourselves and become lost in the activity. If the rock-climber were to worry about his job or his love life as he is hanging by his fingertips over the void, he would soon fall. The musician would hit a wrong note, the chess player would lose the game.

The well-matched use of skills provides a sense of control over our actions, yet because we are too busy to think of ourselves, it does not matter whether we are in control or not, whether we are winning or losing. Often we feel a sense of transcendence, as if the boundaries of the self had been expanded. The sailor feels at one with the boat, the wind, and the sea; the singer feels a mysterious sense of universal harmony. In those moments the awareness of time disappears, and hours seem to flash by without our noticing.

This state of consciousness, which comes as close as anything can to what we call happiness, depends on two sets of conditions. The first is external. Certain activities are more likely to produce flow than others because (1) they have concrete goals and manageable rules, (2) they make it possible to adjust opportunities for action to our capacities, (3) they provide clear information about how well we are doing, and (4) they screen out distractions and make concentration possible. Games, artistic performances, and religious rituals are good examples of such "flow activities." But one of the most important findings of our studies has been that any activity can produce the optimal flow experience, as long as it meets the above requirements. Physicians describe doing surgery as an addictive "body-contact sport" similar to sailing or skiing; computer programmers often can't tear themselves away from their keyboards. In fact, people seem to get more flow from what they do on their jobs than from leisure activities in free time.

The second set of conditions that allows flow to happen is internal to the person. Some people have an uncanny ability to match their skills to the opportunities around them. They set manageable goals for themselves even when there does not seem to be anything for them to do. They are good at reading feedback that others fail to notice. They can concentrate easily and do not get distracted. They are not afraid of losing their self, so their ego can slip easily out of awareness. Persons who have learned to control consciousness in these ways have a "flow personality." They do not need to play in order to be in flow; they can be happy even as they work on an assembly line or are languishing in solitary confinement.

In *Flow* I described individuals who made their lives relatively happy and meaningful by bringing as much flow as possible into their work and their relationships. Some of these persons were homeless drifters while others had suffered devastating tragedies like blindness or paralysis; yet all had been able to transform seemingly hopeless conditions into a serene, joyful existence. But I also remarked on the fact that it is difficult to build a happy life by the simple addition of a series of flow experiences. The whole in this case is definitely more than the sum of its parts. An artist may paint for decades and love every minute of it, yet become depressed and hopeless in middle age. A tennis pro who enjoyed most of his career could end up disillusioned and bitter. To transform the entirety of life into a unified flow experience, it helps to have faith in a system of meanings that gives purpose to one's being.

In the past, faith was usually based on religious explanations. How the world began, why we must suffer, what will happen after we die—these basic questions were answered by the best stories people could make up, in an effort to give order to the chaos and happenstance of existence. The mythical stories of all religions deal with these issues, and they often arrive at the logical conclusion that there must be a God, or a whole pantheon of gods, responsible for our fate. Based on these stories, every religion has developed rules for living, often wise in their consequences, that allow people to lead a coherent existence. The meanings that humankind has invented through religion have played a fundamental, probably irreplaceable role in our evolutionary history. We would be a very different kind of animal if our ancestors had failed to imagine a purposeful, anthropomorphic cosmos.

But now, at the cusp of the second millennium after the birth of the man who has been called the son of God, it is difficult to have faith in the traditional stories. The literal content of sacred texts, of ancient rituals, of rules such as those prohibiting divorce or abortion, seem more and more at odds with other things we have found out about the world. Few now believe that the Earth is flat or at the center of the solar system. Even though an astonishingly large number of people still believe that the Earth did not exist until a few thousand years B.C. and that man was created as he is now out of a lump of clay, such beliefs are likely to become increasingly anachronistic—at least in their literal form—with each new generation.

The passing of traditional beliefs is a dangerous time for any culture. In discarding a literal religious explanation, it becomes easy to discredit the hard-won wisdom often bundled up with it. When the chronology and causality of the Bible become suspect, so do its injunctions against greed, violence, promiscuous sexuality, and selfishness. For a short while those who reject the entire traditional worldview feel liberated, and are exhilarated to be in a new land without rules or restrictions. However, it soon becomes obvious that to live in absolute freedom is neither possible nor desirable. Without rules based on past experience it is easy to make costly mistakes; without a sense of ultimate purpose it is difficult to sustain courage when the unavoidable tragedies of life strike. But where does one find a faith one can believe in in the third millennium?

Flow ended with the proposition that by understanding better our evolutionary past we might generate the grounds for a viable meaning system, a faith that can give order and purpose to our lives in the future. To know ourselves is the greatest achievement of our species. And to understand ourselves—what we are made of, what motives drive us, and what goals we dream of—involves, first of all, an understanding of our evolutionary past. Only on that foundation can we build a stable, meaningful future. It is in order to develop further this contention that the present book was written.

The first chapter, "The Mind as History," introduces the evolutionary perspective, and argues that to understand how our minds work we must take into account its deep roots in the slow unfolding of the past of our species. It reflects on the network of relationships that bind us to each other and to the natural environment, and briefly describes how self-reflective consciousness arose, freeing us to a certain extent from the control of genetic and cultural determinism.

The next chapter, "Who Controls the Mind?," deals with some of the undesirable consequences of the evolution of the self. Free from external control, we are nevertheless often prey to a deep dissatisfaction, an elusive yearning for goals forever beyond our reach—a legacy of the mind's emancipation. We have not yet learned to make it do what we wish, or what is good for us. As far as controlling the mind is concerned, we are like a novice driver behind the wheel of a racing car.

Three sources of illusion stand between us and a clear perception of reality. These are discussed in the third chapter, "The Veils of Maya." They include the distortions due to the genetic instructions, which were once necessary to our survival, but are often in conflict with present reality; the distortions of the culture in which we were born, and those that result from the emergence of the self as a separate entity making its own claims on the mind. Unless we understand how these forces shape the way we think and act, it is difficult to gain control over consciousness.

But our lives are not only directed internally by the instructions of the genes, the culture, and the self. Evolution is the result of competition between organisms for the energy required for survival. The forces of selection are still active around us; oppressors exploit us from above, and parasites from below. The ideas we create, the technological artifacts we produce compete with each other, and with us, for scarce material resources and for attention—which is the scarcest resource of the mind. The necessity of learning how to get along with these external threats is discussed in Chapters Four and Five, "Predators and Parasites" and "Memes *versus* Genes."

"Directing Evolution" is the next chapter. It examines how the principles of evolution apply to the development of culture and consciousness, and it introduces the idea that if there is any meaning to the past, it is to be found in the increase in the complexity of material structures and information over time. It is this feature of the evolutionary process that can provide a meaningful direction to our efforts, a hope for the future.

Chapter Seven, "Evolution and Flow," explains why flow experiences lead to the increase of complexity in consciousness. It argues that in order to have a future worth looking forward to, we must find ways to enjoy actions that lead to greater harmony within ourselves, society, and the broader environment of which we are a part.

In the next chapter, "The Transcendent Self," some case studies of individuals whose lives conform to the evolution of complexity are presented. These are people who enjoy everything they do, who keep learning and improving their skills, and who are so committed to goals beyond themselves that the fear of death has little hold on their minds. Their example suggests what it might mean to live by an evolutionary faith.

Chapter Nine, "The Flow of History," argues that flow not only helps the individual self to evolve, but it also provides the energy and direction for some of the most important transformations of technology and culture. Cars and computers, scientific knowledge and religious systems, seem to have been created more out of a joyous desire to find new challenges and to create order in consciousness than from necessity or a calculation of profit. Based on these reflections, a view of a "good" society that makes flow and complexity possible is proposed.

The last chapter, "A Fellowship of the Future," outlines some practical suggestions about what it might mean to apply the evolutionary faith. If it is true that at this point in history the emergence of complexity is the best "story" we can tell about the past and the future, and if it is true that without it our half-formed self runs the risk of destroying the planet and our budding consciousness along with it, then how can we help to realize the potential inherent in the cosmos? When the self consciously accepts its role in the process of evolution, life acquires a transcendent meaning. Whatever happens to our individual existences, we will become at one with the power that is the universe.

PART I

THE LURE OF
THE PAST

1

THE MIND AND HISTORY

THE PERSPECTIVE OF EVOLUTION

Each year we learn more about the incredible complexity of our universe. The mind staggers at the intimation of billions of galaxies, each made up of billions of stars, slowly revolving in every direction for unimaginable distances. And inside each grain of matter super-colliders reveal ever-receding constellations of strange particles streaking along mysterious orbits. In the midst of this field of stupendous forces a human life unfolds in what is less than a split second on the cosmic time scale. Yet, as far as we are concerned, it is this, our own short life, filled with its few precious moments, that counts for more than all the galaxies, black holes, and exploding stars put together.

And there is good reason for feeling this way. As Pascal said, humans may be fragile as reeds, but they are thinking beings; in their consciousness they reflect the immensity of the universe. In the last few centuries, the human presence has become even more central in the natural world. We have only recently been able to have a glimpse of the millions of years that preceded us, eons during which thousands of organisms replaced one another, struggling to survive in an ever-changing landscape. And we now realize that our unique heritage—the reflective consciousness that lulled us into believing for a while that we were forever destined to be the crown of creation—brings with it an awesome responsibility. We realize that being at the cutting edge of evolution on this planet means we can either direct our life energy toward achieving growth and harmony or waste the potentials we have inherited, adding to the sway of chaos and destruction.

In order to make choices that will lead to a better future, it helps to be aware of the forces at work in evolution; after all, it is through them that we will succeed or fail as a species. My intention in this book is to reflect on what we know about evolution, and to develop the implications of that knowledge for everyday action. If we understand better what we are up against, we have a better chance to live our lives in a responsible fashion, and perhaps to help direct the future toward the most positive goals of humanity.

One result of reflecting on evolution is that one learns to take the past very seriously. *Natura non fecit saltum,* the Romans said: Nature does not progress by leaps and bounds. What we are today is the result of forces that acted on our ancestors many millennia ago, and what humankind will be in the future is going to depend on our present choices. But our choices are influenced by a number of constraints that are part of the evolutionary makeup of every human being. They are subject to the genes that regulate the functions of our body, and to instincts, which, for example, drive us to be angry or sexually aroused even when we don't want to be. They are also constrained by cultural heritage, by systems that teach men to be manly and women to be ladylike, or one religion to be intolerant of the members of another.

While striving to change the course of history we cannot wish away the constraints that the past has burdened us with; to do so would lead only to frustration and disillusion. Knowledge of these forces that determine consciousness and action, however, can make it possible for us to become liberated from them: to become free to decide what to think, what to feel, and how to act. At this point in our history it should be possible for an individual to build a self that is not simply the outcome of biological drives and cultural habits, but a conscious, personal creation. That self will be aware of its freedom and not fear it. It will enjoy life in all its forms, and gradually become aware of its kinship with the rest of humanity, with life as a whole, and with the pulsing forces that animate the world beyond our comprehension. When the self begins to transcend the narrow interests built into its structure by evolution, it is then ready to start taking control of the direction of evolution in its turn. But shaping the future course of evolution is not something that can be accomplished by solitary individuals working alone. Therefore, it is necessary to consider which social institutions are most likely to sponsor positive evolutionary actions, and how we can develop more of them.

This, in brief, is the project of this book. It will first explore the forces from the past that have shaped us and made us the kind of organisms we are; it will describe ways of being that help us free ourselves of the dead hand of the past; it will propose approaches to life that improve its quality and lead to joyful involvement; and it will reflect on ways to integrate the growth and liberation of the self with that of society as a whole. Clearly the task set out for the book is too ambitious to be achieved inside the compass of its covers. Knowledge increases each year; experience matures with time. Writing about such matters is in itself an evolutionary process— slowly changing, never ending—but it is my hope that *The Evolving Self* will serve as a first step in the process.

It is partly for this reason that after each chapter I have listed some questions to stimulate further thinking, followed by blank spaces for you to enter your thoughts in. It is one modest way to show that the argument of the book is not completed, that it is open to be continued by each reader according to his or her wisdom and experience. Writing in books to complete the author's thoughts has been one of the oldest scholarly practices in every civilization. The readers' glosses added to the white margins of pages are as much a part of the culture as what was originally written on those pages. Books no longer have generous margins; hence it makes sense to provide an alternative way for the reader to get actively involved with what he or she reads. I hope it will happen here.

THE GLOBAL NETWORK

Not so long ago my wife and I had the privilege of sitting in on a town meeting in a small Rocky Mountain community. The town was at an altitude of almost nine thousand feet, in a sweet-smelling valley nestled between tremendous peaks. The air tasted as cool as spring water scented with the perfume of resin. Hummingbirds flitted under the eaves, and an eagle circled above the meadows. The meeting took place in the cheerful town hall built of logs and glass, with soaring cathedral ceilings, set on beautifully landscaped grounds. The parking lot glittered with the latest four-wheel-drive vehicles. There were about sixty people in attendance, all eager-looking, forceful individuals who seemed at ease with themselves. Some of them were ranchers, some were nurses and teachers, others had semiretired here from the distant city, or worked at the nearby ski resorts.

At first the meeting proceeded as such meetings do, with the approval of the minutes and comments on pending projects and ordinances. But not much time had passed before a lanky rancher stood up to voice the first complaint. Although he lived fifteen miles north of town, he said, on winter days smoke from the community's fireplaces cast such a pall on the valley that it was like driving into a war zone. Was there anything the council was planning to do to restrict the burning of wood? Next an older man rose to describe the perilous condition of the Blue River, which, as everyone knew, was one of the best places to fish for trout in the entire state. Or rather, had been. Unfortunately, the federal highway department, in order to keep the high pass through which the interstate runs open in the winter, had been dumping tons of sand on the icy road every year. The sand washed into the river, eventually filling in the nooks and hollows where the trout spawn. Few young trout hatch anymore in the Blue River.

Mention of the interstate brought up a question from the audience: What was the current rate of local robberies and burglaries? Was it true that since the new road had been built the crime rate had shot up 400 percent? The sheriff explained that, well, yes, this was one of the prices you had to pay for progress. Before the interstate existed, the riffraff from the city did not want to bother driving this far out through tortuous roads to break into a house. But now that the drive was fast and comfortable, more criminals found the trip feasible. Smoke, trout, and burglaries are the least of our worries, interjected an elderly rancher, who stood up next to speak in a voice cracking with emotion. The real question was, What is going to happen to our water? None of us will survive without it, he said.

The value of our land is tied to the water rights we own. But now the cities to the east and to the west are building giant underground tunnels to suck up the water from under our lands, leaving them dry. The meadows are turning brown and brittle; the herds are thinning out.

As the town meeting went on in this vein, it became progressively clearer that this was not the place I had originally thought it was. At the start I believed I was witnessing the decision-making process of a group of independent, self-reliant, affluent Americans who had the future in their hands. By the end I saw that this small community, proud in its isolation from the woes of the world, was in fact completely enmeshed in economic, political, and demographic processes originating far away, over which the townspeople had little control. And then what I had known for a long time in an abstract sort of a way finally hit home: There is no place left on earth where one can plan one's destiny without taking into account what happens in the rest of the world.

Two other anecdotes may help illustrate this point. A few years ago, a Canadian professor who is a friend of a friend was planning retirement with his wife. Being sensitive and rational people, they decided to retire to the safest spot on earth they could find. They spent years poring over almanacs and encyclopedias to check out rates of homicide and health statistics, inquire about the directions of prevailing winds (so as not to be downwind of probable nuclear targets), and finally found a perfect haven. They bought a house on an island early in 1982. Two months later their house was destroyed: Their choice had been the Falkland Islands.

The other story concerns a relative of a friend, who is an extremely wealthy industrialist. He, too, wanted to retire someplace safe from the congestion and crime of Europe. He bought a small island in the Bahamas, built a splendid estate, and surrounded himself with armed guards and attack dogs. At first he felt safe and comfortable, but soon worries began to appear. Were there enough guards to protect him in case his wealth attracted criminals to loot the island? Yet if he strengthened the guard, wouldn't he become increasingly weaker, more dependent on his protectors? In addition, the gilded cage soon became boring; so he fled back to the anonymity of a big city.

It might have been already true in John Donne's time that "no man is an island," but the truth of this saying is certainly obvious now. And the interconnectedness of human activities and interests is going to increase even faster than we are accustomed to in this third millennium we are approaching. Our actions will affect everyone living on the planet, and we will be affected by theirs. It is together that we shall either prevail or disappear. Yet human consciousness has developed through previous millennia to represent individual experiences, to advance individual interests: At best, we are prepared to love and protect our close kin. A few individuals have been able to stretch their minds to encompass broader interests, understanding that the division between "me" and "the other" is largely arbitrary. By and large, however, our consciousness is not prepared for the problems ahead, regardless of how urgent they are.

How can we best retool the mind for accommodating the challenges of the near future? One possibility, which this book explores, is to review what we know about the evolutionary past and its legacy to our minds. By understanding how human psychology has developed over time in response to changing conditions in the environment, we might find it possible to adapt more rapidly to the increasingly rapid changes demanding action in the future.

AT THE HINGES OF THE NEW MILLENNIUM

Why would someone want to read a book on evolution and psychology? It will not help the reader to invest money profitably, or plan a safe retirement income. It will not help in losing weight, stopping smoking, or moving up the career ladder. It cannot give the townspeople in the Rockies any clear guidance about how to save their trout or their water.

What *The Evolving Self* offers, instead, is a deeper understanding of the direction in which life on earth has been going, and hence a clearer sense of what the meaning of one's own life might be. People who already know what they want out of their lives will probably find what follows superfluous. Those who believe that pleasure and possessions are the only reasons for living do not need to read further, since they will find little in these pages that is useful to them. Religious fundamentalists and adamant materialists alike are not seeking the kind of knowledge that will be explored in these pages, because they are already comfortable in their own beliefs. The ideal reader is someone who is curious about the meaning of life, who is not convinced that any of the existing explanations are exhaustive enough, who is concerned about the state of the world, and who would also like to do something about it. For such an individual, this book might provide ideas that can be translated into a clearer purpose and stronger conviction with which to confront life.

We shall look at the forces that have shaped our present condition on this planet, in order to explore what the future might turn out to be like. Not what it *will* be like, but what it *might* be like. The difference between *will* and *might* rests with us. To a large extent, it is our behavior that will determine which scenario is going to be realized. By acting in concert with positive evolutionary trends we might not become richer, healthier, or more powerful, but we are likely to derive a measure of happiness, or at least of serenity, from knowing that our actions are helping a better future take shape.

When the first millennium was fading into the second one a thousand years ago, people all over Europe were beginning to prepare for the end of the world. They left their homes in droves to camp out on mountainsides and in sanctuaries, hoping to avoid the worst sufferings of the fiery Armageddon they were sure was about to strike. They believed that if the end of the world caught them on a hilltop, after death they would be closer to God, and would be among the first in line to reach the seat of eternal judgment. Many of those who owned land and cattle gave away their wealth to the poor, because according to the Gospels a rich man has as much chance of entering the kingdom of heaven as a camel has of passing through the eye of a needle. For many years afterward people lived in a state of anxiety, looking over their shoulders for the signs of the second coming of Christ that would signal the beginning of the end.

Although for the past half century we have also been haunted by the fear that an explosive grand finale will consume all life on the planet, the reasons for the fear have changed. At the end of the first millennium, people believed that God had promised to end His great earthly experiment a thousand years after the death of His Son.

Now we live with the fear of disintegrating, with devices of our own invention, the very force that keeps matter together, thus reducing the infinite variety and complexity of life on this planet to a bleak, deadly desert.

We have learned much in the past thousand years. We have come to realize that the earth is not the center of the universe, and most people have reconciled themselves to the idea that humans started walking the African plains about four million years ago—after serving time in earlier mammalian roles going back to a tiny shrew who kept stealing the dinosaurs' eggs 250 million or so years ago. We have learned that our vaunted reasoning ability is founded upon a thin overlay of tissue stretched over a solid reptilian brain, and we have come to suspect that when the interest of our blindly programmed genes comes into conflict with our values and even our self-interest, the genes win out.

Our ancestors of the year one thousand were infinitely poorer in terms of material goods, but richer spiritually than we are. Most of them lived in dark, cold hovels without any furniture, often went hungry, and had very little to call their own. If they were able to walk through an average suburban home of today, they would think they had stumbled into a dream palace. On the other hand, whereas our age believes that we are the descendants of apes clinging to a precariously wobbling little planet adrift in a mechanical universe, they believed themselves to be the favorite creatures of an omnipotent God who sent his only Son to die so that they could live forever in eternal bliss.

This worldview gave our ancestors a consoling sense of destiny, a feeling of self-assurance. Even the many nonbelievers and the numerous recreants wallowing in mortal sin could feel that their lives were protected by a safety net. No matter what they did during their lives, at the last moment before death an act of faith could restore them to a state of grace and assure eternal happiness. Our ancestors saw themselves as protagonists of a universal drama. In contrast, we, in the words of Jacques Monod, live in a "frozen universe of solitude." Stripped of our elders' illusions, we are also deprived of their faith.

Is this another illustration, then, of the saying "ignorance is bliss"? Were past ages happier because of their illusions? Although solid evidence on this question is impossible to come by, it does not seem likely that the average person a thousand years ago—or a hundred, or ten thousand years ago—was happier than we are now. Those historians who do try to delve into the mentality of past ages come up with rather grim portraits of what it meant to live in ancient Rome or Victorian England. Johann Huizinga, who wrote one of the most vivid accounts of life in the Middle Ages, characterized it as an almost schizophrenic period, in which people were obsessed in turn by greed and self-sacrifice, their moods swinging between abject fear and spiritual ecstasy.

Whatever their merits, the basic beliefs of an age have an impact on the future of the people who hold them. Perhaps the faith of the Middle Ages provided enough self-confidence to slowly break the ties of religious dogma, and paved the way for the next ages of discovery and exploration. Our current beliefs—or lack of them—will have a comparable influence. Will we have enough courage, enough zest, to allow us to enjoy any future at all—let alone one that is better than the present? Or will our race go out, either with a bang or a whimper, because we can't figure out what life is all about?

What happens in the third millennium depends on what is in human consciousness now: on the ideas you and I believe in, the values we endorse, the actions we take. It depends on what we pay attention to, the environment we create through the investment of our psychic energy. At this point the reader may ask, So what's this got to do with me? I have enough trouble keeping my checkbook balanced, holding on to my job and my family, trying to get some joy out of life. What do I care about the third *millennium?* What is the future of humankind to me?

The thesis of this book is that becoming an active, conscious part of the evolutionary process is the best way to give meaning to our lives at the present point in time, and to enjoy each moment along the way. Understanding how evolution works, and what role we may play in it, provides a direction and purpose that otherwise is lacking in this secular, desacralized culture. It does not mean that we must give up personal goals and subordinate them to some long-range universal good. In fact, the opposite is true. Individuals who develop to the fullest their uniqueness, yet at the same time identify

with the larger processes at work in the cosmos, escape the loneliness of their individual destinies. And in addition, as I hope to
show, history-making is more gratifying than being swept along by
it passively.

But why is this need to reflect on the past and on the future so
urgent in this particular period? We are, in fact, living in a unique
window of opportunity, a crucial threshold of planetary history. If
a traveling space inspector were to return now to visit Earth after an
absence of a few thousand years, it would not believe its eyes. How
did the quality of the air change so drastically? What happened to
those luxuriant rain forests? How did enormous cornfields spread
over the American and Siberian plains? Where did all those sheep
in New Zealand come from, and why are there so few lions and
whales, and no dodo birds left? And it would no doubt be astonished
by the physical changes brought about in so short a time: cement
covering the land, huge structures pointing toward the sky, and
everywhere the signs of unceasing labor that turns mineral, vegeta-
ble, and chemical energy into smoke and waste.

If our imaginary visitor had some historical knowledge about the
phases of planetary evolution, it would soon realize that it was
witnessing a crucial stage in the evolution of Planet Earth: that
period of a few thousand years in which one of the animal species
becomes self-conscious and embarks on the project of transforming
into its own image everything it can lay its hands on. The space
inspector would know, from previous experiences in other parts of
the galaxy, how explosively dangerous this epoch was going to be
for any and all forms of life on the affected planet. Before turning
the spacecraft around for the homebound starlane, it would probably mutter a few words, wishing luck to the awakening species
whose clumsy gropings would result in either destruction or the
slow flowering of a great civilization.

That time, of course, is now. Although some form of human life
seems to have existed for about four million years, it is only about
ten thousand years ago that our ancestors learned that planting seeds
would bring a larger harvest, less than that time since they learned
that metals could be shaped, and even less since they realized that
signs could stand for words and thoughts.

And it is only a hundred or so years ago—less than the wink of an eye in terms of our past—that we began to realize that the future is not ruled by a purposeful providence, but to a large extent is in our hands. Before Darwin and his followers made biological evolution so convincing, most people believed that some all-powerful figure was in charge of the universe, and that despite the prevalence of pain and misery in this world He would eventually take care of us forever in the next one. Evolutionary theory, on the other hand, suggests that each species—including the human—must be responsible for its own survival; there is no supernatural protector who will save it. Although we have hardly had the time to assimilate this bleak intelligence, we are already forced to make decisions that will affect the survival of life on the planet. We do indeed need all the luck that may come our way. But even more, we need to take our predicament seriously, and develop the knowledge that will make a creative response to it possible.

CHANCE, NECESSITY, AND SOMETHING ELSE

But could you, or I, or any single human being, really make a difference to the future? Current understanding of causality suggests that events are determined by random chance's interaction with immutable natural laws. A butterfly flapping its wings over an orchid along the shores of the Amazon River can set in motion a chain of minute atmospheric perturbations that might result in a hurricane's destroying hundreds of condos in Florida. How hurricanes are formed can be explained in terms of atmospheric pressure and temperature differentials; but the flight of the butterfly—and the hundred other causes that dampen or amplify the effects of the initial movement of its wings—may forever remain in the unpredictable realm of random chance.

Caught between unyielding laws of nature and capricious events beyond reckoning, what can we do but go along for the ride? A resigned fatalism seems to be the most rational response to life. In practice this means giving up responsibility, reflection, and choice. It implies following automatically whatever needs and desires the genes happened to code on our chromosomes, at least within the bounds allowed by the society we live in. Taking care of Number

One—our comforts, pleasures, and ambitions—is about all we can hope to accomplish, according to this scenario.

At this point a strange paradox begins to emerge. If everyone takes this attitude—if we all submit to the determining forces of causality—it is unlikely that humankind will survive. Those who have access to resources will keep hoarding them at ever-accelerating rates, the have-nots will rise up to get their share, and the war of all against all will result. Whereas if enough people were to believe that the future is at least partly in their hands, the prospect of survival would be greatly enhanced, for then they would be much more likely to take steps to avoid the cataclysm. But if this is true, then are chance and necessity really the only determinants of our fate? Or is there some other force at work, besides these two, shaping the future?

It has become fashionable to claim that individual action has no significant effect on history. If Socrates or Joan of Arc had not stood up for his or her beliefs, this theory holds, or if Raoul Wallenberg had not given up his life of ease to save thousands of Jews in Nazi-occupied Hungary, well, others might have taken up their causes instead. In any case, their dramatic stands made no real difference in the course of events, which are decided by the vector of social forces, not by individual choices.

This argument may have merit as far as scientific and technological discoveries are concerned. If the Wright brothers hadn't been able to fly their plane—failing as Otto Lilienthal, Samuel Langley, and so many others had done earlier—someone else would have perfected a flying machine within a year or two. Science and technology have thus far followed their own trajectory of development, which human minds have passively agreed to assist. But not all human action is so determined. Truly creative individuals are those who succeed, against all pressures of instinct and worldly wisdom, in visualizing a way of life that will make the lot of others freer and happier.

Breaking out of the fatalistic acceptance of genetic or historical programming requires, at the very least, a belief in freedom and self-determination. A person is unlikely to take risks and work for the common good unless he or she believes that it will make a difference. But is such a person just deluding himself? After all, the

axioms of science postulate that all events must have causes, and so
if a St. Francis decides to distribute his wealth to the poor and retire
to pray with other young men, it must have been because he wanted
to irritate his rich father, or because he was a latent homosexual, or
perhaps because he had some hormonal imbalance.

But one can accept the axiom of causality without becoming
reductionistic. Of the many causes that shaped St. Francis's actions,
a primary one was the belief that his actions mattered, and that he
had a responsibility to change the world around him. This belief, in
itself, is a "cause." The idea of free will is a self-fulfilling prophecy;
those who abide by it are liberated from the absolute determinism
of external forces.

Chance and necessity are sole rulers of beings who are incapable
of reflection. But evolution has introduced a buffer between determining forces and human action. Like a clutch in an engine, consciousness enables those who use it to disengage themselves occasionally from the pressure of relentless drives so as to make their own
decisions. The achievement of self-reflective consciousness, which
humans alone seem to have achieved on this planet, is by no means
an unmixed blessing. It accounts not only for the self-denying
courage of Gandhi and Martin Luther King, but also for the "unnat-
ural" cravings of the Marquis de Sade or the insatiable ambition of
Stalin. Consciousness, this third determinant of our behavior, can
lead either to safety or to destruction.

ARE WE HOPELESSLY BAD?

Only a hundred years ago, the prevalent belief in Western societies
was that mankind, especially in its industrialized version, was the
pinnacle of creation, destined to inherit the earth. The Victorians
and Edwardians thought that their society had reached the heights
of progress. This optimism, however, was only a temporary aberra-
tion in history. Throughout the past people more often characterized their times by a conflicted, even tragic, view of mankind's
destiny. Plato was not alone in believing that the Golden Age was
over. For many Christians, such as Calvin, men and women were
hopelessly corrupt, unable to help themselves without God's grace.
But then, during the nineteenth century, it seemed for a while that

science, democracy, and technology were going to turn the world into a new Garden of Eden. After that brief interlude of self-congratulation we have now swung back to an almost panicked loss of confidence in mankind's goodness and ability to help itself.

Ironically, but not unexpectedly, it is usually those with unrealistically high expectations who are shocked by the perversity of human behavior. A rosy-colored picture of human nature cannot stand up to scrutiny for long. Those who expect priests to be consistently saintly, soldiers brave, mothers always self-sacrificing, and so on, are due for some serious disappointment. To them the entire history of the human race will seem to have been a huge mistake, or as Macbeth said so well, a tale told by an idiot, full of sound and fury, signifying nothing.

Whereas if one starts from the assumption that humans are basically weak and disoriented creatures thrown by chance into a leading role at the center of the planetary stage, without a script and without rehearsal, then the picture of what we have accomplished is not so bleak. Paraphrasing what the trainer said about his talking dog, the point is not that we sing well, but that we sing at all.

It is true that men have been killing one another continuously since the dawn of time, and that those who have managed to grasp power have often tended to exploit those who were weaker. It is true that greed has generally taken precedence over prudence, and that it is now driving us to destroy the environment upon which life depends. But why should it be otherwise? Blaming humanity for such faults is like holding the shark accountable for its bloody habits or the deer for overgrazing its habitat. We may be evolving, but we still have an awfully long way to go before we can overcome what is innate in our behavior.

The human potential and other New Age movements of the past thirty years have tried to restore to men and women the dignity lost to scientific reductionism. In so doing, however, they have often overshot the mark and fallen into the opposite sort of excess. Their often romantic visions of human perfection have encouraged a great deal of wishful thinking, and in the process have set people up for unnecessary disillusion. When New Age thinkers describe what the mind can do, it is difficult to distinguish what is intended as a metaphor from what is offered as fact. "The mind is a hologram that registers the entire symphony of cosmic vibratory events . . . any mind recapitulates all cosmic events . . . [the] mind knows no barriers," writes Sam Keen, an enthusiastic theologian. Fortunately, none of this is true, for if the mind were indeed to register "the entire symphony of cosmic vibratory events"—whatever that means—it would drive us to madness.

The problem with many of the promises of the New Age movement is that, while they reflect some truth about the internal workings of the mind, many people take them to apply equally to the external material world, and there they are bound to be frustrated. Take for instance this creed of a Theta seminar, quoted by William Hulme: "The thinker in all of us is the creator of the universe. . . . Within the dominion of our minds we are surely God, for we can control what we think, and what we conceive to be true becomes the truth." With some serious qualifications this statement might be accepted as far as "the dominion of our minds" is concerned. But many true believers will take the last statement, "what we conceive to be true becomes the truth," to refer to concrete events, not just states of the mind. It is this misplaced concreteness that leads many people to expect material results when "only" spiritual ones were intended. Prayer, meditation, and worship help to bring harmony to our inner lives. But harmony is not what most people are seeking: They pray, rather, to have their health restored, to win the lottery, or to find a lover. Jesus Christ's disclaimer that His kingdom was not of this world tends to be ignored by many eager contemporary Christians.

Rather than claiming Godlike qualities, we might consider instead that 94 percent of our genetic material overlaps with the chimpanzees, and then wonder how some of us have ever built cathedrals, or computers, or spaceships. Then the fact that there are even a few individuals who try to help others will come as a marvelous surprise. If you expect a full glass, a glass with water up to the middle will seem half empty; but if you don't expect any water at all, the same glass will seem half full.

You and I are part of the process of evolution. We are bundles of energy programmed to pursue selfish ends, not for our own sake, but to preserve and replicate the information encoded in our genes. Attila may have believed that he was "the Scourge of God" as he burned and killed his way through Europe, and the Spaniards were half convinced that they were saving the souls of the Indians they were exterminating, but basically they were driven by the same impulses that send birds migrating or lemmings scurrying toward the sea. Looking back now we are horrified at what our forefathers have accomplished, and we conclude that humans are inherently evil. But we have been no better than we should be, and probably no worse.

The time of innocence, however, is now past. It is no longer possible for mankind to blunder about self-indulgently. Our species has become too powerful to be led by instincts alone. Birds and lemmings cannot do much damage except to themselves, whereas we can destroy the entire matrix of life on the planet. The awesome powers we have stumbled into require a commensurate responsibility. As we become aware of the motives that shape our actions, as our place in the chain of evolution becomes clearer, we must find a meaningful and binding plan that will protect us and the rest of life from the consequence of what we have wrought.

THE GOOD AND THE BAD

Over six hundred years ago on two of the walls of the city hall of Siena, the artist Ambrogio Lorenzetti painted a pair of great frescoes: One represented "Good Government," the other "Bad Government." The scene in "Good Government" is similar to the pictures in Richard Scarry's children's book entitled *Busy Busy World*. It shows a city where every house is neat, every garden is full of fruit and flowers, and everyone is doing something useful. Signs of order and prosperity are everywhere. In "Bad Government," by contrast, people are shown arguing and fighting, the houses are neglected, and the crops are struggling against weeds. It is as good a visual illustration as any of what people all over the world mean by good and bad: bad is entropy—disorder, confusion, waste of energy, the inability to do work and achieve goals; good is negative entropy, or negentropy—harmony, predictability, purposeful activity that leads to satisfying one's desires.

Unfortunately, the concepts of "good" and "bad" are often used for selfish purposes, and are given definitions that advance narrow interests. The Sienese wished good government for themselves, but for centuries fought bitterly against the neighboring Florentines. The early European settlers in America—even the most religious ones—attributed evil traits to the natives such as cruelty and savagery, so that they could feel comfortable taking away their land and their lives. William Hubbard, who in 1677 wrote one of the first descriptions of New England natives, called them "treacherous villains" and "children of the Devil." To the Chinese Communists, Americans were imperialist devils; to the Iranians we were just plain devils—while we in return thought of the Ayatollah and of Saddam Hussein as Satan incarnate. "Good" and "bad" are relative terms, and as long as a person identifies exclusively with his or her own body, family, religion, or ethnic group, they will remain so. What's good for me is likely to be bad for you, and vice versa. During the Cold War, a Russian crop failure was seen as a sign of our success, and the drug problem in the United States was taken by the Russians as a sign of their own superiority. When the values that support a moral stance are parochial, it is impossible to reach universal agreement on what is good or bad.

The only value that all human beings can readily share is the continuation of life on earth. In this one goal all individual self-interests are united. Unless such a species identity takes precedence over the more particular identities of faith, nation, family, or person, it will be difficult to agree on the course that must be taken to guarantee our future. At this point our brain is programmed by genes to "take care of Number One," and by society to support its institutions. What we need to do, however, is to change the program so that supporting the needs of the planet as a whole becomes our top priority. But is this possible? How can men and women overcome the drives that were laid down millions of years ago in their genetic code? How can we unlearn the motivations that were taught us from the first hours of life?

The goals and values we now have are appropriate to a species blindly struggling along with other species in the stream of life. They are appropriate to passengers, not to navigators. But whether we like it or not, we are now the pilots of Spaceship Earth. For this role we need a new set of instructions, new values and goals by which to steer a course among the many unprecedented dangers. In this adventure of the mind, the first stage takes us to reflect on what—or who—each of us individually is.

THE EMERGENCE OF THE SELF

The process we have come to call evolution exists because nothing ever stays the same. There are only two choices available to both living and nonliving things: either let entropy get the upper hand, or try to beat the system. Evolution is the second of these two alternatives. With time every form, every structure, tends to decay as its components return to randomness. The cells of the body break up, organs deteriorate, appliances wear out and rust away, lofty mountain chains turn to sand, great civilizations collapse and are forgotten, and even stars die when their energy becomes exhausted. A car will work for a few years, but after that keeping it running takes too much energy to make it worthwhile. When you first buy a house you think you now own a permanent shelter, but if you don't fix the roof, tuck-point the walls, and paint the woodwork often enough the house will start falling apart. The reason for this process of disintegration is entropy, the supreme law of the universe.

But entropy is not the only law operating in the world. There are also processes that move in the opposite direction: creation and growth are just as much part of the story as decay and death. Beautifully ordered crystals take shape, new life-forms develop, increasingly improbable methods of exploiting energy emerge. Whenever order in a system increases instead of breaking down we may say that negentropy is at work.

Every system, whether a rock or an animal, tends above all else to keep itself in an ordered state. In the case of living things, most of what we call "life" consists of efforts to ensure self-preservation and self-replication. A whale will try to remain a whale as long as it can, and before it's too late will try to reproduce as many faithful copies of itself as possible. In order to achieve its end, the whale will have to keep on frustrating entropy by extracting oxygen from the air and calories from plankton, and by protecting its calves from harm and predators.

For negentropy to operate, an organism—an individual body, or a family, or a social system—must always be at work repairing and protecting itself, becoming more efficient at transforming energy for its own purposes. The high points of human history are those discoveries that have made it easier to protect ourselves from the onslaught of entropy. The discovery of fire is justly famous. One of our distant ancestors had the brilliant idea of harnessing combustion to reverse—even if temporarily and locally—the numbing effects of cold, one of entropy's favorite manifestations. The development of ever more efficient, more improbable systems is what we call evolution. Evolution is forced on us by the fact that systems fall apart with time unless they become more efficient. We can't stop and remain in the same place; even to remain still we must advance.

Competition is the thread that runs through evolution. Life-forms displace one another on the stage of history, depending on their success in taking energy from the environment and transforming it for their own purposes. But often species survive because they have found ways to improve their chances of survival through cooperation. Paradoxically, cooperation can be a very effective competitive tool. However, until humans entered the scene, competition and cooperation have been entirely blind and unintentional.

Another way to view evolution is to see it not as the selective survival of life-forms such as dinosaurs or elephants, but of information. From this perspective, what counts is not the external, material shape of the organism, but the instructions it bears. Biological organisms carry extremely detailed scripts coded chemically in their genes, and it is the survival of these instructions that evolution is really all about. Elephants are only a by-product of the genetic information contained in elephant chromosomes. Theoretically one could build elephants provided one had the blueprint of their genes. But without their genetic instructions, elephants would disappear in a single generation from the face of the earth.

Most people have accepted the notion of biological evolution. But genetic information is not the only kind that strives to survive. There are other patterns of information that compete with one another to maintain their shape and transmit themselves through time. For instance, languages are engaged in competition, as are religions, scientific theories, lifestyles, technologies, and even the elements of that realm of consciousness we have come to regard as the "self."

Inside each person there is a wonderful capacity to reflect on the information that the various sense organs register, and to direct and control these experiences. We take this ability so much for granted that we seldom wonder about what it is, and yet, as far as we know, it is a recent accomplishment of evolution that only the human brain has achieved. If we ever think about it, we give it such names as awareness, consciousness, self, or soul. Without it, we could only obey instructions programmed in the nervous system by our genes. But having a self-reflective consciousness allows us to write our own programs for action, and make decisions for which no genetic instructions existed before.

The picture of the self we usually have is that of a homunculus, a tiny person sitting somewhere inside the brain who monitors what comes through the eyes, the ears, and the other senses, evaluates this information, and then pulls some levers that make us act in certain ways. We think of this miniature being as someone very sensitive and intelligent, the master of the machinery of the body. Those who conceive of it as the "soul" believe that it is the breath of God that transformed our common clay into a mortal envelope for the divine spark.

Contemporary neuroscience has a more prosaic view of what the self is and how it evolved. The brain does not seem to have a separate material structure or neurological function that accounts for the phenomenon of "self" or of "consciousness." The capacity for reflection emerged in response to the brain's millions of neuronal bundles, each evolved to perform a limited task, such as seeing color, keeping the body in balance, or detecting certain sounds. As the specialized and disconnected information provided by these neurons bounced around inside the brain, it eventually reached a level of complexity that made it necessary to have an internal traffic cop to direct and prioritize the flow of perceptions and sensations. At some point in the distant past humans succeeded in developing such a mechanism in the form of a consciousness. But the image of a traffic cop is also misleading, in that it again suggests a homunculus, a perfect little manikin—or womanikin—in charge inside the brain. Instead, consciousness is more like a magnetic field, an aura, or a harmonic tone resulting from the myriad separate sensations collecting in the brain.

Once self-reflective consciousness developed, however, the way the brain functions seems to have made an incredible quantum jump. It no longer experienced only separate needs, drives, sensations, and ideas competing for "air time" in awareness, to be admitted there strictly in terms of priorities established by means of inherited chemical instructions. Instead it also experienced the totality of these impulses as forming a distinct self, capable of taking charge of the domain of consciousness, and deciding which feelings or ideas should take precedence over the rest. Having had this experience of something inside us directing consciousness we gave it a name—the self—and took its reality for granted. And the self became an increasingly important part of human beings.

With time this internally created self appeared as real to us as the outside world glimpsed through the senses. Like air, it is always there; like the body, it has its limits. It is something that can get hurt, but it can also soar; it grows, and its powers slowly expand. Although every human brain is able to generate self-reflective consciousness, not everyone seems to use it equally. Some individuals follow the instructions of their genetic blueprint or the dictates of society almost exclusively, with little or no input from consciousness. At the other end of the spectrum are individuals who develop autonomous selves with goals that override external instructions, and live almost exclusively by self-generated rules. Most of us operate somewhere between these two extremes.

But once there is a self—even if it is little used—it begins to make its claims like any other organism. It wants to keep its shape, to reproduce itself somehow even after the body that carries it dies. The self, like other living beings, will use energy from its environment to stop entropy from destroying it. An animal without a conscious self only needs to reproduce the information in its genes. But a person with a self will want to keep and spread the information in his or her consciousness as well. A self identified with material possessions will drive its owner to accumulate more and more property, regardless of consequences for anyone else. The self of Stalin, built around the need for power, did not rest until everyone who might challenge his absolute rule was dead. If the self takes its form from a belief, the survival of that belief will mean more than even the survival of the body—the Christian martyrs felt more threatened by the consequences of compromising their faith than by lions.

It is for this reason that the fate of humanity in the next millennium depends so closely on the kind of selves we will succeed in creating. Evolution is by no means guaranteed. We have a chance of being part of it only as long as we understand our place in that gigantic field of force we call nature. Neither excessive humility nor truculent bombast will serve us well in the future. If the selves of our children and their children become too timid, too conservative and retiring, and try to stop change by retreating into a safe cocoon, eventually they will be overcome by more vital life-forms. On the other hand if we just forge ahead blindly, taking what we can from one another and from the world around us, there is not going to be much left to enjoy on the planet.

Whether life will continue on this world now depends on us. And whether we survive, and preserve a life worth living, depends on the kind of selves we are able to create, and on the social forms that we succeed in building. Certainly there are many momentous tasks looming ahead in these perilous times: from saving the rain forests to protecting the ozone layer, from reducing the number of births to keeping those already born from tearing each other to pieces. But no task is more essential in the long run than finding a way to develop selves that will support evolution. On this depend all the other positive consequences. If there is to be a history, our minds must be prepared to make it.

FURTHER THOUGHTS
ON "THE MIND AND HISTORY"

As a way of pursuing in greater depth the contents of this chapter, you might want to answer the questions that follow. Space is provided after each question for jotting down your thoughts. This procedure is followed in each chapter. And if you write out the answers in more detail in a separate notebook or enter them into a personal computer, you might start to create your own expanded version of this book, which can only suggest a beginning and needs your ideas to be completed.

Interconnectedness

Assuming you had no financial worries, can you think of anyplace where you could retire and hide from the problems of the world? Would you choose a well-armed survivalist camp, a secluded culture like that on Bali, or an isolated island in the Caribbean? And how happy do you think you would be there? Why?

In what aspect of your life are you completely self-sufficient? Assuming that you couldn't count on the cooperation of other people, could you provide yourself with food and water? Could you keep your car running? How much of the information one would need to survive do you actually have?

Evolution

These days almost half the people in the United States still believe that the universe was created about six thousand years ago. Assuming you do not, have you ever tried to visualize the length of U.S. history in comparison with the history of human life as most scientists conceive of it now, or with the history of the earth?

Is there any other age of human history you would rather have lived in instead of now? If yes, why?

Chance and Necessity

Considering your life as it has turned out until now, how much of an element of choice has there been in it? Did you decide personally which schools to attend? Were you able to attend the college of your choice? Did you choose your friends, your partner? Is the job you do a chosen vocation, or more or less an accident? In fact, is there *any* aspect of your life that is the result of a considered choice?

Which has determined more the course of your life, chance or necessity? How can you tell the difference between them? Does it make a difference which one is involved?

Freedom

In what aspect of your life do you feel most free: when you are alone, or with other people? When you work or when you have free time? Is the feeling of freedom due to the knowledge that you can do anything you want, or, on the contrary, to the knowledge that you are doing what you *must* do?

Do you feel the need to enlarge the amount of freedom in your life? Are there times on the job when you feel in a rut, when you are going through the motions without any personal control? How about your home life? What would it take to increase control over an area of life where now you feel control is lacking? What is standing in the way?

Good and Bad

What are the major sources of entropy in your life? What makes you most sad, irritated, or depressed? Whose fault is it?

Under what conditions do you feel the greatest serenity and happiness? Why are these occasions not more frequent?

Self

What is the central organizing principle of your self? Is it fame or fortune, is it the desire to be loved or to be feared, to be envied or to be thanked? What is it that you could not lose without losing your sense of self?

Given what you know about yourself, about what makes you happy, and about the freedoms and constraints of your life, what do you think you can contribute to the making of history? And what would be the consequences if you did nothing?

2

WHO CONTROLS
THE MIND?

In the last few generations it has become clear that the greatest threats to human survival will not be natural ones, but originate from inside ourselves. Not so long ago, a man could do harm only to himself and to those who were close to him. Even a century ago, the range of mischief did not extend much further around a person than the distance of a rifle shot. If a man was evil, or if he lost his mind, the scope of his misdeeds was severely limited. But for the last five decades the chances for a single person to do severe, widespread damage have been rapidly increasing. One demented general could start a war that ends the world, one lonely fanatic terrorist could wreak more havoc than the hordes of Genghis Khan. And just one generation of law-abiding citizens like you and me, through innocent, well-meaning choices, could end up poisoning the atmosphere, or making the planet unfit for life by some ingenious means. For our ancestors, understanding themselves better was a pleasant luxury. But nowadays learning to control the mind may have become a greater priority for survival than seeking any further advantages the hard sciences could bring.

To develop selves capable of dealing with the evolutionary forces rushing us into the third millennium, it is imperative to become better acquainted with the functioning of the mind. You can drive a car all your life without knowing how the engine works, because the goal of driving is to get from one place to the next, regardless of how it is done. But to live an entire life without understanding how we think, why we feel the way we feel, what directs our actions is to miss what is most important in life, which is the quality of experience itself. What ultimately counts most for each person is what happens in consciousness: the moments of joy, the times of despair added up through the years determine what life will be like. If we don't gain control over the contents of consciousness we can't live a fulfilling life, let alone contribute to a positive outcome of history. And the first step toward achieving control is understanding how the mind works.

There is no question that the brain-mind mechanism is one of the most splendid achievements of evolution. Unfortunately, despite its many amazing features, it has also developed several procedures that are less desirable. Every impressive evolutionary adaptation winds up blocking other possibilities: the bat has an exquisitely sensitive sonar but poor eyesight; the shark can't see well either but has a fantastic sense of smell. Our brain is a great computing machine, but it also places some dangerous obstacles in the way of apprehending reality truthfully. The first of these is the nervous system itself. The more that is known about how the mind works, the more we realize that the filter through which we experience the world has some peculiar built-in biases. If we do not understand how these biases work, thoughts and actions are never truly going to be under conscious control.

ETERNAL DISSATISFACTION

That something might be inherently wrong with the way the human mind functions has been suggested in many different ways in different historical periods, depending on the symbolic vocabulary of the age. For instance, Hsün Tzu, the third-century B.C. Confucian philosopher who left such a strong imprint on Chinese thought, based his teachings on the assumption that man is bad by nature. Only through strenuous self-discipline, through ritual, the right music, and worthy role models could individuals hope to be improved. Similarly, one of the central tenets of Christian theology is the doctrine of original sin. According to this belief, we are born corrupted. It is important to note the reason: According to the

Bible, it is because Adam and Eve disobeyed God's orders and ate of the fruit of the tree of knowledge. In other words, the evil at the root of the human condition was the desire to know more. The message seems to be that, if we had only accepted fate, as other animals do, without aspiring to reflective consciousness and free choice, we would still be living in harmony with the rest of creation in the Garden of Eden.

A somewhat similar vision of the human condition underlies the story of Goethe's *Faust*. Getting along in years, the scholar Faust is disillusioned with what he has accomplished in his life. He is tired of philosophy, he is disgusted at the weakness of the body, he snarls at the pursuit of fame, at money, at sex, leisure, wine, and song—he even despises hope and faith. Yet he admits that he feels "the pain of life, earth's narrow way. [He is] too old to be content with play, too young to be without desire." At this point the devil himself appears in the form of Mephistopheles and offers his services to Faust. He promises to fulfill his vague desires and to make him happy in exchange for his soul after death. Faust accepts the bargain, because he is certain not even the devil could make him appreciate what life has to offer. This is the pact he makes with Mephistopheles:

> *If your promises delude me*
> *so that I am contented,*
> *If I get to enjoy it*
> *let my life be ended.*
>
> *If I ever tell you,*
> *"Stop, this is just what I wanted."*
> *You may get your chains out*
> *and take me away forever.*

For a long time it seems that Faust has made a good bargain, because no matter how much wealth, honor, and power the devil provides, Faust always succeeds in finding it boring and meaningless. There is never a moment when he is tempted to say, "Stop, this is just what I wanted!" (Eventually poor Faust does meet his doom—but that part of the story is not relevant to ours.)

Goethe's hero has been traditionally interpreted as representing the psychology of modern or "Faustian" man. But the impulse that drives people ceaselessly to seek new experiences and possessions without ever finding fulfillment might be more longstanding and universal than we realize. In fact, it might be a wired-in function of the nervous system not only for humans but for lower animals as well. This is how the neurologist and anthropologist Melvin Konner expresses it:

> [T]he motivational portions of the brain, particularly the hypothalamus, have functional characteristics relevant to the apparent chronicity of human dissatisfaction. Animal experiments on the lateral hypothalamus suggest . . . that the organism's chronic internal state will be a vague mixture of anxiety and desire—best described perhaps by the phrase "I want," spoken with or without an object for the verb.

If this is true, such a mechanism would be very useful for the survival of the species, because it ensures that we will always be alert and on the lookout for new opportunities, trying to obtain more things, to control more energy—all of which should make us and our offspring more viable. But apparently the price we have to pay for this neat scheme is that, like Faust, we shall never rest contented with what we have achieved—or at least not until we recognize that evolution has set the mind on an endless treadmill.

In everyday life this Faustian dissatisfaction can be easily documented. There is no natural limit to desire. An unemployed person may think that if he made an income of thirty thousand a year he would be happy. But the person who does earn that sum thinks that if he could only make sixty thousand he would be happy, and the one who makes sixty thousand thinks a hundred thousand would satisfy his heart's desire. And so on endlessly. The same holds true for material possessions: the house one lives in is never impressive enough, the car one drives never new enough. Many studies have shown that escalating expectations are the rule in every society where there is a possibility of improving one's lot.

The mind seems to operate under the general instruction to be constantly alert to improving one's chances, because if it is not, someone else will surely take the advantage. The operating principle is that one must always strive for more just to stay even. This mind-set reflects the law of the jungle; a certain amount of built-in paranoia has apparently been useful, and perhaps indispensable, for survival. In many ways, the advance of civilization has consisted in creating small, protected areas of existence where competition and danger are minimized, where we can temporarily feel safe and relax our guard. Tribal dances, religious ceremonies, artistic perform- ances, games, sports, and leisure in general also provide some of these oases of peace. But some people can't even play golf without planning a takeover or worrying about the competition. Wouldn't it be ideal if one could be an ambitious perfectionist when it mat- tered, but then could relax in contented enjoyment? If we begin to understand how we have been programmed, we have at least some chance of overriding the genetic instructions when their demands become intolerable, and of exerting a certain amount of control over this ancient evolutionary force.

CHAOS AND CONSCIOUSNESS

It is generally assumed that, although we might be in control of nothing else, at least we direct what goes on in our minds. Even though most people have become reconciled to Freud's demonstra- tion that our reason is often under the sway of repressed desires, and even though we now know how vulnerable the nervous system is to the effects of drugs and physiological processes, we still tend to believe that we can think whatever we want, whenever we want to.

There is evidence, however, that thought processes are less or- derly than one would like to believe. In fact, it could be argued that chaos, not order, is the natural state of the mind. When no external stimulation engages attention—such as a conversation, a task that must be accomplished, a newspaper to be read, or a program on TV—thoughts begin to drift randomly. Instead of a pleasant, logical thread of mental experiences, disconnected ideas appear out of nowhere, and even if we make an effort to do so, it is impossible to return to a coherent line of thought for more than a few minutes.

One line of evidence for this statement comes from studies of stimulus deprivation. Individuals in solitary confinement—either in prison camps or in experimental deprivation tanks—where they are cut off from any meaningful pattern of sound, sight, or activity, soon begin to lose track of their thoughts, and describe having bizarre, uncontrolled fantasies and hallucinations. The mind needs ordered information to keep itself ordered. As long as it has clear goals and receives feedback, consciousness keeps humming along. This is why games, sports, and ceremonial rituals are some of the most satisfying activities—they keep attention ordered within narrow boundaries and clear rules. Even the experience of working at a job, which people often claim they hate, has these characteristics of order and continuity. When they are missing, chaos returns.

Another relevant finding is that in normal, everyday life, people report feeling most listless and dissatisfied when they are alone with nothing to do. Paradoxically it is when we are ostensibly most free, when we can do anything we want to, that we are least able to act. In these situations the mind tends to drift, and sooner or later it hits on some painful thought or unfulfilled desire. Most of us are unable, in such circumstances, to just pull ourselves up and think instead about something useful or cheerful. For many people in Western society the worst part of the week is Sunday morning between ten and noon. For those who don't go to church regularly it is the least structured part of the week, with no external demands to be met, no habits to channel attention toward some goal. One has breakfast, reads the Sunday papers, and then what? By noon most people make a decision; they will watch a game on TV, go out for a drive, paint the back porch. The decision gives the mind a new direction, and unpleasant thoughts that have arisen recede again below the threshold of awareness.

Ironically, most people who work experience a more enjoyable state of mind on the job than at home. At work it is usually clear what needs to be done, and there is clear information about how well one is doing. Yet few people would willingly work more and have less free, leisure time. Those who do are pitied as "workaholics." Generally unnoticed is the fact that the work we want to avoid is actually more satisfying than the free time we try to get more of.

There is a reasonable evolutionary explanation for this condition, too. If we could be contented just sitting by ourselves and thinking pleasant thoughts, who would be out chasing the saber-toothed tiger? Or driving two hours on the congested expressway to work? It is probably better that we need ordered external input to keep the mind in order; this way we ensure some congruence between objective and subjective reality. If we could dream up satisfying fantasies regardless of what happened outside our head, we would run into trouble. If imagining having sex felt as good as the real thing, we would soon cease having children. So the fact that the mind experiences unpleasant disorder when not engaged in goal-directed action is an important safety feature.

Again, however, it is one thing to recognize the wisdom of such a development for the continued well-being of the species, and another to accept its personal consequences. After all, if we aim at controlling consciousness, we should be able to function at least somewhat independently of external stimulation. Is there some way to free ourselves from the intrusion of this evolutionary safety device?

There are two ways of avoiding the random drift of consciousness that is usually experienced as a painful sensation of either anxiety or boredom. One is to impose order on the mind from the outside. By getting involved in a task, or by talking with another person, or even by following a TV program, we structure our attention and can follow a more or less linear pattern. The other way to achieve order is to develop an internal discipline that makes it possible to concentrate at will. This is much more difficult, and it takes meditators, yogis, artists, and scholars many years to learn how to do it. In either case, the mind is not going to fall into ordered and enjoyable patterns of experience unless one spends energy to give consciousness shape. There are innumerable ways of achieving this goal, but all of them involve developing personally chosen habits. These could involve training the body through jogging, yoga, or martial arts; developing hobbies like woodworking, painting, or playing a musical instrument; or taking up focused mental activities like reading the Bible, doing mathematics, or writing poetry. Any purposeful activity that requires skills will prevent disorder from taking hold of the mind, and forcing it into frenetic escape.

WHY IS HAPPINESS SO ELUSIVE?

There is another bias built into the way the mind works that makes it difficult to find contentment. We saw before that when attention is not occupied by a specific task, like a job or a conversation, thoughts begin to wander in random circles. But in this case "random" does not mean that there is an equal chance of having happy and sad thoughts. What happens instead is that the majority of thoughts that come to the mind when we are not concentrating are likely to be depressing. The reasons for this are twofold.

In the first place, considering all the possible things to think about, the negative possibilities always outnumber the positive ones. There are just more "bad" things in our lives than "good" ones, simply because the kinds of outcomes we define as "good" are generally rare and unlikely. For instance, if I think about my health, there is one positive scenario—good health—and hundreds of negative ones, represented by various diseases. If my mind wanders, chances are that it will light on one of the numerous negative outcomes. If I am moving into a new house, there is a chance that everything in it will be in order. But there are hundreds of things that could go wrong: the roof might leak, the plumbing might not work, the wiring might be faulty, and so on.

It is also important to note that, other things being equal, the higher the goals, the higher the probability of disappointment. As one raises one's expectations, the probability of success gets automatically smaller. Which is easier to achieve for the average overweight man, a weight of 180 or 200 pounds? If my goal is to stay at 180, I am more likely to get depressed when thinking about my weight than if I aim for 200. If my ambition is to earn a quarter million dollars a year, the possibility of being unhappy with my income will be greater than if I aim for half as much. Thus one of the simplest ways to decrease the frequency of negative thoughts is by selectively moderating expectations. This is not to say that high ambitions necessarily produce unhappiness. But we often carry so many high expectations in so many areas of life that disappointment is a forgone conclusion.

The second reason that the freely roaming mind usually attends to negative thoughts is that such a pessimistic bias might be adaptive—if by "adaptation" we mean an increased likelihood of survival. The mind turns to negative possibilities as a compass needle turns to the magnetic pole, because this is the best way, on the average, to anticipate dangerous situations. Positive outcomes are gratifying, but they will take care of themselves, so we don't need to allocate scarce psychic energy to their contemplation. By dwelling on unpleasant possibilities, however, we will be better prepared for the unexpected.

The bias toward negative outcomes is well illustrated by the attraction that any kind of disaster has for most people. A traffic accident, a fire, a street fight will immediately draw a crowd of avid spectators. Attention is attracted to violence and danger, whereas it skips over the normal, the peaceful, the contented. The media are very aware of this propensity, so newspaper stories are filled with atrocities, and television shows revel in gore. As a result, the average child is estimated to witness over seventy thousand murders on television before he or she grows up. What the long-term consequences of such a visual diet are going to be remains to be seen.

When the mind dwells on something negative, it creates conflict in consciousness. This conflict—or psychic entropy—is experienced as negative affect. Feeling a bald spot on my head causes me to think about all the unpleasant consequences of getting old, and it makes me feel depressed. Or my mind may drift to office politics and the way certain colleagues are trying to advance their careers at my expense; this makes me angry and apprehensive. Or I might idly wonder why my wife isn't home yet, and this makes me feel jealous and worried. Depression, anger, fear, and jealousy are simply different manifestations of psychic entropy. In all cases, what happens is that attention turns to information that conflicts with goals; the discrepancy between what I desire and what is actually happening creates the inner tension.

Negative emotions are not necessarily bad. Many great paintings were created, many great books were written, in order to escape depression. Anger has led revolutionaries to build more just social institutions. The fear of lightning led to the invention of the lightning rod. But while negative feelings last, they take over consciousness and make it difficult to control thought and action. Moreover, the subjective experiences of fear, anger, and so on are unpleasant; thus the more often we have them, the more miserable life becomes.

The species mind is not only Faustian in its discontent, but almost Victorian in its prurient fascination with the downside of life. Because of this, if we let our individual consciousness be directed by genetic instructions that have been advantageous in the past, the quality of our life is likely to suffer in the present. Those who always worry about what can go wrong might be well prepared against dangers, but will never know how enjoyable life can be. The best strategy involves finding a balance between what's good for us in general and what's good for us as unique individuals living in the here and now. We cannot reject the genetic instructions for para-noia; at the same time we cannot follow them blindly, or we will miss what makes our particular life meaningful.

THE LIMITS OF REASON

For as far back as we know (which isn't very far), people have tried to figure out the meaning of their inner lives. Thoughts and feelings are mysterious things. Where do they come from? Are they real? Where do they go? The Greeks believed that feelings and thoughts originated in the chest, the Hindus located them at different centers along the spinal cord, and the Chinese held that we think with the heart. To explain why there is consciousness, some cultures be-lieved that the spirits of dead ancestors spoke from within the living, others considered it the voice of gods or demons.

It took a long while for people to conceive of the mind as something separate from the body, and to realize that mental pro-cesses could be controlled. The general attitude seems to have been that thinking is something that happens spontaneously, like breath-ing or sweating. Mental life was thought to be part of the holistic functioning of the body, no more under our control than digestion. The Roman saying *Mens sana in corpore sano,* or a sound mind in a sound body, is a reflection of the belief that thinking is inseparable from physical functions. The harmony between mental and physical activity was particularly stressed in Eastern cultures, where the split between body and mind was never as great as it became in the West. The yoga emphasis on the right diet, the right body posture, and correct breathing, all of which are believed to affect the content of thoughts, emotions, and the ability to concentrate, is just one exam-ple.

But by the time the Greek philosophers began their systematic investigations into the nature of being, it was already clear that thought processes followed their own rules, and could be shaped and directed at will. With the right mental training, a blind poet could write the most glorious verse, and a lame philosopher could conceive the most brilliant thoughts. In the wake of these philosophers, the mind was quickly perceived to be more important than its physical container. When St. Francis taught in the thirteenth century, he referred to the body as "brother ass," the envelope of flesh and bones that laboriously carried the mind on its journey (and of course, also the soul—but that's a slightly different story).

The high point for this dichotomy was reached in the seventeenth century, after René Descartes's relentless analysis of mental processes. Descartes believed that the rational stream of thought could proceed independently of anything else—of the body and its needs, of previous learning, cultural values, even self-interest. He demonstrated the feasibility of his claim by spending years in a drafty peasant cottage on a gloomy beach in Holland, during which time he formulated a prodigious number of elegant theories, ranging from optics to calculus to the first systematic forays into epistemology. For a while the rules Descartes developed were tremendously liberating, because they promised that if we just sat and thought things through, every human being could arrive at the same truths.

Unfortunately, it soon became obvious that the brain is not insulated from the rest of the body, and that it does not function merely as a logical-geometrical machine for performing deductive operations. This conclusion was prompted in part by the continuing evidence of irrational human cussedness, in the shape of senseless wars, onerous dictatorships, pointless revolutions, and the abundance of other forms of seemingly irrational behavior. It was given conceptual form by the writings of Sigmund Freud, who showed that the thoughts and actions of supposedly serious and sane individuals were ruled by repressed memories of childhood events. When I disagree with my boss about his proposal for a sales campaign, for instance, I might be using market projections and demographic trends in very logical ways, but the real reason for my objecting is that the boss reawakens in me the hostility I felt for my father. The numbers I use in my argument are simply rationalizations, and could just as easily be interpreted to make the opposite point if I felt differently about my boss. So much for the autonomy of rational processes.

Another attack on the pure independence of thought came from Marxism. This doctrine emphasizes the role of material self-interest in shaping our supposedly rational arguments. It claims that medieval philosophers could not separate their ideas from the interests of the Church that supported them; that scientists and philosophers of the Enlightenment were propounding ideas that were congenial to a mercantile class; and that nineteenth-century thinkers did not just follow the voice of reason but were influenced by the needs of the capitalist ruling classes. And, presumably, Marxist scholars let their own thinking be shaped by the demands of Communist bureaucrats. What seems like rational argument, according to this perspective, is usually a disguised ideology—an attempt to transform selfish needs into universally valid truths.

And no sooner has Marxism lost some of its former widespread intellectual appeal than new assaults on reason have sprung from the fertile soils of Europe. In the past few decades deconstructionism and postmodernism have taken on the task of debunking reason where Freud and Marx left off. Deconstructionism is the latest form of a perspective that has emerged at regular intervals throughout history, according to which there is no way of knowing anything beyond direct experience itself. If I try to tell you about the sufferings of my childhood, the words I use will bring a first level of distortion into the tale, and your interpretation of my words will distort the story even further. Neither logic nor scientific discourse can avoid mystifying through their attempts at communication. There is no way to get at reality through words, all generalizations are suspect, and the sharing of meanings between minds is an illusion.

Of course the rationalists have not surrendered. Undeterred by the often childishly romantic exaggerations of those who deny the validity of any claims to objective knowledge, they go their merry way assuming that there is order in the universe, and that the mind is equipped to recognize it. In their efforts at unequivocal truth, the rationalists sometimes succumb to the tendency of simplifying consciousness into a caricature of itself. The current followers of the Cartesian approach are the cognitive scientists who believe that by

studying how computers work they will discover how we think.
The similarities are often instructive, but by believing that computers are like mirrors in which we can see reflected the workings of
the mind, many cognitive scientists have come to mistake that
reflection for reality.

If we consider all that we have learned in this last century, it seems
fair to say that Descartes was right in believing that the mind can
follow universal rational principles, but (and it's a huge but) only as
long as universal rational principles are followed. If this sounds
tautological, it is not by accident. We think like computers whenever we think like computers. But certainly this particular function
represents only a small aspect of how we think. Every normal person
can learn the rules of chess—provided he or she wants to—and
when playing chess can appear to behave as rationally as any autom-
aton. Logic, however, is only a small part of what takes place in the
consciousness of a human chess player. There is also sensory pleasure
in handling the well-turned pieces; there is a relief at escaping from
the burdens of the real world into a manageable, self-contained
activity; there is the excitement of beating an opponent; and there
is joy in being able to meet a difficult challenge. All of these feelings
are present in the mind when playing chess, and without them who
would bother following the logical rules? The computer, in contrast, has no choice about whether to play or not.

It is a logical fallacy to conclude, as Herbert Simon and other
prophets of the new cognitive sciences do, that if they program a
computer so that it will derive a scientific discovery such as Newton's laws of motion, this means that the computer operates just as
Newton's mind must have when he came up with those laws. We
can be sure that when Newton wrote down his laws his consciousness contained at least as many nonrational elements as a chess
player's, and that these feelings and intuitions were more important
than logic in the genesis of his discovery. That a computer will
obtain Newton's results in a few seconds (provided it is fed prese-
lected information and the right rules—all of which assumes previous knowledge, and therefore is not at all comparable to the original
situation) is no more surprising than the fact that anyone can shoot
in a few seconds a photographic replica of the Sistine frescoes that
took Michelangelo a dozen years to paint. Yet it would be difficult

to argue that by understanding how the camera works we can understand how Michelangelo thought.

Rational thought works well within the boundaries of rational "games" such as chess, geometry, or calculus, all of which have clear rules and limited assumptions. A war game can be played out logically in a strategy room, much less so on a field of battle. Economists are very clever at modeling economic behavior according to all sorts of assumptions—but it is foolish to expect to find those behaviors functioning predictably in reality, where the assumptions don't hold. It is easy for priests to follow religious rules in the nicely ordered church rituals, but it is very difficult for them to do so in the complexity of private life. Baseball players behave in predictable and orderly ways during a game, but if you took away the umpires, their behavior would soon degenerate.

It is good to have rational, logical structures by which to order thoughts and actions. Much of what we call civilization consists of attempts at rationalizing life, so that actions can be predictable and reasonable. But civilization is a fragile construction that needs constant protection and care. Without it, the mind will not behave logically. And there is no guarantee that evolutionary pressures by themselves will produce increasingly rational behavior. For instance, it could be argued that war used to be more rational in the past, when armies fought primarily to impress rather than to annihilate each other, campaigns stopped to allow crops to be harvested, battles ended at sunset, and civilian casualties were considered bad form. Economic behavior, likewise, seems to have been more rational in the past, when acquiring property was not the only goal that motivated people to act. If we want more rational behavior, we cannot expect it to happen by itself; we must invest psychic energy in creating and preserving ordered systems of rules.

But suppose we could reduce all choices to the binary logic of the computer, and somehow find a way to abide by a perfectly rational program of action, binding on each member of society. Would that ensure a rosy future? That, too, is unlikely. Reason works best in closed systems where there are accepted rules, and outcomes can be predicted in advance. Building an engine or a bridge to specifications, playing chess or baseball, or solving a problem that has a standard solution are activities that lend themselves to the analytic steps of the mind.

The future, however, is not constrained by rules and predictable outcomes. We need to cultivate more than logic if we want to thrive in it. We must foster intuition to anticipate changes before they occur; empathy to understand that which cannot be clearly expressed; wisdom to see the connection between apparently unrelated events; and creativity to discover new ways of defining problems, new rules that will make it possible to adapt to the unexpected.

Logic can be programmed into a computer because its rules do not change easily with time. But human evolution cannot be tied to strict rules. It must remain flexible so as to seize whatever opportunities are presented in the kaleidoscopic landscape of its environment. Intuition, empathy, wisdom, and creativity are themselves part of the human evolutionary process—they change with time as events, and our understanding of them, change. If we programmed these qualities into a computer, they would become obsolete almost immediately because with each generation the conditions that affect human consciousness change in subtle but important ways. For example, attitudes toward women that a few decades ago were perfectly acceptable may now seem blatantly sexist. This change was not logically preordained, but has been the result of many discrete human experiences. The computer would not know how to rewrite its programs because it takes a mind dependent on a body, as it lives in a unique historical and cultural milieu, to figure out how to compute that which is not yet rational.

THE ADDICTION TO PLEASURE

If excessive rationality is dangerous, so is an excessive confidence in the wisdom of the body. Our ancestors have switched time and time again from trusting their minds to trusting their senses, first embracing Apollo, then Dionysus. The sociologist Pitirim Sorokin has described these changes in worldview in his researches on the history of culture, which he saw as alternating between *ideational,* or value-ruled, phases, and *sensate,* or pleasure-ruled, phases. In our own era we have witnessed one transition, which started during the

Belle Époque at the turn of the century, picked up momentum after World War I, accelerated after World War II, and reached its peak in the late 1960s. The current sensate phase is characterized by an increasing legitimation of materialism (people were probably just as much materially oriented before, but few cared to admit it openly), a gradual rejection of behavioral repressions and moral codes that are seen as hypocritical and benighted, a loss of faith in permanent values, a narcissistic self-centeredness, and an unabashed search for sensory satisfaction.

One popular formulation of this worldview has been the "Play-boy philosophy" inspired by Hugh Hefner, the midwestern publisher of the first widely distributed magazine of the new sensate age. It found responsive chords in the many sects, therapies, and lifestyles that have sprouted on the West Coast during the last two generations and that extol the limitless reach of human potentials. The basic message of this movement is that we should do what feels good, because the body knows best. Any attempt to interfere with pleasure is suspect, part of a conspiracy to make our lives more miserable.

This thesis would not have made much difference as long as it remained a "philosophy," except that it coincided with a historical period during which many of its tenets could actually be implemented. Material affluence kept lurching forward. Cars, contraceptives, hot tubs, and a plethora of conveniences made it possible for many people to feel that they could indeed satisfy every whim without fear of consequences.

As it turns out, however, there is ample evidence suggesting that our body does not know what is good for it. The increasing number of drug addicts, alcoholics, victims of sexual diseases, unwanted pregnancies, and overeaters demonstrates that doing what feels good can easily lead to feeling very bad indeed. Rats who have a choice between eating and stimulating electrically the pleasure centers of their brains will choose the stimulation and die of hunger. Monkeys addicted to heroin will work till they die of exhaustion to get another fix. Similar behavior on the streets of our cities shows how easily the brain succumbs to pleasure.

Pleasure, according to current understandings of evolution, is an experience felt when one does something that in the past had been useful for survival. It is the result of a chemical stimulation of the appropriate neural receptors, usually by substances that the organism has needed for optimal functioning. For instance, when our very distant ancestors lived in the sea, their bodies became adapted to a salty environment. Although the human race has been terrestrial for many millions of years, it still needs a constant supply of salt to replenish the physiological balance of the body, maintain the internal water metabolism, and keep up the electric potential across cell membranes that is necessary for the heart to pump blood. With time, the taste of salt has become pleasurable, a lucky adaptation that ensured that we would seek it out and consume the necessary amount.

This was fine in past environments where salt was scarce. Traders took chunks of it over enormous distances and exchanged it for ivory and precious metals; wars were waged to get more of it; salt mines were among the most prized possessions of the early empires. Because it was so expensive, it was difficult to overdose on it. The pleasure of salty taste was neatly balanced by its scarcity. But as our ancestors learned to extract and concentrate salt more efficiently, it became more readily available and therefore cheaper. Now one bag of potato chips can provide more salt than diets of the past contained in many days. Salt still tastes good, but now we consume far too much of it and endanger our health in the process.

The same pattern holds true for fats, sugar, alcohol, and other substances that can easily become addictive. Because at one time they were good for us, we learned to enjoy them. But after the advent of culture, conditions started changing more and more rapidly, and the pleasure centers in the brain did not have the time to adapt. In just one 40-year period after 1860, the total world production of sugar increased by 500 percent. And by 1990 there were about 17.7 million Americans with alcohol problems, and 9.5 million chronic users of illicit drugs. Our genes did not have the time to learn that too much salt, sugar, cocaine, or alcohol is unhealthy. Because they never had to worry about the presence of too much of these substances before, no defenses had been built up against excess. As a consequence, pleasure became a misleading guide to behavior.

What is true for chemical substances is also true for behaviors that are pleasurable because they help survival, but can become dangerous if they are overindulged. The anthropologist Lionel Tiger argues that sex, the exercise of dominance and power, and social interaction are all pleasurable because they aided survival in the past. For instance, a solitary Stone Age person would have had trouble finding a mate with whom to procreate, and would have soon been eaten up by the big cats roaming the savannah. Only those individuals who felt pleasure in the company of the group, and never strayed far from other people, survived. Thus we all descended from extroverted ancestors—the survivors—and our brains are wired to experience pleasure when being with others. But sociability, like other useful adaptive behaviors, can in our own time be easily overdone and then become unhealthy.

Evolution has apparently provided us with an efficient mechanism to make us do what is good for us—the experience of pleasure. But to save effort (and evolution is always about saving effort, because entropy is so powerful and energy is so difficult to obtain), it did not provide a complementary mechanism for sensing a golden mean and avoiding excess. As Tiger says, paraphrasing the historian Santayana, "Those who do not learn from prehistory are condemned to repeat its successes." The brain won't tell us when enough is enough.

The only way to avoid becoming dangerously dependent on pleasure is to use the mind. Only through conscious reflection can we determine how much of what seems good is actually good for us, and then adopt a discipline that makes it possible to stop at the threshold. This is precisely what religions have tried to do: provide cultural instructions for holding to the golden mean. For example, Christianity, Islam, and Buddhism, three of the oldest and most widespread faiths, all advocate very strongly the moderation of unchecked appetites. The seven deadly sins of Christianity warn against indulging in excessive pride, too many material possessions, inordinate sex, too much food and drink, anger, and laziness. Similarly the Four Noble Truths of Buddhism state that (1) suffering is an essential part of existence, (2) the cause of suffering is desire for sensory pleasure, (3) release from suffering involves the elimination of desire, and (4) elimination of desire is achieved by following the Noble Eightfold Path—which in turn is a system of self-discipline whereby one learns to control the boundless cravings of the body. Religions, however, may no longer be able to impose the necessary limitations, so until credible new cultural instructions are discovered, each of us is left to find the golden mean that will prevent pleasure from taking over our lives.

STRESS, STRAIN, AND HORMONES

Because of its susceptibility to pleasure, the body has been held in suspicion by most religions and philosophies since antiquity. In opposition to the blind desires of the body, salvation has often been sought in the rational processes of thought. But getting the body to listen to reason has never been easy. Two extreme views have developed about the mind-body, or mind-brain, relationship. One is the currently orthodox view that thoughts and feelings are caused directly by electrochemical or hormonal events in the brain; thus phenomenology is an epiphenomenon of neurophysiology. In other words, what we feel and think is strictly the consequence of physiological processes over which we have little or no control. Then there is a position 180 degrees removed, held by stalwart Scientologists and such, which claims that the mind is entirely independent of its biological hardware. Not only that, but it can even directly affect physical phenomena outside the body; it can make dollars appear in a bank account, remove cancers, lift buildings in the air, and so forth. The truth, as always, is a bit more complex, and lies somewhere between these extreme positions.

Clearly anything the mind experiences must be based on neurophysiological processes in the brain. The question is whether the interpretation of these experiences in consciousness can in turn affect the underlying chemical networks. Several scientists believe this to be the case. For example, Roger Sperry, who won the Nobel Prize in 1981 for his discoveries with split-brain patients and who pioneered hemispheric lateralization studies, believes that although consciousness is generated by the electrochemical properties of the brain, in certain important respects it becomes independent of its origins, and can in turn influence further thoughts and actions. Thus events in the mind can become causes in their own right.

One form of this mutual interaction that has been much studied is the case of stress. Stress can be measured in terms of a variety of physiological changes, ranging from the release of adrenaline, sweating of the palms, dilating of the pupils, accelerated heartbeat, increased blood pressure, and so forth. These changes have a positive adaptive value in that they prepare the body to fight or flee an external threat. But excessive or prolonged stress can be harmful because it throws the internal balance of the body off. Stress increases when we meet external stressors like a strange man in a dark alley, a deadline on the job, or a lump in the armpit. The standard argument connecting these facts goes something like this: An external stressor causes the physiological stress reaction, which in turn—if excessive—causes physical impairment. The practical lesson some people derive from such a conclusion is that to stay healthy they have to remove external stressors, whether it is the job, the wife, or the car that doesn't work.

However, the amount of stress one experiences does not depend on the stressors alone. There are many ways in which control of consciousness can help mitigate the effects of external causes. It is well known, for instance, that the stress reaction often does not set in until after the danger has passed. Helicopter gunners in Vietnam showed no physiological signs of stress during their missions, when their lives were in constant jeopardy; when the chopper landed back at the base, however, their hormones started flowing. This occurred because, when the danger was present, the soldiers were able to block it out temporarily; as soon as they returned to the base, the realization that they could have been killed was allowed back in consciousness, and it hit them with a vengeance. While an immediate stress response might have been useful to ancient warriors fighting with sword and spear, the modern warrior sitting in a high-tech cockpit is probably safer inhibiting the flow of adrenaline till later— the unchecked hormonal reaction might easily lead to a crash.

How we interpret threat also determines the severity of the stress reaction. Highly neurotic persons, or those prone to depression, typically see events more negatively, and react more strongly to stressors that would bother others much less. It is true that a person might get more easily depressed because of genetic predisposition, but it is also true that one can learn to modulate one's interpretations of events. The lesson from this conclusion is that to stay healthy one need not change the external stressors—just one's mind.

If adrenaline is one of the hormones that plays a major role in stress, testosterone is the one most implicated in the dominance behaviors traditionally associated with masculinity—preening, boasting, swaggering, becoming aggressive, and starting fights. It seems that this chemical was developed through evolution to ensure that men—who have a larger dose of it than women—will protect their offspring and territory from all comers. It has been reported that in primate groups the most dominant males tend to have the highest levels of testosterone, and the meekest individuals the lowest levels. One might extrapolate from this observation that testosterone has something to do with the establishment of social hierarchy and stratification.

It is also easy to jump to the conclusion that testosterone *causes* dominance and masculine behavior. While this is probably true in part, the opposite also appears to be true—in other words, behavior and experience modify physiology. If one removes a meek monkey from the bottom of the male pecking order of his group and puts him with a group of female monkeys, he becomes more assertive, and the level of testosterone in his body increases. Conversely, if a dominant monkey with a high testosterone level is taken away from his companions and placed in a different group with an already established, strong dominance structure, the immigrant male will have to take a position on the lower rungs of the hierarchy, and as a consequence his testosterone level will decline. Clearly, dominance is not simply a reflection of hormonal level: the effects of the environment and one's view of one's hierarchical position are also involved in a complex circular causation.

It should be added that dominance hierarchies in primates are not formed by the most macho males beating everyone else into submission. Usually the contrary is true: it is by backing off from confrontation that the meeker animals allow the more assertive ones to achieve their position of dominance. What are the implications of this tendency for human evolution? With us, too, genes and hormones affect temperament, and temperament is an important factor in determining social status. In some organizations like the Marines, railroad companies, the AFL-CIO, or General Motors, a high level of assertiveness probably helps advancement—but mostly because the extroverted, assertive types are deferred to by the less pushy ones. And once power differentials are established, the behavior, the thought processes, and presumably the hormonal levels that are typical for different positions reinforce the assertiveness of the dominant, and the submissiveness of the subordinate.

This pattern, however, is not inevitable. By changing the values and rules of an organization people with a different makeup could also get respect and power—and this, in turn, is likely to have physiological consequences. To a certain extent this is already happening as a result of affirmative-action programs that have placed increasing numbers of women in leadership positions. Even GM and Conrail are realizing that the principles of organization that suit a baboon troop might not be the most efficient ones for running a complex corporation.

If testosterone and other chemicals prime males for the kind of kinetic and assertive behavior that evolution has selected out as adaptive for one-half of the species, estrogen is involved in regulating the behavior of the other half. During most of evolutionary history, gender specialization was simple: men had to produce, women reproduce. Production involved mainly hunting and defense, and males acquired the hormones to facilitate those tasks. Reproduction involved having strong, healthy babies that would grow to maturity, and females developed the hormones for it. Whereas male hormones are triggered when an external threat or confrontation requires a quick and forceful response, the female ones follow an internal rhythm tied to the reproductive cycle. The release of androgens and estrogen, which help females to be receptive to males, also make them critical and selective to ensure the best match for their own genes. After conception had taken place (we are talking here of the millions of years during which adult females were almost invariably pregnant), hormones helped predispose the future mother toward protective nurturant behavior.

Just as the effect of male hormones is not always adaptive to the contemporary social environment, so is the effect of female hormones sometimes problematic. Women's reproductive cycles are still operative, but in technological societies, where most women conceive only once or twice in a lifetime, they have lost much of their function. Until recently women had to start as many babies as possible just to have one or two who survived. Two hundred and fifty years ago, the mother of Louis XVI had eleven miscarriages and eight live births during the fourteen years of her marriage; of her five sons, only one survived. This was by no means an unusual situation during the millions of years of human evolution. Today, lower infant mortality rates have made the monthly preparation for pregnancy serve very little purpose. Just as men's testosterone-induced feistiness can be embarrassingly out of place in a boardroom or a laboratory, the behavioral changes induced by the menstrual cycle in women can seem willful and arbitrary.

We meet again one of the central paradoxes of evolution: the adaptive skills of the past, which have made it possible for us to exist in the first place, do not necessarily make life easier or happier now. Macho hunter types find fewer and fewer niches in the modern economy, and many of them may become bitter outcasts from the system. Too much testosterone today is more likely to result in criminality rather than leadership. Similarly, earth-mother types will suffer from frustrated fertility in an overpopulated world. To the extent that all of us are programmed to be hunters or mothers, we must all somehow come to terms with this awkward heritage.

It is fashionable these days to try to deny our evolutionary heritage. Now that men don't go out hunting every morning, the argument goes, they don't need to be any more assertive than women. Or, given that we have decided that all men are created equal, we no longer need dominant individuals. On the one hand, feminists try to erase the evolutionary past by insisting that women can—and should—be as aggressive and dominant as males. On the other hand, some men attempt to develop nurturing behaviors and approach the traditional feminine ideal.

But it's wishful thinking to believe that the instructions deposited in our genes through the ages by natural selection can simply be altered in a few generations by good intentions alone. Many parents must have had an experience similar to that of one of my colleagues at the University of Chicago, a neuroscientist who had two children, a boy and a girl, in the late sixties. Convinced that sex-typed behavior was the result of culturally stereotyped child-rearing practices, she did her best to bring up both babies the same way. Being a successful professional, the mother expected that she would be a good role model for her children. Both infants were handled medium-roughly, talked to in the same tones, dressed in similar clothes. At the appropriate time both children were given trucks and dolls to play with. Yet, no matter how hard she tried to instill non-sex-specific behavior, the boy kept pushing aside the dolls and the girl delicately ignored the trucks. She now ruefully concedes that the son has turned into an outgoing, aggressive young man and the daughter into a seductive, sensitive charmer.

Trying to deny the bred-in-the-bone differences between people is one of the silliest conceits of our times. Pretending that we can be anything we want to be without taking into account how physiology controls the mind is not only useless but dangerous, because it only breeds disillusion, hypocrisy, and finally cynicism. It is not surprising, for instance, that in the last few years there has developed a "men's movement" in dialectical opposition to the 1960s attempts to ignore the facts about masculine biology and its psychological consequences. Even though some of the manifestations of this movement are equally silly in their reactionary earnestness—dancing naked in a forest clearing to the beat of drums is not a very original solution to yuppie alienation—the need they point to is not trivial. Certain basic drives cannot be eradicated, and if they are not satisfied in a meaningful, creative way, they will clamor for satisfaction regardless.

On the other hand, it is essential to realize that "human nature" is the result of accidental adaptations to environmental conditions long since gone. Our genetic programming is inevitably bound to give us distorted views of reality now that the external conditions have changed. Only by transcending the limitations of physiology, and not letting testosterone or estrogen determine entirely the way we act and think, will we free ourselves from the tyranny of the past. But to do so requires patience, good will, and, above all else, a more thorough understanding of the way the mind works.

FURTHER THOUGHTS
ON "WHO CONTROLS THE MIND?"

Eternal Dissatisfaction

In what area of life do you feel the greatest discontent? Looks, money, relationships? Let's suppose you have achieved what you wished for; if you wanted to be rich, imagine you are now a multimillionaire. Do you think you would be happy? Is there anything else you would still want then? How many of the rich people you know or have heard about seem happy and contented?

Do you have to keep striving to achieve more in order to be happy? Or does the pursuit of ambitions interfere with your present chances to be happy?

Chaos and Consciousness

Does disorder in consciousness ever bother you? Do you spend time ruminating about problems, feeling sorry for yourself? If and when this happens, what do you usually do? Do you turn to entertainment, to chemical mood-lifters, or do you get involved with some activity, like work or playing golf? What works for you?

How well can you control your attention? Do you need pills to fall asleep and stay awake? Does having a TV or a radio in the background help keep your mind on track? Do you have a system for focusing your mind when reflection is needed—such as writing in a diary, making lists, or meditating?

Elusive Happiness

Do you sometimes feel happy for no reason at all, or only when everything is going your way? Can a grand view, a beautiful tune, someone else's good luck make you happy, or is happiness limited to the satisfaction of your personal goals?

What do you usually do when something you hoped for does not turn out? Do you tend to feel bitter and stew in disappointment, or does it spur you to do something about it?

The Limits of Reason

When you try to argue a point logically, to what extent do you think that your reasoning is influenced by self-interest? Think of the last discussion you had with your partner, or co-worker. Did your personal comfort, or hopes for advancement, or just the need to be right, have anything to do with the arguments you advanced? Is there any situation in which your logic is completely objective?

If you made a list of all the things you know for certain under four headings: (1) those things that you know from direct experience, (2) those that logically follow from self-evident truths, (3) those that you believe because you were told, (4) those you "just know" because of an intuitive gut-level feeling, which one of the headings would have the longest list?

The Addiction to Pleasure

To which pleasures are you addicted: sugar, alcohol, opiates, the endorphins produced when working out, or television? What are the consequences of this addiction, both pro and con? What would it take to become free of it, and how would it feel? What could you choose to take the place of the former addiction?

Stress, Strain, and Hormones

Can you recognize when your body interferes with control over consciousness—e.g., when being hungry makes you nervous and snappy? Have you developed ways of regaining control?

Do you feel that if your body tells you that something is good or bad, then it must be so? If, for instance, you feel a surge of anger at someone who cuts in front of you in a line, do you feel you should act out the anger? Or if you are sexually attracted to someone, you should try to have sex, regardless of prior attachments?

3

THE VEILS
OF MAYA

The brain is a wonderful mechanism, but it is also deceptive. To guarantee that we don't relax too much, it forces us to strive after forever receding goals. To keep us from settling for daydreams, it begins to project unpleasant information on the screen of consciousness as soon as we stop doing something purposeful. It makes us feel good when we do things that in the past have served survival, but it can't tell us when pleasure trespasses the threshold of danger. Whether we like it or not, it primes us for actions that made sense when people lived in caves, but are now out of place. These are some of the biases built into the machinery of the brain, and in order to gain control of consciousness we must learn how to moderate their influence. But they are not the only obstacles that stand in the way of freeing the self. We normally allow a whole series of illusions to stand between ourselves and reality. Built out of genetic instructions, cultural rules, and the unbridled desires of the self, these distortions are comforting, yet they need to be seen through for the self to be truly liberated.

ILLUSION AND REALITY

A recurring theme in many cultures has been that reality as it appears to us is a deceptive illusion. What we see, think, and believe are not the true outlines of the world. Reality presents itself through a series of veils that distort what lies behind them. Most people look at the illusory veils and are convinced they see the truth, but actually they are only deluding themselves. Only by patiently lifting what the Hindu called the veils of Maya—or illusion—do we get a closer glimpse of what life is really about. This idea is not unique to India, however. Many religions and philosophies the world over hold that commonsense appearances are deceptive and must be seen through to understand the nature of reality. Twenty-four centuries ago, Democritus is supposed to have said: "Nothing is real, or if it is, we don't know it. We have no way of knowing the truth. Truth is at the bottom of an abyss." Christianity did not deny the reality of the material world, but only its importance. All the action that really mattered took place outside this existence. Those who took the events in the physical realm too seriously ran the risk of being deluded by trivial and transient concerns, and thus forfeited the eternal realm of the spirit.

But why should we be concerned, at the threshold of the third millennium, with what ancient religions and philosophies have said about reality? What did they know about truth? It might seem anachronistic that in discussing evolution and the future one should pay any attention to Hindu myths or Christian worldviews. If one takes evolution seriously, however, one appreciates how important the past is in shaping the present and the future. Just as the chemical structure of the human chromosome began to determine, millions of years ago, both the truths and the illusions that we are destined to experience, so, too, do the symbolic representations created by past thinkers help to reveal as well as to conceal reality. The task for us today is to separate the genuine insights of religions and philosophies from the inevitable errors that crept into their explanations. It would be indeed an act of sinful pride to assume that present knowledge is in every way superior to that of the past, and to dismiss what the ancients learned as backward superstition.

"Evolutionary epistemology" is a branch of scholarship that applies the evolutionary perspective to an understanding of how knowledge develops. Knowledge always involves getting information. The most primitive way of acquiring it is through the sense of touch: amoebas and other simple organisms know what happens around them only if they can feel it with their "skins." The knowledge such an organism can have is strictly about what is in its immediate vicinity. After a huge jump in evolution, organisms learned to find out what was going on at a distance from them, without having to actually feel the environment. This jump involved the development of sense organs for processing information that was farther away. For a long time, the most important sources of knowledge were the nose, the eyes, and the ears. The next big advance occurred when organisms developed memory. Now information no longer needed to be present at all, and the animal could recall events and outcomes that happened in the past. Each one of these steps in the evolution of knowledge added important survival advantages to the species that was equipped to use it.

Then, with the appearance in evolution of humans, an entirely new way of acquiring information developed. Up to this point, the processing of information was entirely *intrasomatic,* that is, it took place within the body of the organism. But when speech appeared (and even more powerfully with the invention of writing), information processing became *extrasomatic.* After that point knowledge did not have to be stored in the genes, or in the memory traces of the brain; it could be passed on from one person to another through words, or it could be written down and stored on a permanent substance like stone, paper, or silicon chips—in any case, outside the fragile and impermanent nervous system.

The immense increase in our power to control the planet was made possible by the extrasomatic storage of information, a skill that we acquired in only the last few seconds of evolutionary history. At first information was stored in songs, myths, and stories that our ancestors told one another around campfires. Legends encapsulated centuries of useful experience in a few rhymed lines, proverbs, or cautionary tales. The young members of the tribe no longer had to learn only from their own experiences what was dangerous and what was valuable in their environment; instead, they could rely on the collective memory of past generations, and possibly avoid repeating their mistakes. This knowledge helped them to achieve a certain amount of control over the environment, and freed their time to learn the various technologies—such as making weapons, building fires, and working metals—that were also being transmitted extrasomatically.

Of course myths and legends did not just convey useful information; they also passed on an enormous amount of what nowadays would be called "noise"—that is, irrelevant details, or details that make sense only in certain specific historical situations. This is inevitable because anyone who wants to pass on a personally experienced truth usually cannot distinguish the essential element of that truth from its incidental features. For example, suppose a father in our own culture wants to explain to his son the love he felt when he married his wife. Because discussing emotions among males is embarrassing, and because external events are more "real" and easy to describe, the father might recall the wedding primarily in terms of what music was played in the church, the number of guests at the reception, the number of bottles of wine consumed, and so on. The central message concerning his feelings for the bride may hardly be mentioned. So what the son might learn from the father's story is that the significance of weddings depends on music, guests, and drinks, missing the most important part of the message altogether.

When the experiences and thoughts of a culture begin to coalesce into a systematic view of what life and the world are about, religions make their first appearance on the stage of evolution. It is no exaggeration to say that religions have been the most important extrasomatic organs of knowledge created by humans up to now—with the possible exception of science, which is a way of checking objectively the information one obtains, and so allows its users to systematically reject erroneous conclusions. Although religions lack this feature of self-correction, and thus generally fail to adapt to new knowledge and to grow with time, they do have certain other advantages over science that should not be dismissed. Perhaps most important is the fact that religions have existed for centuries, and have had a chance to retain information that is important for human survival for a longer time than science. For this reason alone it would be fatuous to ignore religious insights, especially when, as in the case of the veils of Maya that disguise reality, they recur over and over in very different cultural contexts.

The notion that reality is well hidden from view is not one that only ancient thinkers have entertained. Current scientific thought is beginning to explain, in its own terms, what earlier thinkers may have meant by the metaphor of Maya. The social sciences, for instance, have provided ample evidence to show how different truth appears, depending on where one happens to be born, what sort of early experiences one is exposed to, or what kind of occupation one ends up pursuing.

For example, anthropologists have demonstrated in any number of studies how successfully cultures can inculcate their values and worldviews. Most human groups believe that they are chosen people situated at the center of the universe, and that their ways of life are better than anyone else's. The Amish live in an Amish world, the Zulus in a world of Zulus. Both take it for granted that their understanding of the world is the only one that makes sense. One unfortunate consequence of this attitude is that, believing too strongly in the reality of our culture's world, we miss the larger reality behind it. Many people don't object to toxic waste as long as it is not dumped in their neighborhood. Substances become poisonous only when they threaten one's world. If my world is limited to Chicago, then all the toxins outside the city are not poisonous—as far as I am concerned, they don't exist. The larger the group with which one identifies, the closer to ultimate reality one gets. Only the person who sees the entire planet as her world can recognize a toxic substance as poison no matter where it is dumped.

Similarly, sociologists have pointed out the ways in which reality is socially constructed. As people interact with parents, friends, and co-workers, they learn to see the world from the vantage point of those particular interactions. The world looks very different from a businessmen's club than from a union hall, a military barracks, or a monastery. The chiefs of staff live in a world centered around the Pentagon, where megadeaths, body counts, and fat contracts with defense industries are the main features of the landscape. Theirs is a different world from that of car salesmen, football players, or professors. But it is not just the differences in social position or in ways of making a living that so often result in conflicts of interest, what Marxists call the class struggle. It is that people in different positions in the social system end up living in different physical and symbolic environments—in what are, in effect, alien worlds. Considering how powerful the forces of culture and society are in shaping what we see, what we feel, and what we believe, it is not surprising that the Hindus thought we were all living under spells cast by demonic wizards.

Psychologists find comparable biases at the individual level. Each person, equipped with a more or less unique set of genes and experiences, develops a "cognitive map" of his or her world that makes navigation among its shoals easier. In the same household one child might learn to see the world through rosy glasses, while the other will learn that it is bleak and dangerous. Some children, born with a great sensitivity to sound, will grow up paying attention to the auditory environment and not see many of the colors, lights, and shapes that surround the more visually sensitive child. One person is more interested in quantities, another in feelings; one is open and trusting, the other retiring and suspicious. These individual differences develop with time into habits and then into ways of thinking about and interpreting experience. Such "maps" are useful because they provide consistent directions to those who use them, but they are hardly accurate in the sense of presenting an objective, universally valid picture of reality. In fact, in the same situation two persons using different cognitive maps will see and experience entirely different realities.

The relativity of knowledge is not a concept that only the "soft" social sciences have explored. Even physics, once the paragon of a mechanical and absolute science, has in the last century given up hope of providing unambiguous accounts of what is actually out there—for it turns out that even the most elementary, concrete sense data give unreliable information. Mountains, trees, and houses are not made up of solid matter, but of billions of unpredictably twitching particles. As Democritus already suspected centuries ago, the world we can see is only the part that registers upon the senses. There are all sorts of things happening around us about which we have no idea because they are beyond our perceptual threshold. The eyes, ears, and other senses provide just the minimum of information needed to survive in an average environment. But they leave out so much. It's enough to see a puppy almost going out of its mind with excitement as it explores scents in a meadow to realize how much information we routinely miss.

Why can't we then just make bigger and more sensitive instruments so as to get at those elusive events outside our ken? As physicists have come to realize, every instrument, every measurement gives only a biased view, dependent on the instruments themselves. Reality is created as one tries to apprehend it. Heisenberg's famous uncertainty principle, which describes the logical impossibility of determining both the position and the velocity of a given atomic particle at the same time, was just the first rumble in what has become a veritable earthquake threatening the formerly solid edifice of the physical sciences. Ilya Prigogine, a Nobel laureate in chemistry, expressed the difficulty of getting an accurate picture of absolute reality as follows: "Whatever we call reality, it is revealed to us only through an active construction in which we participate." And the physicist John Wheeler said: "Beyond particles, beyond fields of force, beyond geometry, beyond space and time themselves, is the ultimate constituent [of all there is], the still more ethereal act of observer-participation." In other words, no matter how complex the theory, how precise the measurement, the fact is that it is we who have developed the theories and the measuring instruments—hence, whatever we learn is going to be dependent on our perspective as observers. The limitations of the human nervous system, the particular history of the culture, the idiosyncrasies in the symbol systems used are going to determine the reality one sees. The inelegant acronym used by computer programmers, GIGO (Garbage In, Garbage Out), is applicable to epistemology in general. The output is always a function of the input.

When the Australian aborigines tried to explain the monsoon that each year came to their land from the sea amidst thunder and lightning, they pictured it as a huge snake mating in the clouds and giving birth to rain. Given what they knew, this was the most meaningful account for what they were experiencing. The modern explanation is based on temperature differentials, rate of vapor condensation, wind velocity, and so on. This story sounds much more sensible to us than the one about the giant snake, but would observers looking at it a few hundred years hence not find it equally primitive?

Does this mean, then, that it is useless to worry about what is true, because no matter how much one tries the answer will always be distorted? Many people end up agreeing with this notion. The step from relativism to cynicism is easy to take, yet it is not the best direction in which to go. If we refused to take seriously the reality available here and now because it isn't the absolute truth, we would surely regret that decision in short order. Even though reality can only be seen through distorting glasses, it is better to make do with what one can comprehend, rather than disdain it because it falls short of perfection.

But isn't it discouraging to know that, no matter how much we strive to understand, ultimate reality will always remain hidden? Only if the search for truth is motivated by the desire to reach an absolute, definitive answer. The person looking for certainty is bound to be disappointed. He will be like Faust, who after spending his life studying theology, philosophy, and the sciences despairs at the discovery that he has not learned one single truth he can confidently hold on to. If on the other hand we realize that the partial truths we uncover are all legitimate aspects of the unknowable universe, then we can learn to enjoy the search and derive from it the pleasure one gets from any creative act—whether it is painting a picture or cooking a good meal. In this case, however, it is a question not just of a painting or a meal, but of a way of seeing, of creating an entire world. Shaping one's own reality, living in a world one has created, can be as enjoyable as writing a symphony.

No person who ever lived could apprehend reality as a whole, nor is it imaginable that someone will ever do so. Like evolution itself, the quest for truth never ends. Certainties are always revised, and entirely new vistas open up when we least expect it. Imagine the revolution in understanding when the first farmers discovered that a single seed planted would yield hundreds of new seeds, or when the Copernican view of the planetary system displaced the Ptolemaic view.

But creating a new reality, a personally valid world, is not easy. It is much easier to accept the illusory certainties provided by the genes and by the culture, or to reject all effort and seek refuge in a radical cynicism that denies the value of any effort at understanding. Although the reality we must seek will not contain *the* truth, it must have *a* truth contained in it. A creative product is never random or arbitrary; it must be true to something deeply sensed or felt inside the person. And in order to get to that kernel of inner certainty, one must learn to peel away the various veils of Maya.

There is an old Indian parable that I like to repeat to graduate students who are trying to find topics for their doctoral dissertations. It involves a young disciple who approaches an old and skilled sculptor with a request.

"Master," he says, "I want to become a famous sculptor. What should I do?"

"Well," replies the master, "tell me, what kind of a statue would you like to make?"

The young man thinks for a while, and concludes: "More than anything else, I would like to sculpt a beautiful elephant."

At this the master places in front of the young man a block of stone and a few tools: "Fine. Here is some marble, a mallet, and a chisel. All you have to do now is carve away everything that does not look like a beautiful elephant."

Thus ends the story. Simple? In a way, of course it is, and yet also infuriatingly difficult. How do we know what is *not* the elephant? How do we know which is the veil, and which is the reality it conceals? We cannot know in advance. Only after he starts carving does the sculptor begin to sense what must be cast away, and what must be kept; it takes much longer still to know whether he is getting an elephant or just a shapeless lump of stone. Only after many trials does one realize how difficult the simple task actually is. One must painstakingly match one's preconceptions against actual, ongoing experience to begin separating truth from illusion.

This chapter will discuss three major sources of distortion that interfere with a truthful apprehension of what goes on in the world. They include genetic programming, the cultural heritage, and the demands of the self. These distortions are "inside" each one of us—no human being is immune to the illusions they foster. The next chapter will review three "outer" obstacles to a true perception of reality. By taking these six veils into account we will find it easier to see beyond the appearances, and create a personally meaningful world with what we see there.

THE WORLD OF THE GENES

In the previous chapter we have seen that the brain is built so as to be susceptible to a variety of pleasurable sensations that can be harmful in excessive doses. More generally, it is by now beyond any serious doubt that how we experience the world is limited and structured—but not determined—by the chemical instructions encoded in the genes. These instructions have been passed on more or less unchanged for many millions of years from ancestor to ancestor, and down to our parents. What they tell us to do is to follow the best strategy for survival that our ancestors were able to develop. They tell us to search for food when hungry, defend ourselves if attacked, be interested in members of the opposite sex, and so on.

Genetic instructions are rather generic—they apply to average situations, and prompt us to act in ways that generally tended to be useful in the past. Infants are born with the ability to recognize human faces, because these are the most important features of a baby's early environment. Similarly, babies are programmed to imitate adults, because that is the surest way for them to become independent and survive. These instructions are solidly embedded in the brain, and their effects are automatic. However, when a person is confronted with a new situation, the wisdom of the genes is no longer reliable. An infant will imitate an abusive adult as well as a well-meaning one. Evolution has not been able to build an accurate detector for letting us know which behaviors are worth imitating and which are not. Mammals might be genetically equipped to avoid snakes, but not unscrupulous bond salesmen.

As humans have come to depend more and more on cultural rather than genetic instructions for survival, they have had to unlearn much that was useful in the past. New, artificial rules have had to be adopted instead, such as learning to control anger, to curb sexuality, to tolerate long periods of sitting at desks thinking—often against the promptings of "nature." Yet, despite all this domestication, the voice of the gene is still strong, and the way we experience the world is to a large degree determined by it. Even if a man has learned not to act out aggressive or sexual impulses, much of his inner life, much of his psychic energy, is tied down in emotions and thoughts prompted by instincts. This is the first veil of Maya, and unless one learns to see through it, reality will always be obscured by the needs and desires in the genetic program.

Generally we assume that instincts, drives, and visceral needs constitute the most genuine core of personality, that they are the essence of who we are. But lately evolutionary biologists have begun to argue that the individual person, as far as the genes are concerned, is only a vehicle for their own reproduction and further dissemination. The genes don't really care about us at all, and if it helped their reproduction, they would just as soon have us live in ignorance and misery. Genes are not our little helpers; it is we who are their servants.

The chemical instructions that predispose an unwed teenager to become pregnant were not designed to make her happy or successful in the complex society in which she now lives. They are just a mechanism for making sure that the information in her chromosomes is going to be copied and passed down to another generation. In the past, when the life span was short and infant mortality high, genes that were able to stimulate a young girl to become pregnant as soon as she could bear a child had a better chance of spreading than genes prompting more demure behavior. Whether this was actually good for the individual girl or not is beside the point. The teenager is, of course, blissfully unaware of all this, and obeys the call of nature in the mistaken belief that what feels good at the moment will also be good in the long run.

The genes are programmed to protect us only for as long as we produce viable offspring; afterward we might as well be dead meat. While it is true that our interests as individuals and as carriers of genetic instructions often overlap, this is not always the case. For instance, genes are not interested in how long people live past the time their children are old enough to survive on their own. In fact, it would be to their advantage if the parents died as soon as possible after their children are out of college, so they wouldn't take up room and resources that could be used by still another generation. Not a very friendly bunch, these genes, yet we keep mistaking their interests for ours. As long as we cannot tell the difference between those interests, our minds will not be free to pursue their own ends, but will have to obey garbled commands from the past.

Each person creates the world he or she lives in by investing attention in certain things, and by doing so according to certain patterns. The world constructed on the blueprints provided by the genes is one in which all of a person's attention is invested in furthering the agenda of "reproductive fitness." This is a simple goal: How can I get enough out of the environment to make sure that I reproduce and that my children will also have children? In less complex organisms, like many species of insects, practically the entire life span is dedicated to the project of laying a clutch of eggs; promptly afterward, the parents expire. Like every other organism, the butterfly has evolved to see only those things that will either help or hinder the survival of its offspring. Its world is made up of flowery shapes that provide nectar, and shapes that resemble predators that are best avoided. Poets make much of the majestic eagle soaring freely among the snowy peaks. But the eyes of the eagle are generally focused on the ground, searching for rodents lurking in the shadows. The lives of much of humanity could be summed up in similar terms.

Let us take the example of Jerry, an imaginary young lawyer. On what does he spend his life? Most of it is directed by the requirements of his genes. As he wakes up in the morning, he will spend close to an hour washing, dressing, and sprucing up in an attempt to make his appearance attractive yet at the same time somewhat intimidating—a red power tie might help in that department. Then he spends a few minutes having breakfast, the first of several meals during the day that will boost his spirits and energy by replenishing the sugar level in his bloodstream. The car he drives to work, and the way he drives, are also indirectly influenced by the instructions in his genes. He might drive a Volvo because it is safe, a Ford because it is practical, or he might choose a car that is full of power, or one that projects the image of success. And why does Jerry spend eight, ten, twelve hours a day working? So that he can satisfy his nesting instinct and buy a comfortable house, attract a desirable mate, have children, accumulate some property to pass on, and afford a large insurance policy to protect his offspring.

In all probability Jerry would not say that he spends his psychic energy the way he does because he is trying to humor his genes. He would say that he *chose* to wear the red tie because he likes it better than the others, and drives the Volvo because he feels good driving it. Perhaps he could back up his choices with reasons based on personal experiences, or with objective evidence. In that case, more power to him. But all too often people do not consider options; they do not pause to reflect on alternatives. They simply take the script provided by the genes, and enact it according to the specific directions given by the culture they happen to be born in.

As a teenager I spent a year or so attending a high school in the working-class neighborhood of a southern Italian city. My classmates came from families uprooted by World War II who had moved from traditional farming communities to try their luck in the new urban slums growing up around the factory districts. During the time I spent with them, I felt like an anthropologist visiting a strange tribe; not only their values, but also the ways they looked at the world were so very different from what I had been used to. Although quite a few of the boys (the classes were still segregated by gender) became my friends, I never ceased to wonder at the fact that roughly nine out of ten ideas that went through their heads were about sex. If an unknown teacher or student walked into the classroom for the first time, the boys would comment loudly and at length about his or her primary and secondary sexual characteristics, and speculate about how he or she would be in bed. The high point of the week for these fourteen-year-olds was Wednesday, when the nearby whorehouse gave daytime student discounts. Even though not everyone had access to heterosexual adventures, most of the conversation revolved about real or imaginary exploits. There were also several stable homosexual couples who took their relationships very seriously and with a certain romantic flair.

Not that the school I describe was unique. Teens everywhere must learn to struggle with the hormones flooding their bodies—and their brains—with urgent instructions concerning sexuality and reproduction. It has been estimated that American teenagers think of sex on an average of once every twenty-six seconds—not because they want to, but because the sensations coursing through their flesh make it impossible to do otherwise. Whatever the actual frequency of sex-related thoughts, the point is that psychic energy is not free to go wherever we wish it to go; left to itself, it turns in the direction it was programmed.

Food has a similar grip on the mind. We cannot spend more than a few hours without starting to think of eating. My studies of the psychology of everyday life suggest that average people spend between 10 and 15 percent of their waking life either eating or thinking about food. For people with eating disorders the figure is twice as high—almost one-third of the day is filled with preoccupations about food. In extreme cases, not being able to curb one's hunger can kill. It is uniformly reported by people who have spent time in concentration camps that the prisoners who die first are those who cannot get their minds off food, and are willing to do anything to obtain it. A friend who spent years in the Soviet gulags tells that in one of the camps the kitchen staff amused itself by dumping potato peelings—the only even remotely edible refuse—right next to the latrines, where they would be immediately contaminated with excrement. To eat these raw potato skins was suicide—yet there were always several inmates who could not restrain themselves, and heedless of warnings gorged themselves on the peelings, usually to die soon thereafter of intestinal infections.

Problems of this severity we do not have. Yet in reading popular magazines one gets the impression that even in our society most people are still engaged in a constant battle against obsession with food. It seems that a new diet makes its appearance every week, promising deliverance to the overweight masses. Celebrities discuss their weight-watching strategies with the seriousness once reserved for the salvation of the soul. Sedentary employees in the United States consume as many as 8,000 calories a day—almost three times what the body actually needs—and this inevitably leads to weight gains dangerous to health. Clearly we are far from having gained control of our appetites.

Does this mean that it is better to question every move we make, and try to repress sexual desires, or try to stop eating, or refrain from having children, because these are not really *our* goals, but are ones that have been implanted in our minds by selfish genes? Such a course of action would of course be self-defeating. There is no way to escape the facticity of biological existence. It would be presumptuous to try second-guessing the wisdom of millions of years of adaptation, even if it were possible to do so. At the same time, survival in the third millennium will require that we understand better how we are manipulated by chemicals in the body.

As a first step, as we go through daily routines, it is liberating to stop and reflect why we do the things we do. It helps to know, if I get a third rasher of bacon for breakfast, that I am not just exercising free choice or indulging a passing whim, but am probably being manipulated by the instructions of a hungry three-million-year-old gene. It does not matter whether I go ahead and eat that third rasher or not. What counts is that, even if only for a few seconds, I have interrupted the automatic determinism of the genes—that for the moment, I have lifted the first veil of Maya.

Reflecting on the source of impulse, of habits, is the first step in getting control of one's psychic energy. Knowing the origin of motives, and becoming aware of our biases is the prerequisite for freedom. But it is not enough to know how genetic instructions keep us doing what they wish us to do. The second veil is the one with which culture and society—the human systems we are born into—shroud reality, covering up alternatives in order to use our psychic energy for their own ends.

THE WORLD OF CULTURE

Peasants living in the tiny hamlets of the Hungarian plains occasionally told visitors: "Did you know that our village is the center of the world? No? You can check it out for yourself easily enough. All you have to do is go to the square in the middle of the village. In the middle of the square is the church. If you climb its tower, you can see the fields and forests spreading out in a circle all around, with our church in the center." The fact that the neighboring villages also thought they were at the hub of the world didn't matter—after all, what did foreigners living on the periphery of the universe know? Their delusions were not to be taken seriously. These traditional peasants based their views on perfectly sensible bits of information: When they were looking down from the church spire the village did in fact look as if it stood at the center of the world, and the traditions they learned in infancy from their elders held a stronger truth value than anything they learned later. From their isolated vantage point, the reality they knew made perfectly good sense.

Unfortunately, every isolated culture must come to the same locally plausible yet ultimately erroneous conclusion. When living in Calabria, in the far south of Italy, I spent many frustrating hours debating other teenagers who claimed they were much more civilized than the people who lived far north in Naples, or in Rome: "After all," they said, "everyone knows that the farther south you go, the higher the level of civilization." It did no good to point out that in that case the tribes of equatorial Africa were much more civilized than the Calabrians. It only confused them and made them surly. For every human group not only believes itself to be at the center of the universe, but also that it has unique virtues that make it somehow superior to any other group.

Every culture instills a similar prejudice in its members. The Greeks called everyone who did not speak their language "barbarians," because the sounds they made were unintelligible gibberish—*bar bar*—to their ears. The Chinese believed that only their culture deserved to be called civilized, and the Navajo word for their own tribe means "the people." We are certainly not immune to such myopia. Some of it is just amusing. When I used to take the old Chicago streetcar No. 22 to college, I passed by three different diners advertising "The Best Fried Chicken in the World." Other examples of ethnocentrism are less amusing. During the Gulf War, the U.S. media complacently crowed about the few casualties suffered in the conflict, almost never calculating in the equation the enormous Iraqi losses. Every ethnic group in the U.S. holds on to its own version of superiority. Some African-Americans lay claim to the Egyptian civilization, and preach the superiority of the "sun people" over the fair-skinned "ice people." Even the states of the Union, so recently constituted, have had time to develop this kind of bigotry: Coloradans sneer at people sporting Texas license plates, the good people of Wyoming look down on Coloradans, and in Montana they are not so sure about people from Wyoming.

The sense of importance and invulnerability one gets from one's culture is illusory but convincing. It is good to feel at the center of the universe. Someone who first comes to the United States finds it difficult to believe how self-assured in their unique destiny most citizens of this fortunate country are. One almost envies those Americans who serenely believe that because they are protected by the Constitution they need not worry about anything drastic ever happening. Then one remembers that before World War II it was the Germans who were supremely confident in their destiny, what with all those great scientists, composers, and poets they had produced in the past. The Russians are able to forgive themselves many faults because the deep sensitivity of their souls is so obviously more valuable than the mundane virtues cultivated in other cultures. The Italians are often bitterly self-critical, but they know deep down that no one understands life as well as they do. The French look down the length of their rational noses at the rest of the world; the British feel set apart by the fair common sense that breeds only in their insular haven. And if you think such prejudice is peculiar to Western imperialism, all you have to do is talk to a Chinese, Japanese, Hindu, or Ethiopian to get quickly disabused. Of course these claims about Americans, Russians, and so on are egregiously stereotyped generalizations, but then so much of social behavior *is* ruled by stereotypes.

If ethnocentrism seems to be an inevitable outcome of belonging to a culture, there is probably no other way of being. Survival and self-esteem depend on those among whom we are born. By now, to be human we need the instructions transmitted through culture almost as much as we need genetic instructions. How else would we talk, read, count, think? The genes cannot teach these skills; we must learn them from women and men who speak our language, from the knowledge stored in books and other symbols systems. But in the process of teaching us how to be human, culture begins to make its claims. Just as genes use the body as a vehicle for their own reproduction, a culture also tends to use individuals as vehicles for its own survival and growth. In order to ensure this end, it must convince us of its superiority.

A well-acculturated person is someone who is willing to sacrifice even his or her life for the sake of country, party, or religion. He is someone who intuitively knows that the native hills are more beautiful, the native food more tasty, the songs more melodious, the old people wiser than in any other part of the world. He knows that strange languages are barbaric, alien habits are ridiculous or repulsive. It is well-acculturated people who keep traditions alive; without them cultures would be in a state of constant flux and they would soon lose their peculiar characters.

Cultural loyalties often push people to act with even greater disregard for their best interest than genetic instructions do. It is difficult to see how the continuing saga of mutual murder between Serbs and Croats, between Catholics and Protestants in Ireland, between Armenians and Azerbaijanis, Cambodians and Vietnamese, or the various warring tribes in South Africa benefits the parties involved. A Capulet who derives his identity from ancestral hatred of the Montagues cannot refrain from jeering when he meets an enemy walking across the piazza, even if he gets stabbed to death as a result. Worse yet, hundreds of gang members die each year on the West Side of Chicago for the same reason. Sometimes they are killed only because they are wearing insignia that identifies them with the wrong group, such as a cap pulled down on the left side of the head, or a bracelet on the right wrist.

Excessive acculturation leads one to see reality only through the veils of the culture. A person who invests psychic energy exclusively in goals prescribed by society is forfeiting the possibility of choice. It is easy to see this danger in the case of a simple society, such as the Gusii of West Africa. According to Robert LeVine, the anthropologist who has studied the life course of this tribe, the Gusii value three goals above all else, and devote almost all of their energies to reach them. One is to own as many head of cattle as possible, because wealth is reckoned in terms of the size of one's herd. Two is to have as many children and grandchildren as possible, because social position depends on the size of one's network of relatives. The third goal is to gain spiritual power, which to a certain extent follows from wealth and social position, but also requires personal actions that evoke fear and respect from one's peers. Wealth, esteem, and the ability to instill fear are all forms of power that make a man more likely to accumulate the resources needed to have many children and grandchildren.

There is very little room for poetry, romance, or flights of the imagination beyond these goals. Stripped to its bare outlines, the world of the Gusii does not look that much different from the world as structured by genes. Although the Gusii have their own rich and unique cultural traditions, the main goals of survival, reproduction, and dominance that organize their lives are transparently an extension of similar goals shared by nonhuman primates and by other lower species.

The requirements of our own culture are more complex and less clearly tied to biological antecedents, but they can be equally restrictive. If we ever came to the point where a majority of people could not imagine any goal worth living for except making money, if respect—and self-respect—rested solely on social comparison based on material achievements, then the world revealed by even the most technologically advanced culture would become as constraining as that of the Gusii.

It is true that at first glance the opportunities for leading different lifestyles in our society appear to be extremely varied and diverse. If you wish to live as a religious fundamentalist, an Amish, or a Hare Krishna, you can do it. If you want to be a swinging single in an urban high rise, or camp out with hippies on a riverbank, there are many opportunities for that, too. There are communities of scholars, scuba divers, vegetarians, sun worshipers, each with its own values and lifestyles. But does this diversity imply a complex cultural integration? Usually it does not; the many different subcultures lead parallel existences, each well insulated from the influences of the others.

And those aspects of the culture that are common to almost everyone are not much more sophisticated than those of the Gusii. The culture that spans most of our society looks up to the likes of Donald Trump, Ivan Boesky, and Michael Milken because they have amassed large herds of dollars; worships General Norman Schwarzkopf because he bombed the enemy into submission; pays millions to a basketball player because he jumps higher than anyone else; and swoons at the feet of entertainers who serve as symbols of youth, beauty, and a happy life, even though the person behind the smiling mask is more often than not a confused and unhappy wretch. The landscape of this world is seen by millions of people each night on television screens. It is a world of a few simple ideas repeated incessantly, in as many different ways as possible.

It is dangerous to take too seriously the picture of the world as painted by one's culture. First, to do so limits the scope of any individual's potential. For example, an educated woman living in an Arab country cannot but feel that she has to sacrifice many personally important options in order to preserve the integrity of her culture. Second, excessive identification with a particular worldview inevitably leads to blindness to other cultures, and eventually to hostility toward the "other." Nationalism, religious bigotry, and ideological intolerance have served as justifications for all the major wars in the past few centuries, and now that the planet is becoming ever more congested, these divisive forces become increasingly explosive. Finally, to accept the cultural worldview unquestioningly is dangerous simply because it blinds us to larger realities. Those who automatically dismiss everything that falls outside the prejudices of their group are condemned to live forever in a paltry world.

But railing against the limitations of one's culture is just as useless as inveighing against the lack of vision displayed by genetic instructions. Even though one might disagree with many of the values and practices the culture supports, the benefits of living within a reasonably civilized social system are so high that a blanket rejection is senseless. Being grateful for the culture that made one human does not, however, imply accepting it at face value. Some of the greatest figures in history were those who cared enough about the development of human potentials to take issue with the society in which they lived, even when that society was at the height of its success: Socrates questioned the basis for civic loyalty; Cato and Cicero criticized the mores of the Roman elite; and Joan of Arc, Martin Luther, and Mahatma Gandhi challenged the status quos of their own times.

Creative geniuses are often marginal people, individuals whose vision was greatly expanded because they were forced to move from one cultural world into another, and thus were able to see the relativity of both. Of the seven "creators of the modern era" whose lives Howard Gardner describes, only one, the dancer and choreographer Martha Graham, ended up living in the country where she was born—but she traveled so widely that one might say she was de facto multicultural. Sigmund Freud studied in Paris and then had to leave Vienna for London; Einstein moved from Germany to Italy, Switzerland, back to Germany, and then to the United States; Gandhi spent many years in England and South Africa before returning to India; Picasso left Spain for France; Stravinsky had to abandon Russia and lived in various places of exile, including Hollywood; and T. S. Eliot fled from the banks of the Mississippi to London. The common element of such peregrinations is probably not a coincidence, but points to the fact that it is easier to see reality in new ways when one leaves the cocoon of one's native culture.

On a more modest level, it is important for each person to

recognize that the values, rules, habits, and attitudes we inherit are useful and necessary, but are not absolute. It is dangerous to leave the critical evaluation of the culture to a few specialists; such a responsibility should, rather, be widely shared. If the great majority accept passively whatever public opinion and tradition decree, it becomes easy for a few unscrupulous interest groups to manipulate the rules in their favor.

To lift the second veil of illusion involves realizing how partial a view of reality even the most sophisticated culture affords, and it need not involve more than that. It is not essential to reject familiar values and practices. Only too often, those who adopt a countercultural stance end up being just as controlled, or more so, by their rebellious values as they would have been by the mainline ones they abandoned. The strident fanaticism of religious reformers like Calvin; of revolutionary leaders like Danton, Marat, Lenin, or Stalin; or of the current heralds of Maoism, deconstructionism, and postmodernism, can be just as limiting as the orthodoxy they sought to overthrow.

Nevertheless, it is liberating to question the descriptions of reality of one's culture, and especially those presented by the media. As one opens up the newspaper in the morning, it is well to remember that what one reads represents a necessarily biased view. Colonel McCormick, the legendary publisher of the *Chicago Tribune,* is often quoted as saying that a dogfight in the Chicago Loop was more newsworthy than a major war in China. As long as we realize that the media present the world *sub specie culturae,* we are less likely to be deceived.

And during the rest of the day it is also useful occasionally to take off the distorting glasses that we have grown accustomed to wearing, and look at what is happening from a different perspective. To what extent have I accepted other people's definition of who I am and what I could be? How ignorant am I of the values held by people of different cultures? Or more prosaically: Do I actually like the highly advertised values of my car? Is the company I work for deserving of my loyalty? Is working seventy hours a week really the best investment of my life energy? Is a slim figure, a youthful look the highest peak of human accomplishment? It was for asking similar questions that Socrates had to drink hemlock, and Savonarola was burned at the stake. But Socrates and Savonarola spoke out in public squares to convince their fellow citizens of the rightness of their alternative visions. To see more clearly the nature of reality, however, one need not become as ardent an activist; it is enough to raise such questions in the privacy of one's own mind. Just by doing so one begins to be freed from the illusions that are the side effects of being a cultural being. It will be possible then to see through the second veil.

THE WORLD OF THE SELF

Instinctual desires and cultural values work their way into consciousness from the outside, so to speak. The first start as chemical impulses that we interpret as true needs, the second begin as social conventions that we internalize as inevitable. The third distortion of reality begins in the mind and works itself out: it is the side effect of being conscious—the illusion of selfhood.

As we have seen earlier, self-reflective consciousness is a recent development in human evolution, but exactly how recent, no one knows. Certainly the genetic instructions are much older; probably cultural instructions also developed earlier than the advent of self-reflection. It has even been proposed that it was only about three thousand years ago that people began to realize that they were thinking. Before that point, ideas and emotions passed through the mind on their own, without any conscious control. A Greek warrior or a Sumerian priest followed instinct and convention; when a new idea occurred to him, he believed it was sent by a god or spirit.

It is unlikely that we will ever be able to determine with any precision when people started to realize that they could control their mental processes. Unlike arrowheads and pots, traces of self-reflection cannot be dug out of the remains of early settlements. The event was so inconspicuous that it left no evidence: not with a bang but a whisper did the era of consciousness begin. Whenever the ability developed, it was one of the most momentous events that happened on our planet. Not even the asteroids alleged to have put an end to the age of the dinosaurs some 65 million years ago brought so great a change into the world.

Why was this event so important? Partly, of course, it was because conscious manipulation of mental content made new inventions and new technology much easier to envision, and to adopt once invented. But even more significantly, once the mind realized its autonomy, individuals were able to conceive of themselves as independent agents with their own self-interest. For the first time, it was possible for people to emancipate themselves from the rule of genes and of culture. A person could now have unique dreams, and take an individual stance based on personal goals.

While the self brought the gift of personal freedom, it also spun another veil, as thick as the two earlier ones: the illusions of the ego. Selfishness is an eternal part of living, and ruthless bullies must have been abundant long before men and women started to control their own minds through the ability to reflect. But once the self developed, it brought its own distortions to bear. Let us consider Zorg, the imaginary leader of a group of hominids far enough in the past to be prior to the advent of self-reflective consciousness. Zorg knows he is the leader because if he decides to walk in a certain direction the tribe will follow. Likewise, if he snarls, the others cringe. When prompted by hunger or sexual desires, Zorg takes advantage of his dominant position to take more than his share. Occasionally he may throw a tantrum and hurt some of his fellows. He is clearly selfish, but his selfishness lacks an essential component that only a person with a reflective ego can have: Zorg is not ambitious, and he does not try to accumulate power in an abstract sense. His bids for dominance are the result of genetic instructions and the feedback he receives from others; they are temporary, context-driven attempts. He does not even try to accumulate more property than his peers; after all, hunter-gatherers own no real estate, and movable goods are a great burden to carry around.

It could be said that Zorg's perspective is severely limited by what biology and culture allow him to experience. But he remains free from all those biases that are the by-product of a mind conscious of itself. The Pharaohs, the rulers of Mesopotamia, of the Indus River valley, of ancient China, were different from Zorg not only in that they had immensely greater resources to draw upon, but also because each had a sense of his own unique individuality. And once an ego is present, its foremost goal becomes that of protecting itself at all costs. Thus tens of thousands of Egyptian slaves had to give up their lives to build the pyramids so that the Pharaoh's ego could live on; the thousands of statues buried in the tombs of the Chinese emperors were laboriously shaped for the same purpose.

On a smaller scale, insatiable egos were devouring the psychic energy of people in almost every ancient human group we know about. When the chieftain of one of those nomadic troops of horsemen who were constantly swooping down from the steppes of Central Asia to ravage the more settled regions of Europe and Asia happened to die, he was buried with his horses, weapons, and jewelry—and also his women and servants, so they could serve the dear departed in the afterlife.

The *Iliad*, that most revered epic of the European past, gives an excellent description of how the ego of a Greek warrior worked. The poem begins with a meeting of the leaders of the Greek army that is besieging the enemy city of Troy. The siege has lasted for many years and so far has been a fiasco; the Greeks are tired, homesick, and ravaged by disease. The council is trying to resolve a squabble between two great chiefs that is threatening to disrupt the Greek alliance and end the war in an ignominious retreat. Agamemnon, leader of the largest of the army's factions, claims that the meager spoils the Greeks have won so far have been distributed unfairly: Achilles got more than he deserved. Achilles, the young prince whose reckless valor has made him the most admired among the Greeks, objects heatedly that he is entitled to all the prizes he has won. Agamemnon insists that, unless he is granted Briseis, a Trojan princess who had been awarded to Achilles, he will pull out with his troops. The other leaders fear that if Agamemnon and his many soldiers leave, the war will be lost, so they reluctantly force Achilles to give up the girl. The rest of the *Iliad* tells of the consequences of this action: sulking Achilles refuses to fight any longer; without him the war turns even worse for the Greeks; the gods descend from Olympus to take sides with the various factions and against each other . . . and so on and on, until the proud towers of Troy finally fall, engulfed in flames.

The point is that the conflict that sets the stage for the *Iliad* is a contest between two men caught in the need to satisfy their egos. Neither Achilles nor Agamemnon particularly values the wretched

Trojan princess: she simply happens to be a symbol, a prize that publicly identifies the best man. But the two great warriors are ready to ruin themselves, their families and friends, in order to protect the idea of self nurtured in their minds. As soon as a hero becomes self-conscious, he identifies his whole being with his reputation. And once he does that, in order to continue existing, he must keep up his reputation at whatever cost.

The example from the *Iliad* also illustrates that, with the advent of reflective consciousness, the ego begins to use possessions to symbolize the self. As William James clearly saw: "A man's Self is the sum-total of all that he can call his, not only his body, and his psychic powers, but his clothes and his house, his wife and children, his ancestors and friends, his reputation and works, his land and horse and yacht and bank account."

The problem is that the more the ego becomes identified with symbols outside the self the more vulnerable it becomes. James goes on to write that the sudden loss of one's possessions results in a "shrinkage of our personality, a partial conversion of ourselves to nothingness." To prevent its annihilation, the ego forces us to be constantly on the watch for anything that might threaten the symbols on which it relies. Our view of the world becomes polarized into "good" and "bad"; to the first belong those things that support the image of the self, to the second those that threaten it. This is how the third veil of Maya works: it distorts reality so as to make it congruent with the needs of the ego.

The ideas that become central representations of the self are those in which a person invests the most psychic energy. For the Greek warriors it was honor, for the early Christians it was religious faith. There were times when Christians forced to choose between death and rejection of their faith chose death, because annihilation of a self built upon a religious foundation would have been worse. In the thirteenth century the Cathars of southern France let themselves be killed by the thousands rather than give up their worldview, a view that other Christians believed to be heresy. Of the major religions today only Islam seems to command this degree of total allegiance. At least in technological societies, people rarely build their egos around religious faith any longer.

Currently the symbols of the self tend to be more of the material kind. Scratch the paint on someone's new car, and he's liable to kill you. If psychic energy is invested in a home, furniture, a retirement plan, or stocks, then these will be the objects that must be protected in order to ensure the safety of the self. The advantages of identifying the self with possessions are obvious. The man who drives a Rolls-Royce is immediately recognized by everyone as someone successful and important. Objects give concrete evidence of their owner's power, and the ego can increase its boundaries almost indefinitely by claiming control over greater quantities of material possessions. But the more the self becomes identified with external objects, the more vulnerable it becomes. After all, nobody can really control fame and fortune—not an absolute ruler like Alexander the Great, not a multibillionaire like Robert Maxwell—and for those who depend too much on them to define who they are, any threat to acquisitions will threaten the core of being. It is for this reason that religious and philosophical systems have always been so ambivalent about material strivings, and prescribed instead the development of a self that has a value independent of external accomplishments.

Objects are not the only external symbols by which the ego represents the self. Kinship and other human relationships are also very important. We invest a great deal of attention in those who are close to us, and thus they become indispensable to our sense of who we are. Especially in societies where fewer material possessions are available, ties with others are the central, defining components of the self. Even the war described in the *Iliad* started because Paris, one of the sons of the Trojan king, eloped with the wife of Agamemnon's brother. The symbolism of her leaving was intolerable to the egos of the principals involved.

Human relationships seem a much sounder basis for building an image of the self than material possessions. Unfortunately the temptation to use other people to aggrandize one's ego is also quite strong, and many people find it difficult to resist. Parents who are overprotective of their children, lovers who are exceedingly jealous, paternalistic employers, revolutionaries ready to sacrifice lives for the good of humankind often do not care much for the well-being of the people with whom they interact. The effort to "help" or "protect" is often a way of demonstrating the ability to control, and therefore the power of the self.

Because the ego is such a source of trouble, there have been many efforts made to abolish it. Some of the Eastern religions have come up with the most radical prescriptions to this effect. Their arguments are quite logical: If a person refuses to invest psychic energy in goals, gives up desires, and does not identify with any idea, belief, object, or human relationship, then in a certain sense he or she becomes invulnerable. By our nature we want certain things to happen; when our desires are frustrated, we suffer. By giving up expectation and desire—in effect, by giving up the self—one can no longer be frustrated. Whatever happens will be acceptable. A vulgarized version of this solution seems to have imbued the attitude of many young people these last few decades. The expression "It's no problem," and the statement "I'm O.K., you're O.K." are distant cousins of that detached stance.

Could the radical project of ridding oneself of the self succeed? It is unlikely that a society would survive if a majority of its people were to become entirely selfless. And even if one were successful in giving up desires, one must at the same time by necessity also give up hope, ambition, and striving for a better, or even for a different, future. The person without an ego—if he or she actually exists—is a great rarity, an exemplary specimen that is a useful model to show us that this also is a possibility. But it is not likely to be the way of the third millennium.

If there are to be a thousand years longer in which we will evolve, however, it will be necessary to find better ways to build selves. The type of ego that might pull us through is one secure enough to forgo desires beyond what are necessary. It will be one that relies on possessions that are not scarce. Instead of competing for the same symbolic resources, as Achilles and Agamemnon did, it will be satisfied with what is unique about itself and its experiences. And despite greater individuality, it will be a self identified with the greatest common good—not only with kin and country, but with humanity as a whole, and beyond humanity, with the principle of life itself, with the process of evolution. It is difficult to see at this point how humanity can survive otherwise.

The first stages toward constructing such a self involve clearing the mind of the illusions that drain psychic energy and leave us impotent to control our lives. These illusions are the inevitable consequence of being born of flesh, in a human culture, with a brain complex enough to have become conscious of its own workings. They are inevitable, but they are not inescapable. To become free of the facticity of existence, at first we need only to step back and reflect on what makes us function. As we begin to see behind our acts the control being exerted by genes, by the culture, and by the ego, and as we realize the extent to which we are following their instructions, we might become discouraged and hopeless. But the harsh winds of reality are bracing as well. The realization that many of our actions are not of our choosing is the first step toward the development of a more authentic, more genuinely individual agenda.

People who lead a satisfying life, who are in tune with their past and with their future—in short, people whom we would call "happy"—are generally individuals who have lived their lives according to rules they themselves created. They eat according to their own schedules, sleep when they are sleepy, work because they enjoy doing it, choose their friends and relationships for good reasons. They understand their motives and their limitations. They have carved out a small freedom of choice. Typically they are not people who want much for themselves. They may be ambitious dreamers, great builders and doers, but their goals are not selfish in any of the three senses of serving the goals of the genes, the culture, or the ego. They do what they do because they enjoy meeting the challenges of life, because they enjoy life itself. They feel that they are part of the universal order, and identify themselves with harmonious growth. It is this kind of self that will make survival into the third millennium possible.

But before thinking through how an evolutionary self can be created, it is necessary to spend more time looking at the conditions that make such a self so difficult to attain. In addition to the obstacles built into the mind by genes and by culture, our freedom to apprehend reality is curtailed by competition with other people, and with the products of our own thoughts. In the next chapter, we shall review how evolutionary pressures often produce differences in power between individuals, differences that can easily turn into oppression and exploitation. And Chapter 5 will deal in more depth with how the fruits of technology and of the human imagination drain scarce physical and psychic resources. These factors outside the mind can prevent the free exercise of control over our lives as effectively as any of the internal impediments; therefore, it is useful to become better acquainted with them.

FURTHER THOUGHTS ON "THE VEILS OF MAYA"

Illusion and Reality

What kind of information do you trust the most? Think of something you are absolutely sure of. How do you know it is true? For example, what direct evidence do you have for facts such as the following: (a) the earth revolves around the sun, (b) you have experienced love, (c) Picasso was a great painter, (d) there is (or there is not) life after death?

It's a good exercise to occasionally look at an object that comes into your view as if you don't know what it is, as if you do not even know its name. Can you look at a chair or a lamp in a room without prejudice, as if you were seeing such a thing for the first time, and refuse to think of it as "chair" or "lamp"?

The World of the Genes

What is attractive to you about people of the opposite sex? Of the same sex? Why?

Eating and sex are two of the basic needs we all have. How much of your psychic energy do these two needs consume? How much energy does it take to keep to a diet and to repress sexual desires? How can you free up some energy that is under the control of these needs?

The World of Culture

What about your family, your city, your country—in what ways do you think they are better than other families, cities, or countries? In what ways are they worse?

Have you ever tried to understand what life must feel like to a mother of small children in Bangladesh, or in Ethiopia?

The World of the Self

When a person gets in front of you in a line, do you get very upset? Do you get jealous easily of other people's good fortune? Do you feel that you should always have the last word in an argument? Do you keep grudges for a long time? How much psychic energy could you save by not letting these feelings overcome you?

If you were to represent the self by drawing a series of five (or ten) concentric circles, like a bullseye, with the one in the center representing that which is most essentially "You," how would you label the circles? What would you write in the middle one—a value? a quality? a possession? a relationship?

4

PREDATORS AND
PARASITES

The previous chapter reviewed three sources of illusion that interfere with the ability to see clearly and to act freely. If we can understand better what our built-in motivational biases are, it was argued, we shall no longer be under the total control of the body, the culture, or the ego. But this is not enough for becoming active partners in the construction of the future. There are other obstacles that first need to be confronted. In contrast to the veils of Maya, which are internal, these obstacles arise out of interactions with other people. They are the results of the competitive pressures inherent in evolution. All of us have a built-in incentive to take advantage of other people in order to advance our own interests. We all try to gain as much power as possible, to extract as much energy as we can from the environment, to make our lives more secure and comfortable. Therefore oppression and parasitic exploitation are constant features of evolution. But oppression and exploitation also distort the perception of reality, both for those who win and for those who lose out in the process.

THE FORCES OF SELECTION

Evolution is directed by natural selection. Nobody can predict how "natural selection" will work, or describe it a priori. It is only after a certain species of animals dies out that we say, "Oh, it was eliminated by natural selection." The conditions that make one kind of organism survive but not another are still too complex and changeable to make predictions about their chances possible. Not so long ago, the human race seemed slated for a brilliant future. If any life-form was going to survive, we certainly seemed to be it. But now it is possible for a drunk officer in some missile silo to press the wrong button, and then natural selection might give the prize to the cockroach.

We exist because organisms who carried our genes in the past were able to pass them on from generation to generation all the way to the present. But not only genes evolve; so do *memes,* that is, patterns of behavior, values, languages, and technologies. The information contained in memes is not passed on through chemical instructions on chromosomes, but through imitation and learning. When you learn the tune of "Greensleeves," or the way to tie a shoelace, or the words of the Declaration of Independence, you are part of the process of selection that transmits memes through time.

Selection always involves a choice between two or more alternatives. In natural selection, an organism that produces many viable offspring will have more of a chance to transmit the instructions in his or her body than another who has fewer offspring; thus the first will be able to make more copies of itself and populate the earth. Currently the rate of birth for Turkish guest workers in Germany is much higher than that for native Germans; if the trend were to continue, natural selection would slowly replace German genes with Turkish ones. The same trend exists in the United States, where the birth rate for Hispanics is higher than that for Anglos.

A few years ago, during a trip to rural Finland, my wife and I stopped at a farm next to a small village hidden between misty lakes and boundless fir forests. It was a perfect setting for a Nordic myth. One expected blond Vikings to stride forth from behind the mossy rocks, singing verses from the *Kalevala*. But instead, we noticed little tykes with distinctly Asian features who seemed quite at home in the subarctic landscape. Our Finnish host ruefully responded to our puzzlement. For many years now the output of the farms in this region could not compete successfully with agricultural products imported from warmer climates. Like so many farmers in the Western world, the locals were paid by the government for letting their land remain unproductive. But the life was poor and boring compared to that in Helsinki. The region's men still clung to the fields, because a man's self was too closely identified with his farm, but more and more of the young women left to work in urban electronic factories.

Without women, of course, the old, traditional life of the Finnish villagers was sure to end. What to do? Bright middlemen soon filled the market niche. They advertised tours to the Philippines for the equivalent of ten thousand dollars, with a bridal show included. You could go and choose a woman willing to follow you across the world, provided that you paid a little extra to her family. How did these poor immigrants adjust to the harsh land, the foreign ways, the language they could not understand? Not very well. But it was their children who were now running in the cold forests, bringing new genes to places where for centuries there had been no biological change. What does this do to the selection for or against Finnish genes?

The catch is that, as far as we know, there is no such thing as specifically "Finnish" or "Filipino" genes. Humans belong to the same species, and the chemical instructions we carry are so well mixed that there are very few genetic traits unique to a given culture or ethnic group. In fact, geneticists now figure that chimpanzees and humans share over 94 percent of their genetic instructions—yet, *vive la différence!* The relevant consideration for our species' future is not so much whether the gene pool of the Finns will be diluted by Filipino genes, or that the United States will be slowly invaded by Hispanic (or Slavic, or Asian) genes. The more germane possibility is that foreign memes will displace the original meme pool. To the extent that Hispanic parents teach their children the Spanish language and their native customs and values, the English language and the attendant cultural habits might lose out. (Of course, English memes in America are not really "original," since they displaced the many native American cultures in the last few hundred years.)

The evolution of memes is now probably much more critical than genetic evolution in determining our future. Therefore, it is essential to understand better how we select the information contained in memes. Each one of us is involved in this process, and to the extent that we know what we are doing, we can participate in setting its direction. But before we can turn to consider what a positive evolutionary direction might look like, it is useful to consider some of the peculiar dangers of cultural—or mimetic—evolution. As we shall see, many of the features that make natural selection seem "red in tooth and claw" are repeated in similar form in the selection and transmission of memes.

POWER AND OPPRESSION

One feature that distinguishes humans from other animals—perhaps as characteristic as speech or upright posture—is the fact that we find so many ways to oppress and exploit one another. Distinctions of wealth, status, and knowledge make it possible for some individuals to live off the psychic energy expended by others. "Power" is the generic term to describe the ability of a person to have others expend their lives to satisfy his or her goals. Power can be based on money, property, fear, or respect; it can be wielded by a person or by a group. Power can be dangerous, for as Lord Acton saw it, "Power tends to corrupt; absolute power corrupts absolutely." Even with the best of intentions, a powerful individual, group, or country will eventually assume that it has the right to live better than those less powerful. The average person living in the United States uses up many more natural resources than one born in India or China. Whether we like it or not, we have the potential to control the lives of strangers possessing fewer resources, and therefore to exploit them, to a degree unprecedented in history.

When there are great differences in power, exploitation takes place even when people have the best of intentions. For example, in the newly rich Gulf countries like Kuwait, it is natural for the citizens to refuse to do menial jobs like cleaning streets, driving trucks, building houses, or even becoming policemen and soldiers. On the other hand, thousands of Pakistanis and Filipinos are eager to do these jobs, for much lower wages than a Kuwaiti would expect to be paid. Therefore it makes a good deal of sense to admit millions of third-world "guest workers" to do the dirty work. This scenario, of course, is familiar to every relatively wealthy country, from Sweden to Italy. In the United States it is the reason for the steady influx of unregistered workers from Mexico and Eastern Europe.

There is nothing wrong with such voluntary readjustments of populations. As long as both parties are content, there is no question of oppression or exploitation. Unfortunately such an equilibrium remains stable only for a short time. A Turkish worker in Germany, or a Mexican worker in the U.S., will soon begin aspiring to the social benefits available to the more powerful citizens. Health insurance, social security, pension plans, unemployment benefits, voting privileges—all the perks of living in a powerful society begin to be contested. Of course the citizens of the host country tend to become indignant at such aspirations—after all, the guests were invited in precisely because they didn't expect much in the first place. At this point, the stage is set for a conflict with charges and countercharges of exploitation.

To avoid such an outcome, many of the richer nations have adopted various policies that allow them to use cheaper labor without creating a troublesome underclass. For instance, thousands of young people arrive each year in Switzerland from Spain, Portugal, and practically every other country to wash the dishes and clean the rooms in the innumerable hotels that provide that nation with its most reliable source of cash flow. These guest workers receive visas that entitle them to work for a number of months just short of what it would take to be eligible to begin drawing health care and other social benefits; at that point they have to return home. After a year they can return, but again only for a period just short of getting coverage. Plans such as these are of course very sensible, yet they are not entirely free from exploitation.

In the past, the United States has been able to absorb huge waves of poor immigrants without establishing a permanently disenfranchised underclass—with the possible exception of the African-American and Native American populations. To what extent this country will retain its capacity to maintain a reasonably classless society remains to be seen. By all accounts, the gap between the haves and the have-nots is increasing. If present trends continue, with time, inheritance of wealth and status is likely to play an increasing role in determining who will be able to use his or her psychic energy freely, and who will be exploited.

For most of human history—the millions of years that Zorg and his fellows roamed the earth in hunting and gathering bands—it was practically impossible for one individual to establish a firm control over another. If the dominant male of a band became too brutal, the others left and joined another group. Leaders could use their size and strength to intimidate followers, but brute strength alone is never a very satisfactory means of domination. In any case, there was very little to control. Except for more food and more sex, what could Zorg desire? If he tried to appropriate his fellows' stone axes or pots, he would soon get exhausted dragging them along on his daily hunting expeditions. If he tried to get others to work for him, they would soon disappear over the horizon, leaving Zorg to fend for himself. So for the longest stretches of human evolution, the exploitation of men (and women) by men was not a rewarding proposition. It probably happened quite often on an occasional basis, but it was impossible to establish in any lasting form.

The situation changed dramatically when farming became the main form of subsistence in the last fifteen thousand years or so. First of all, farming tied people down to a specific territory. Whereas hunters could always move on, it was much more difficult for farmers to relocate. They had too much psychic energy invested in their fields, and any good land in the immediate area was probably settled by someone else. Second, agriculture—as opposed to hunting and collecting—produced a surplus that could be stored away. This meant that through skill or good luck some people amassed more food than others. At that point, inheritance of wealth became possible, and under the right conditions it could bring about permanent caste or class distinctions. Third, farming required relatively specialized knowledge and ownership of land and tools. Some individuals inevitably were able to acquire more productive land or make better tools, and since they produced more food, they accumulated wealth. Putting these three conditions together, the scene was set for permanent, institutionalized exploitation.

The rest, quite literally, is history. Those who happened to be wealthy, or who owned means of production—that is land, tools, beasts of burden—were able to employ others who lacked the means of making a living for themselves. By and large, the rich had few scruples about using the psychic energy of the poor for their own benefit. After all, wealth was like a new cultural virus for which humanity had not yet developed antibodies—those would come only later, with the development of laws, religious restraints, the organization of labor unions, and so forth. In the meantime, very shortly after the agricultural revolution, or by roughly eight thousand years ago, all over the world new social forms arose, based on despotic rulers who had amassed enough surplus to hire great armies, build fantastic cities, and erect huge tombs to transmit the memory of their own unique existence down the generations.

Thus ended equality. As soon as memes began to play a larger role in human affairs, it became possible for some people to exploit others. Marx was not far off when he wrote that human history is the history of class conflict. Once certain groups became entrenched in their ability to control others, the seeds of conflict were sown. Where Marx was wrong was in the extreme oversimplification of this conflict. His idea was that history followed a slow, linear progression from tribal societies, where all men were equal, to slavery, then to feudal systems, to mercantilism, and to unrestricted capitalism, which was destined to self-destruct, thus setting the stage for a new, classless society that would do away with exploitation—the dictatorship of the proletariat. But differences in power are not as easy to erase as Marx had naïvely believed. During the seventy years in which the "dictatorship of the proletariat" ruled the Soviet Union, a powerful clique of ruthless politicians and bureaucrats became more of a burden on the backs of the citizenry than the old Czarist court had been.

Also, exploiters alternate much more rapidly than Marx would have thought possible. For example, within this century the control over resources in Central Europe has changed hands at least three times. In 1945, with the help of Soviet troops, the disenfranchised proletariat took away the property and the power of the then-ruling propertied classes. In countries like Poland, Rumania, Czechoslovakia, Hungary, Yugoslavia, and Bulgaria, if your parents or even grandparents had been members of the middle class, you were now considered a "class enemy." You would have been blacklisted from most jobs, and probably not have been admitted to a university. But since 1990, ownership and power are again being redistributed. Clearly, some of the old Communist Party officials are going to come out on top again in the new market-driven regimes, because they were the only ones with the opportunity to hoard resources and information; nevertheless, the change is bound to be quite drastic. Perhaps the new power elite will be less exploitive than the former Communist one was; still, it is quite certain that many people who will be unable to profit from the changes will feel that their life energy is being consumed by a new class of capitalist entrepreneurs. After all, even in a democratic, egalitarian society such as Finland people speak in hushed tones about the twenty or so families who control the country.

Oppression is a condition in which the psychic energy of one person is controlled by another against his or her will. To a certain extent, we all have to do things we don't like because someone more powerful wants us to do them. American teenagers spend the largest part of the day in school, and 70 percent of the time they wish they weren't there (the remaining 30 percent of the time they are not in the classroom but in halls, cafeteria, or student center, and at those times they don't feel as strongly constrained). The same pattern holds true for many American adults with respect to their jobs. But these are not really examples of oppression, because students and workers hope to derive some future benefit from alienating their psychic energy in the present.

The purest example of oppressive exploitation is slavery. What makes it intolerable is not so much that slaves have to work hard—modern executives might work even harder—but that they cannot control their attention freely. They cannot choose where to be, what to do, whom to marry. Thus they are deprived of the basic condition of humanity—control over psychic energy. Not surprisingly, the Greek philosophers concluded that slaves were not really human because they lacked freedom of choice.

But there are many other ways to exploit psychic energy short of slavery. Everyone would prefer to have his needs and desires satisfied without having to work for them. Whenever we can get away with doing so, we will take the opportunity. The teenager who expects his parents to buy him a new car at the slightest excuse, the husband who lets his working wife do all the housework, the CEO who uses company income to pay himself outlandish salaries and bonuses are all familiar attempts to have other people spend their lives making one's own more comfortable.

Oppressors often start their careers as protectors, and only later turn into exploiters. One interesting example is the historian Leslie White's account of how the feudal system developed in Europe. According to White, after the powerful Roman Empire collapsed, most of its land returned to semi-autonomous farmers living in isolated villages. These farmers could generally defend their independence against potential enemies, who were not that much better armed or trained than they were. But then, between the sixth and the eighth centuries, a fateful technological innovation changed the balance of power, and hence the politics and the lifestyle of the entire continent. The innovation was the stirrup, adopted from the nomads of the Asian steppes.

Before stirrups were in use, it was easy for mounted soldiers to slip off the backs of their horses accidentally. Therefore, they could not be heavily armed, or any slight loss of balance would bring about a fall. But with stirrups, a horseman could wear increasingly heavy armor and still keep his seat. Soon knights in shining armor began to roam the land, and they were almost indestructible. The farmers realized that if they wanted to keep their crops safe, their only defense was to have knights of their own. In many villages the farmers themselves chipped in to buy the expensive gear—lance, sword, mail shirt, body armor, helmet, gauntlets, and so forth—so they could outfit a strong local lad and make him their protector. This scheme worked for a while, but soon the freshly minted knight realized that if he wanted to exploit his former patrons there was nothing the farmers could do about it. After a few generations the knights and their descendants developed into a separate caste, with their own specialized skills, ideology, and lifestyle, living handsomely off the labors of those who had originally created them.

Oppression is often made possible by a new technological advance—sometimes as dramatic as the introduction of farming, sometimes as apparently trivial as the stirrup. Whenever a new meme makes it possible for some individuals to get an edge over others, exploitation is sure to follow. To keep control over our own psychic energy, it becomes essential that we understand how power is being used. We cannot be free unless we learn to protect ourselves from other people's ambitions, and unless we refrain from exploiting others.

THE EXPLOITATION OF WOMEN AND CHILDREN

Some power differences are built into our biological makeup, and therefore lend themselves more easily to oppression. Whereas in many insect species it is the females that have the advantages—males often live only long enough to mate, whereas females have long and varied careers—among mammals the physical advantages tend to run in the opposite direction. For instance, in many mammalian species males tend to be considerably larger and stronger than females. This "sexual dimorphism" seems to have an adaptive value. Males specialize in protecting the young, therefore they need to be strong; if females spend most of their time taking care of infants, they can afford to be smaller and less threatening. If both sexes were large, more food would be needed to keep everyone fit, so under conditions of scarcity it is easier for species that are sexually dimorphous to survive. Human beings, like most other mammals, fit this pattern.

Unfortunately this sensible physical differentiation, which should benefit both males and females equally, can be easily corrupted. In many societies, the physical power advantage males have is exploited to give them control over women's lives. In much of Asia the patriarchal system leaves women with few choices over their own destiny. Infanticide in China and other parts of the world is still rather common, and it is female babies that are most often killed. Extreme forms of exploitation are also prominently directed against women. According to some estimates, each year one million Asian girls are sold or lured into the equivalent of slavery. In the poorer regions of Asia—India, Bangladesh, the Philippines, Burma, Thailand, Sri Lanka—prostitution rings are among the most profitable enterprises. The flesh trade is made possible by the vast disparities in wealth between these and the rich countries such as Japan and the oil kingdoms.

Although women are often forced against their wills to give up control over their bodies and the freedom of their minds, many of them are lured into prostitution by promises of getting well-paid jobs as "entertainers." They accept in the hope of being able to send money home to their families, only to find out too late that they have put themselves in the hands of ruthless exploiters. There are now about 300,000 imported Asian women selling sex in Japan, but few of them end up making any money; it is the pimps and brothel owners who get rich. In China, a farmer can buy a kidnapped concubine for $300; an Arab can buy one in India for even less.

The other class of persons who are at a physical disadvantage—at least temporarily—is children. In most historical periods, they have been shamefully exploited by adults who needed extra pairs of hands to do work, and who could count on the collusion of the more powerful segments of society. Here an Anglican curate describes the typical fate of a young boy in an English textile factory during the heyday of the Industrial Revolution, in the middle of the last century:

> He . . . had been found standing asleep with his arms full of wool and had been beaten awake. This day he had worked seventeen hours; he was carried home by his father, was unable to eat his supper, awoke at 4 A.M. the next morning and asked his brothers if they could see the lights of the mill as he was afraid of being late, and then died. (His younger brother, aged nine, had died previously. . . .)

Conditions in many parts of the world are no better for children even today. The investigative reporter Uli Schmetzer estimates that in Asia 40 million children below age fifteen have to work in miserable conditions, most of them for more than eight hours a day, many for as long as fourteen hours. According to some estimates, by 1990 about 13 million children in America lived below the poverty line. Child abuse and neglect reports have increased from an estimated 669,000 in 1976 to 2,178,000 ten years later, a 300 percent increase. The situation is even worse in much of the rest of the world. According to a recent United Nations report, about 10 million children below the age of five die each year from illnesses like diarrhea or respiratory infections that could be easily treated with rehydration therapy and antibiotics; 150 million are clinically malnourished; about 100 million live by their wits alone in the streets; and many more are abused, exploited, and forced into prostitution.

Women and children are made potentially helpless by their relatively inferior physical strength. This of course does not mean that their exploitation is inevitable, but it does make it easier for unscrupulous oppressors to take advantage of their superior power. Because of this, in all societies, even the simplest ones, roles are different according to gender and age. All men might be equal, and all women, but men and women will have different rights and different responsibilities, and these rights and responsibilities will differ according to age. Some cultures have evolved in such a way as to give women more power than others, and some treat children very well while others ignore or abuse them. One of the few unequivocal achievements of cultural evolution has been to make blatant forms of sexual and child exploitation less likely. But such gains are fragile and tenuous, and they must be defended at every step of the way. Oppression can take many different forms. For instance, contemporary feminists are justly suspicious of the practice of "putting women on a pedestal," because an idealization of femininity has often been used to mask the effective relegation of women to domestic and decorative roles.

Of course, not all the biological disadvantages are on the side of women and children. Children eventually grow up, and women tend to live longer than men—in our society, on the average about seven years longer. Consequently, women end up inheriting a larger share of property. This seems to have been the case even in medieval Europe, where most of the civilian contracts and deeds were in the names of women. And even if the notion is nowadays unfashionable, one should not underestimate the power that women have in society owing to their nurturing role. The line "The hand that rocks the cradle is the hand that rules the world" has a subtle psychological truth to it, as so many powerful men who are still dependent on their mothers demonstrate.

INDIVIDUAL DIFFERENCES IN POWER

But of course exploitation does not thrive only on differences in gender and age. Each man is different from other men in terms of an almost infinite list of variations, and so is every woman different from other women. What traits one happens to inherit will make it either easier or harder to maintain one's freedom from the encroachment of other people's wills. Whatever the Declaration of Independence might have meant by the self-evident truth that all men are created equal, it could not have meant that this is so in terms of natural endowment. While it is a worthy social goal to assume that all individuals have equal rights to certain social goods, their equality in terms of health, strength, physical attractiveness, intelligence, skin pigmentation, temperament, and character—among other traits—is visibly otherwise.

And in every known society such variations are used as indices of power. In hunting societies physical agility coupled with prudence will lift a man to leadership; among the Huns and Tartars ruthless visionaries were held in high esteem; intelligence, stealthiness, and steadiness allowed men to rise to the top in the great bureaucracies of China and the Middle East. In our culture, we tend to promote employees who are "aggressive" but cheerful, enterprising yet conforming. In every culture, good looks and extroversion add to a person's ability to attract the attention of other people, and therefore potentially to control them.

Personal qualities are not the only reason why one person becomes more powerful than another. Luck also plays a major role. Being at the right place at the right time often explains why this particular businessman became rich rather than another, why this physicist won the Nobel Prize or this general won the war. Claudius stuttered and limped, and although he was of royal blood, nobody in Rome dreamed he would one day become an emperor. Fortunately for him all of his relatives were homicidal maniacs, who diligently killed one another off until only he was left to shoulder the purple.

Nonetheless, luck aside, probably the factor that most helps determine the ease with which a person will gain power and increase his or her chances of influencing the future is personality. Although psychologists are by no means unanimous in agreeing whether there are traits that help a person to be uniformly successful in different areas of life, it seems clear that if you are an extrovert, have strong self-esteem, and look at the world with optimism, you will have a better chance of becoming successful and leading a satisfying life. Some of these traits appear to be temperamental, that is, largely determined by genetic inheritance; on the other hand, they can all be influenced to a certain extent by early environment. A child who at birth is inclined to be an optimist is likely to turn into a neurotic adult if treated with cruelty.

One well-established trait is "personality strength," studied for many years by the German survey researcher Elisabeth Noelle-Neumann. People who score high on this trait (which is related also to extroversion and self-esteem) tend to be more active and successful personally and professionally than people low on the scale. They also tend to take positions of leadership and influence, especially individuals on the lower rungs of the socioeconomic ladder. In other words, for those who are rich and well educated, a strong personality is not as crucial a determinant as it is for those who are poor and not well educated, because wealth and status will compensate for a weak personality. But if you are poor, a strong personality helps to get ahead in life. Strong personalities from all classes are curious, try many new things, and enjoy influencing others, and are thus especially well equipped to affect the evolution of memes, for their beliefs, ideas, and habits will be represented more frequently in the future. One encouraging finding of these studies is that people with strong personalities seem to be less selfish and more concerned with helping others than those whose personalities are less strong. Apparently whatever trait makes for success and influence also includes a feeling of responsibility for the community.

All too often, however, when one achieves a position of power, it becomes easy to take advantage of it. Whether it is luck, intelligence, or personality strength that propels a person to a position of eminence in the social system, the opportunities for saving psychic energy at others' expense are almost irresistible. The successful businessman finds it self-evident that his time is more valuable than that of his chauffeur, secretary, his less fortunate friends, the pastor of his church, or his wife and children. Why should he be particularly concerned about these less worthy individuals? And why should he not receive more money for his efforts, much more money than most people could even imagine? Powerful politicians begin to believe that the rules binding less eminent mortals to the social contract do not apply to them as well. President Nixon and his retinue thought themselves above the law, but they were of course amateurs compared to potentates in most other societies. Respected academicians are tempted to exploit graduate students, while artists of renown find they can dispense with social graces and abuse the bourgeoisie.

Fortunately there are always exceptions to show that corruption is not inevitable. Great feats of courage are admirable, and so are useful contributions to science and society, but the most marvelous human accomplishment is to refrain from abusing one's privileges.

Is conflict based on individual differences inevitable? Probably so. In evolution a positive change can happen only if there is selection, and selection works only when differences exist between individuals—that is, if one trait is better adapted to the environment than others. As long as all individuals survive equally well, and produce a similar number of offspring, there is going to be nothing to choose from, and every generation will look like the preceding one. Differences are the starting point of selection, and therefore of evolutionary change. Consequently, almost all evolutionary biologists stress the importance of competition between different individuals as the engine that propels evolution. Competition, however, need not involve aggression or exploitation, or even latent conflict, for in evolutionary terms, competition refers simply to the fact that some organisms reproduce more successfully than others. Even cooperation can be a very effective competitive strategy, which explains why social systems bound by laws and division of labor have evolved everywhere on the planet. But we need not concern ourselves too much about how conflict and competition affect biological evolution. The question is how they affect human evolution as a whole, and that nowadays involves primarily changes in ways of thinking—the decisions we make on the basis of our goals and beliefs.

THE TRANSMISSION OF INEQUALITY

Generally we do not resent it when a person acquires a great deal of power if it was earned because of superior effort or unusual talent. But inequality becomes much less tolerable if it is based on inherited wealth or status. Yet one of the first instincts of someone who has control over power is to try to pass it along to family and descendants. This effort, too, is a time-honored adaptive instinct that became magnified in the course of cultural evolution. As long as we could leave our offspring only our genes, differences in what any child could inherit were minimal, and confined to the range of physical variations present in the genetic pool. One boy would be relatively stronger than the rest, one girl more alert than her peers, but that was the luck of the draw.

Real inequality, and the attendant feelings of envy and jealousy, comes about when the elements of power begin to be passed on through cultural inheritance. One of the earliest methods of pooling resources and increasing one's power has been through selective marriage practices. Rich and powerful men married women from rich and powerful families, thus guaranteeing that their children would begin life with advantages. As long as like marries like, inequalities are not only preserved but they also become exaggerated with each generation. The concern for keeping power within one's family ultimately leads to formalized practices that encourage social division. For instance, Romans were forbidden by law to marry provincials so as not to dilute the highly valued rank of "citizen."

In our society we no longer have laws against miscegenation (although some states did prohibit interracial marriages up until the Supreme Court ruling of 1967). But in effect "selective mating" continues to be a very strong practice. Like still tends to marry like as far as income, education, political preferences, religion, and race are concerned. Perhaps the most important effects of this trend are not on the genes the offspring will inherit, but on his or her memes. A child born to an educated, well-to-do white couple is going to learn different values and develop a different self-concept from a genetically similar child born to an interracial couple of the same social standing, or to a couple with a different level of education and income. The more homogeneous the couple's background, the more the child's memes are likely to resemble those of the parents.

Because some of the most important memes—the basic world-views and values—are transmitted through the family, it follows that, with time, selective mating results in the equivalent of *cultural speciation,* in which members of social groups become differentiated and even segregated by virtue of their cultural backgrounds. This process makes it practically impossible for an Amish boy to marry a Catholic girl, or for an extreme liberal to marry a staunch conservative—almost as if they belonged to different species who cannot mate with each other because they are biologically incompatible. As long as selective mating keeps the memes segregated, the cultures continue to remain distinct, and the child born to the liberal couple will learn to see the offspring of conservatives as a potentially enemy alien.

Of course, marriage practices are not the only way to keep power in the family and to pass it along to one's descendants. Tax and inheritance laws have always played an important role in politics because they determine to what extent economic power will be concentrated or distributed. One of the first laws the Communists passed after coming to power in Russia was to prohibit parents from leaving property to their children, so that all citizens would start life on an equal footing. (Unfortunately, the powerful Communist functionaries soon found a way to subvert that law, and nepotism became almost as flagrant in the U.S.S.R. as it had been under the Czars.) During the 1980s, under the Reagan administration, changes in the tax laws increased economic inequality in America to a startling degree, making the rich richer and the poor poorer. When control over resources becomes highly polarized, the affluent, even with the best of intentions, become de facto oppressors. They need not actively seek to prevent their less well-off peers from getting a good education or living in a nice neighborhood; the invisible hand of the market will do it for them.

Returning to the question of whether exploitation is inevitable, one must conclude that some inequality in the access to resources, in the control of psychic energy, and in the ability to influence the future shape of culture is indeed unavoidable. In any complex social system, some individuals will be more fit, by virtue of temperament, training, or background, to occupy certain positions than others. In large organizations such as Motorola or Nissan, each of which employs about twenty thousand technicians, a few engineers will be better able than others to apply their skills to the opportunities available in their respective companies. They will be paid better and advance further, and their ideas will be incorporated in new products. Colleagues left behind will envy them, and many will resent the fact that they have to work for them. Each organization in effect selects the "fittest" among its employees. It is important to realize, however, that such fitness is not based on some absolute advantage that the successful engineers possess. The person who makes it to the top at Motorola may be a failure at Nissan, and vice versa. One set of skills might fit one company culture, a particular economic climate, a specific marketing strategy, but not another.

Even though some people will always succeed in controlling more resources than others, does that control necessarily lead to exploitation? It is probably true that unless we take steps to prevent it, control over resources will tend to result in control of other individuals. "Eternal vigilance," Jefferson said, "is the price of liberty." This implies, among other things, that if we don't take care, our freedom to dispose of psychic. energy will be diluted. Our savings, the product of years of work, will lose their value if people who spend more than they earn cause an inflation. Our job may be suddenly discontinued because investors can realize higher profits by manufacturing in a third-world country. The value of our tiny plot of real estate will fluctuate depending on the buying and selling of large landowners. All of this can happen without any malice or the slightest bad intentions; it is simply the way the market works, when it is manipulated—as it always is—by those who own a large share of it.

What can we do to prevent this from occurring? Again, as with the sources of illusion, the first step is simply to become aware of the real state of affairs. Is anyone using your energy without adequate return? Your boss, your spouse, the power company, the government? Examining in detail who or what is in a position to decide how you invest your time, and therefore control the content of your consciousness, is a good start. The next step is to figure out whether you want this situation to continue, or not. If not, can you do anything about it, and what will be the consequences of your actions?

From the very beginning of its history, America has attracted people who had been oppressed in their native countries, and had decided to take control of their own fate. To the early English settlers escaping religious persecution, the Irish escaping from the famine, the Poles who did not want to fight for the Russian Czar, to the Southeast Asians fleeing Communist terror, the United States beckoned as a land where one could make a living and be free. From an evolutionary perspective, the population of the United States is largely a selection of those individuals, from among the people of the earth, who have refused to be exploited. Thus the meme for freedom has become concentrated in the American culture, and this, more than any other single trait, determines its uniqueness.

However, although we don't have Czars or commissars, exploitation is not entirely absent from our society. And those who don't feel in control of their lives here cannot emigrate elsewhere, because it is unlikely that they will find a country where the degree of personal liberty would be effectively greater than what they already have. So the choice is either to find a different lifestyle with fewer constraints, or to fight back—depending on which course provides the most freedom for the least investment of psychic energy.

One way of handling an oppressive situation is illustrated by the case of Jeff, a manager in a utility company, who was responsible for the distribution of electricity in a populous Western region. He had advanced rapidly in the company, partly because of his skills, partly because he was willing to spend sixty to seventy hours each week on his job. At forty Jeff was making a salary higher than anything he had hoped for, and there still remained one or two possible promotions if he was willing to continue to invest time and energy at the expected rate. But he also had a wife and three children whom he rarely saw. Jeff began to feel that his entire life was flowing into his job, and this no longer seemed to make sense. He tried to talk to his superiors to determine if he could cut down on the workload, but was informed that company policy required full commitment from its executives. So Jeff began to look for alternatives, and now he runs an outdoor-equipment franchise, spends many hours each week at home fixing up the old Victorian house he and his wife bought, and can often be found at a nearby creek fishing with his children.

Jeff's solution seems to have worked for him, and for thousands of others in a similar situation who have opted out of the so-called rat race. It is not the best solution for everyone, but it is an example of a feasible solution when one begins to feel exploited by one's job. The point is not to be browbeaten into the belief that you are powerless. It is in the interest of those who control our energy to make it seem that the status quo is natural, right, and impossible to change. It is in our interest to figure out that this is not always true.

PARASITIC EXPLOITATION

A friend who is a biologist and who spent many years in Africa studying the native fauna tells how sad it is to do an autopsy on a freshly killed lion. Most of us hold an idealized picture of the king of the jungle—strong, majestic, and free. But if one looks closely, the powerful lion turns out to be a living shelter for hundreds of different parasites, mites, ticks, and worms making themselves at home in his mane, his eyelids, his tail, his nose, and his throat, down to his gullet and intestines. The lion might look healthy and powerful, but internally he is consumed by legions of vermin. For every complex organism, survival is a constant battle against less complex life-forms that make a career out of using its energy for their own ends.

At the psychological level, a parasite is someone who drains another person's psychic energy, not by direct control, but by exploiting a weakness or inattention. There are innumerable forms of parasitization, and it is useful to be aware of some of them so as to guard against spending our lives working unwittingly to make someone else comfortable.

If oppression is a form of exploitation wherein someone who has more power takes away the freedom of someone who has less, the opposite happens in parasitization. The parasite usually extracts energy from a person who—at least in some respect—is more powerful. For example, suppose tomorrow you win a few million dollars in a lottery. The sudden windfall has increased your power, because now you can hire others to work for you, or you can control them indirectly through interest on capital. As a result of this good fortune, you can now relax, right? Wrong. You will immediately attract a host of individuals who can't wait to siphon off as much of the potential energy you control as possible, and use it for their own benefit. Salesmen, poor relatives, insurance agents, investment brokers, fundraisers, scam artists, and people with pitiful sob stories will suddenly appear and clamor for their share. Lucky individuals who have had money, power, or fame for a long time are chronically surrounded by such would-be parasites.

In some ways this behavior is very natural. As noted before, entropy is the most universal law of nature; it states that complex systems tend to break down, that heat will flow from the warmer to the colder body, that order will decompose into disorder. Parasites are the living manifestation of entropy. They find ways to attach themselves to more complex organisms and exploit their energy with little effort of their own, often harming or killing their hosts in the process.

At the level of cultural evolution, parasites are attracted mostly by wealth and fame. Rock singers attract groupies, wealthy widows attract shady characters, rulers attract sycophants, celebrities of all kinds attract hangers-on. A person surrounded by parasites may need to spend a great deal of his or her energy to avoid being taken advantage of, instead of enjoying life. It is no wonder that so many religions and philosophies make the point that the accumulation of worldly goods fails to bring contentment.

It is true that such relationships are often at least in part symbiotic. Both partners gain something, and the exploitation is not just one-way. The rock singer would feel ignored without an obsequious entourage, and the ruler would feel less powerful without a retinue. (It is an indication of how widespread parasitism is that there are so many synonyms for it: groupie, sycophant, hanger-on, entourage, retinue. . . .) Parasitism is not always easy to distinguish from symbiosis, which occurs when each partner contributes to the other's well-being. But when someone is trying to make you believe that you need him, and you suspect that it's not true, you are probably looking at a would-be parasite.

THE STRATEGY OF IRRESPONSIBILITY

The parasites who drain energy from the more advantaged don't always do so consciously. Individuals who have no access to more complex skills often harm others thoughtlessly in the process of ensuring their own survival and comfort. In biological evolution, parasitism often manifests itself as a selfish strategy that provides individual advantages at the expense of collective well-being. One typical example involves deceptive strategies that result in differential access to reproduction. Because in biological evolution the replication of one's genes is the bottom line of survival, it is inevitable that with time some individuals will evolve ingenious ways to gain sexual access to more members of the opposite sex, giving them a chance to leave more offspring to the future. Thus there will be males who learn to make themselves attractive to females even though it is not to the females' advantage to succumb to their charms, and females who attract a larger than average number of males.

An extreme case of such exploitation involves the child-rearing practices of the cuckoo, which deposits its eggs in the nests of certain other species of birds, leaving the adoptive parents to struggle to feed the baby cuckoos at the expense of their own progeny. Similar practices exist in cultural evolution. Currently we are fast approaching a point in the United States where there will be more children born out of wedlock than legitimate children. This is not primarily a "moral" issue, but rather a question of biological and cultural selection. Fathers and mothers who cannot take responsibility for the nurturing of their children are in effect exploiting the psychic energies of the rest of society in order to transmit their own genes into the next generation. To avoid this form of exploitation, most cultures around the world, from Africa to the Pacific islands, have established protocols to guard against a man or a woman starting to produce children unless the community has some solid evidence that he or she is able to nurture them to adulthood. The expectation of chastity in unmarried women, the elaborate dowries a girl had to have in order to find a husband, or the steep bride-wealth a groom had to provide his prospective father-in-law were not just quaint primitive practices, but very effective means by which communities saw to it that only those individuals who had the ability—and social support—to embark on the energy-intensive task of child rearing would in fact have children.

A form of parasitism that is perhaps unique to cultural evolution is fiscal irresponsibility. A charming illustration of this is the ancient fable of the ant and the grasshopper. During the balmy summer days, the ant was busy hoarding every scrap of food he could find, and storing it in his home. The grasshopper enjoyed the beautiful weather, hopping around and fiddling his tunes night and day. Whenever he met the ant scurrying about with his load of food, he would laugh and taunt the workaholic friend. But when winter came the ant was snug in his home, while the grasshopper jumped around hungry and freezing, looking for food in vain. And of course he was furious at the ant for not sharing his supplies.

Aesop's fable does not in any way represent accurately the situation in the world of insects, but it is quite applicable to certain forms of human exploitation. Much of history has consisted of periods in which some people worked hard to save property, while others squandered their opportunities in careless living. As time passed, the ones who had squandered became incensed at the injustice of owning so little. Often a revolution followed, so that the savings of the ants were redistributed among the grasshoppers. Nowadays one needs no revolution to accomplish this; cycles of inflation and devaluation of money accomplish the same result. The person who invested his psychic energy for many years to create savings, will have that psychic energy siphoned off by people who accumulated debts, went into bankruptcy, and destroyed banks and the worth of the currency in the process.

Just in my own memory, this process has repeated itself twice. All of my grandfather's savings, his pensions, insurance, property, and government bonds were swallowed up without a trace during the great inflation that followed World War I. In an identical pattern, whatever my father succeeded in accumulating during his life was either forcibly taken away, voided, or lost its value as a result of World War II. It is true that these events took place in Europe, and war was their immediate cause. But the United States is not immune to such trends. How safe are your investments? Your pension plans? Even social security gets periodically raided, and we cannot be certain that the various safety nets we laboriously create to ensure our future well-being are not being gnawed away right now by hordes of industrious parasites.

It is probably impossible to rid ourselves of parasites entirely. They are too much a part of life, the dark underside of evolution. Like strains of viruses that mutate quickly just when we think we have found an effective drug to combat them, cultural parasites are adept at changing strategies as soon as we have found a way to neutralize their old ploys. "You make the law," says a cynical Italian proverb, "we'll find the loopholes." It is more than ironic that in the recent savings-and-loan fiasco, which is a better example of successful parasitism than anyone could invent, it is often the individuals most responsible for defrauding the public who are profiting from the efforts to repair the damages. It is typical for a businessman who has defaulted on tens of millions of dollars' worth of loans from various banks to be given new interest-free loans and other financial incentives by the Resolution Trust Corporation, the federal agency created to manage the bailout, so he can buy properties previously owned by S&Ls, even though other buyers are offering to pay more for them. This is an example of a case in which parasitism has become so much a part of the system that it routinely drains a huge amount of energy away from its stated goals. When a society becomes riddled with parasites to such an extent, it will become incapacitated like the proud lion laid low by lice and fleas.

EXPLOITATION THROUGH MIMICRY

Oppressors can be resisted and parasites disarmed, but there is another way to have one's psychic energy exploited, and that is by individuals who appear to be something they in fact are not. In many ways this is the most insidious attack on our freedom, because it is often so difficult to unmask. While we are ready to resist people who act as parasites, we are often eager to cooperate with those who appeal to us under false pretenses, and then take advantage of the relationship to defraud us.

Mimetic exploitation can take place quite innocently, without any intention to do harm. For instance, a long time ago I used to know Cardinal W., who had a powerful position at the Vatican.

Cardinal W. was a pleasant gentleman in his eighties, but without any obvious qualifications that could justify the high office he held. What he did have, however, was a stupendous white beard that seemed spun of silver and moonlight, a face with features as delicate as Wedgwood china, and eyes of the purest blue. Anyone who saw him was immediately overwhelmed by the sensation that he was in the presence of a saint, an impression that must have helped Cardinal W. greatly in the slow ascent to the pinnacles of the Catholic Church. Even though it was widely rumored that every morning it took his sister over an hour to comb out W.'s beard, a session during which the cardinal could be quite vicious, just seeing him seated in his scarlet robes, with a serene demeanor, one was quite ready to forget the backstage reality for the sake of appearance.

Surely everyone has met business executives whose main strength was that they knew how to dress well; or that they spoke in an impressive, fruity baritone; or had a reassuring smile. A professor with a British accent immediately gets extra points for scholarship, and a woman with a good hairdresser for wit and worldliness. These, too, are examples of innocent mimetism, where the agent is not consciously trying to deceive, but gains power advantages simply because the audience is so ready to be duped. Then there are the equally numerous instances in which the agent uses false coloration with the direct intent to secure an advantage fraudulently. One type is the seducer—the Don Juan who exploits women by convincing them of his undying loyalty and affection. Another is the con man who cultivates the appearance of a respectable businessman to embezzle retired persons' savings. A third is the professor who uses the cover of an academic title to extract sexual favors from his students.

Mimetic exploiters usually take on the coloration of the positive image of a more complex identity. They obtain trust by pretending to be among those who work hard to reduce the chaos of existence. For almost two thousand years the Christian Church represented the most advanced institution in the West, because it offered the most detailed and integrated rules for living and for dying. The very success of Christianity's symbolic system allowed untold numbers of ambitious, unscrupulous, or inept men and women to infiltrate its ranks and acquire power by becoming priests, monks, or nuns. For centuries the population of Europe devoted a large part of its energy toward enriching the clergy, without ever learning to distinguish between priests who had genuine spiritual wealth to share and corrupt priests who simply went through the motions but did not help bring order to the lives of the faithful.

In most cultures religion has provided the best-articulated explanation of reality, the one that tried to make sense of the chaotic totality of human experience. From Outer Mongolia (where at some point over half of the male population resided in Buddhist monasteries) to Thailand, Iran, Quebec, Morocco, and Brazil, the priesthood has provided hope and direction to the populace. In exchange for this spiritual leadership, monks and priests have been given respect and resources. This has made the priesthood a logical target for mimetic parasites. Despite all the recent publicity about spurious spiritual leaders who surround themselves with Rolls-Royces and burrow into luxury estates at the expense of their flocks, there always seems to be enough of a supply of faithful who cannot distinguish even the most obvious fakes from genuine sanctity.

According to an expert who has helped more than three thousand individuals escape from religious cults in which they were trapped, whenever a cult develops around a "perfect master" who claims to know a series of steps that must be taken to reach enlightenment, one should expect trouble. The guru may start out with a genuine interest in helping others, but if he achieves power over his followers, he will find it easy to begin exploiting them—and few such leaders can resist the temptation. One of the dangerous mimetic ploys is for the corrupt guru to insist that his followers surrender their selves. To prove that he is moving to a "higher" self, the disciple hands over his savings to the teacher, or lets himself be beaten and humiliated. Under the guise of spiritual enlightenment much material harm can be done. And the psychological effects, when a person realizes he's been misled, can be devastating.

Another profession subject to such abuses is the military. In almost every known culture, warriors are accepted by the rest of society because they promise security; all too often, however, the protectors turn into exploiters. Until recently an officer in uniform, especially if decorated with medals, was accorded deference and respect. Even now, almost any exorbitant sum, as long as it is earmarked for defense, will pass muster. If a toilet seat must cost

$8,000, so be it; if the Strategic Defense Initiative will cost a hundred billion, can we afford not to pay for it? Security is such a comforting concept that anyone who promises to give us a piece of it can walk away with our wallets.

It is ironic that past success is usually the reason why a person or institution can become so easily a mimetic exploiter. The American military and the industrial complex that supported it could justly claim great credit from the rest of society for having won World War II. But once power and legitimacy had been acquired, it became progressively easier for the military-industrial complex to exploit its position of preeminence, even without actively trying to do so. President Eisenhower, himself one of the leading figures of the victorious U.S. military machine, warned of this danger after his retirement from active politics in the early 1960s.

It has been calculated that by 1990, an American family of four paid the Pentagon $4,200 a year. The equivalent contribution of a Japanese family for national defense was $500. The American government spends 65 percent of its research and development funds on defense, the Japanese, who were mercifully restrained from building up a strong military after WW II, only 5 percent. Conversely the United States spends less than 4 percent on energy development and 0.2 percent on industrial development; the Japanese allocate about 600 percent and 2,500 percent more of their government R&D funds to these goals, respectively. Meanwhile, and not coincidentally, all the indicators show that the Japanese are increasing their edge in manufacturing and industrial capacity. In the past, the menacing hulk of Soviet Russia provided at least some excuse for allocating resources to the production of dangerous and useless hardware. But defense expenditures do not show signs of decreasing appreciably even though the U.S.S.R. has broken up into its numerous ethnic components. It is difficult not to interpret these trends as an indication that defense has become a dangerous mimetic exploiter in our society.

Even science, that most respected of institutions, is not immune to becoming an instrument of abuse. Now that science offers the most credible explanations of reality, it might become especially vulnerable. For every genuine work of scientific research, hundreds of stupefyingly trivial studies are completed. Thousands of useless conferences take place every year—usually in busy centers of scientific activity such as Acapulco or Hawaii—and thousands of articles no one will ever read are published in obscure journals edited for the sole purpose of allowing the editors and their friends to add to their publication lists. But as long as the external forms of the scientific method are respected, it is very difficult to separate the good work from the useless. And science is dangerous in part because it is easy to learn how to mimic it—probably easier than it was for a medieval monk to mimic sanctity.

The institution that understands mimetism best must surely be advertising and its sister disciplines, such as public relations. The goal of the advertiser is to connect in the mind of the potential consumer product X with something desirable, such as health, sexiness, a clean kitchen, or a serene old age. It is absolutely irrelevant whether the connection is true or false as long as it is effective; if the product sells, the ad has justified its existence. Of course the public must be in collusion for this deception to work. Millions must have felt more ruggedly self-confident smoking a Marlboro even though they never roped a calf or had a tattoo on the back of a hand. Advertising—like other forms of mimetic exploitation—works in part because we are willing to pay for the privilege of dreaming pleasant dreams.

Mimetism has been widely adopted in biological evolution as well, but there it is much more difficult to carry out. Nevertheless there are some spectacular examples, like the famous angler fish that hides in the fissures of coral reefs, invisible except for a wormlike appendage that grows out on a slender thread sticking out of its forehead. The angler fish has to put little energy into catching its prey because small fishes, attracted by the wiggling counterfeit worm, will swim right up to it. At that point the angler fish just opens its large jaws, and the unsuspecting visitor gets swallowed up along with the onrushing water. This is quite a successful adaptation, but it is staggering to imagine how many thousands of years it took for natural selection to slowly perfect the lure of the angler fish. In cultural evolution mimetism takes no time at all: a scoundrel can put on a clerical collar or a police uniform and be immediately trusted.

This form of exploitation, like the ones described earlier, can work only if we all agree to allow ourselves to be deceived. It would be lovely if the universe made sense and God watched over every one of our steps, if security could be bought through armaments, if youth and beauty were just a matter of the right hair treatment. Thus, we choose not to look too closely at the credentials of those who make such promises, lest we be disillusioned. As many thinkers, from the novelist Dostoevsky to the sociologist Pareto, have pointed out, we generally prefer our illusions to reality, even though the illusions may lead to tragic consequences. People whose lives are most beset by entropy are, unfortunately, particularly vulnerable to this form of exploitation. When there is little hope or solace, we will cling to whatever promises to introduce even a little order into our experience. It is the poor, the sick, the lonely derelicts who are most vulnerable to the dulcet tones of the televangelist, or to the boastful promises of the political extremist.

Whether we let ourselves be duped by oppressors, parasites, or pretenders is our choice. While it may be impossible to be entirely free of their wiles, it is also clear that if we wish to advance successfully into the third millennium it is mandatory that we understand how much of our psychic energy is channeled away by those who drain our lives to enrich theirs.

FURTHER THOUGHTS ON "PREDATORS AND PARASITES"

The Forces of Selection

For most people, a central concern in life is the fear of oblivion after death. For that reason the ability to leave some legacy to the future is an important component of their peace of mind. Is it for you? And what do you consider more important to leave behind: a memory of yourself and your accomplishments, children who will carry on your biological blueprint, or values that might help influence how future generations act and think?

Would it bother you if a race different from yours were eventually to take over the world? Which one of these two scenarios for the year 3000 makes you feel more uneasy: (a) most of the people in the world are Chinese; (b) no one speaks your language or believes in your values any longer.

Power and Oppression

Traditionally, people have been oppressed by political leaders who control behavior, administrators who keep exacting taxes, employers who use psychic energy without giving adequate remuneration, and patriarchs who rule families with iron fists. In which aspect of your life, if any, do you feel exploited by some powerful person or institution? What can you do about it?

Those of us who were born in the technologically advanced "first world" automatically inherit advantages that are envied and resented by many third-world natives, who feel exploited by us. Their trees go to make our furniture, their air is fouled by our emissions, they are forced to trade nonrenewable raw materials and labor for cheap manufactured products. Do we have any responsibility to ameliorate this state of affairs? And if yes, what can you do about it?

The Exploitation of Women and Children

Setting aside for the moment the often extreme rhetoric of militant feminism, it is clear that women and children have been often vulnerable to exploitation in complacently patriarchal societies. In the family, on the job, in social situations, it is easy for a person who has more power to begin taking advantage of the one who has less. Do you unwittingly participate in this form of oppression, either as the victim or as the abuser?

We have strict child labor laws to protect our children. But does that mean that children are free from exploitation? For example, we devote more energy to train young people to be consumers—to buy toys, watch TV, buy records—than to be autonomous individuals. What are the likely consequences of this type of education? Is there anything that can be done about it?

Individual Differences in Power

Unfortunately, a mechanism for finding a perfect match between individual abilities and social rewards does not exist. A few people get much more than they deserve, while many get less. Do you feel that some of your qualifications are not recognized in the social milieu in which you live? For instance, do you have skills that are not used on your job? How can you better utilize such skills, either at work or in some other activity?

The Transmission of Inequality

Is it right for parents to be able to pass on unearned power (e.g., property, money, status) to their children? At what point does the need to enhance oneself through one's descendants begin to conflict with the common welfare? Is evolution better served by polarization of power—i.e., letting the rich get richer and the poor poorer—or by a reshuffling of power in each generation?

Parasitic Exploitation

It is easy to get incensed about parasites that prey on us—such as viruses, cockroaches, welfare frauds, or drug dealers. But some might claim that humanity as a whole and at its best is a parasite of the planetary ecosystem, living off Gaia while destroying its complexity as we use up resources, limit the life-forms to those that are compatible with us, and generate toxic by-products. What examples would you give to show that humankind is "better" than lice or ticks?

In terms of social parasitism, to what kind of exploiters are you most likely to be vulnerable: Anonymous bureaucrats who control your taxes and real estate assessments? People who have a delightful way of laughing? Flatterers? Brokers who promise quick profits? Personable workers who fail to deliver on their obligations? Shiftless relatives? Insensitive friends? Egocentric partners? How much psychic energy could you save if you immunized yourself better against them?

The Strategy of Irresponsibility

Selfish individuals who are able to ignore other people's needs generally benefit by advancing their own interests at others' expense. What are some examples of exploitation through irresponsibility that bother you most, and what could be done about them?

The anthropologist Margaret Mead once wondered why we require drivers' licenses before allowing people to drive, but require no proof of competence before allowing young people to become involved in the much more difficult and responsible job of parenting. In societies prior to ours, young people could not become parents unless the prospective bride and groom were "guaranteed" by their respective families, who, through the practice of a "dowry," placed in escrow considerable property and labor commitment to support the new union. What ways are there now for society to protect itself against irresponsible reproduction?

Exploitation Through Mimicry

Do you sometimes accept more or less at face value the claims of persons who are good looking? Well dressed? Who look wealthy and prosperous? Who act and talk smoothly? Who claim to follow the word of God? Who say they are willing to die for their country? Who appeal to scientific proofs? And have you ever regretted having trusted someone for any of these reasons?

Next time you are leafing through a glossy magazine or are watching a series of TV commercials, stop at each ad and try to identify its mimetic strategy. How does the ad try to attract your attention? What desirable condition does it associate with the product it tries to sell? What sort of ads attract your attention most, and how do they influence your actions?

5

MEMES *VERSUS* GENES

The conclusion to be drawn from all that has been discussed so far is that many of the greatest dangers on the path to the future are the result of previous adaptive successes: the organization of the brain, the emergence of a primitive self, the genetic instructions that helped us survive through past millennia, and the competition with other people that is the result of the selective forces on which evolution is based. All of these achievements helped the human race survive, but unless we understand how they affect us today, they may also help us destroy ourselves in the future. And there remains one more danger we must consider: the threat of the artifacts we have created to make our lives more comfortable.

If humankind yields its brief primacy on the planet to the cockroach, it will not be because natural selection has found our biological equipment wanting. Rather, it will be because we have done something terminally stupid, like drowning in our own waste or blowing ourselves up to the last man, woman, and child. Some people, however, would argue that this could never happen. A race that has produced such marvels of art, science, and technology as ours has is too smart to exterminate itself.

This optimistic argument is based on the assumption that the memes we have created—the great conceptual systems like geometry or democracy, the marvels of technology like space probes or electronic melon-ripeness testers—are tools in our evolutionary struggle, our servants in survival, our best line of defense against the ravages of chaos. Like the hammer that extends the power of the arm, or the car that increases mobility, artifacts help us adapt and survive. We like to think that with their help our species will prevail. But a radically different interpretation is also possible.

THE COMPETITION OF MEMES

The term "meme" was introduced about twenty years ago by the British biologist Richard Dawkins, who used it to describe a unit of cultural information comparable in its effects on society to those of the chemically coded instructions contained in the gene on the human organism. The name harks back to the Greek word *mimesis,* or imitation, for as Dawkins pointed out, cultural instructions are passed on from one generation to the next by example and imitation, rather than by the shuffling of genes that occurs between sperm and ova. Perhaps the best definition of a meme is "any permanent pattern of matter or information produced by an act of human intentionality." Thus a brick is a meme, and so is Mozart's *Requiem.* Memes come into being when the human nervous system reacts to an experience, and codes it in a form that can be communicated to others. For instance, when a family decides to name its pet Shredder, because the puppy likes to chew up everything in sight, they have created a new meme—although admittedly not a very important or permanent one. The invention of electricity, or life insurance, qualifies as a meme that has a much wider diffusion and greater impact.

At the moment of its creation, the meme is part of a conscious process directed by human intentionality. But immediately after a meme has come into existence, it begins to react with and transform the consciousness of its creator, and that of other human beings who come into contact with it. Once electricity is discovered, for example, it begins to suggest hundreds of new applications. So even though memes are initially shaped by the mind, they soon turn around and begin to shape minds. The question is, once free of their creators, do memes continue to serve our purposes?

What if, instead of being extensions of ourselves ready to help as required, memes were actually competing with us for scarce resources? What if the survival of our genes is most threatened not so much by other biological organisms but by information contained in memes? Although these questions may appear fanciful, they are worth considering. It is possible that one of the most dangerous illusions we must learn to see through is the belief that the thoughts we think of and the things we make are under our control, that we can manipulate them at will. The evidence seems to suggest the contrary. The information we generate has a life of its own, and its existence is sometimes symbiotic, sometimes parasitic, relative to ours. In Dawkins's words: "A meme has its own opportunities for replication, and its own phenotypic effects [concrete manifestations], and there is no reason why success in a meme should have any connection whatever with genetic success."

There is no question that ideas and artifacts evolve, in the sense that they will start varying from one another, and some will be selected in preference to others, and then transmitted to a new generation. Most people assume that this cultural "evolution" is simply an extension of human evolution. After all, they argue, ideas and objects could not survive without us, and therefore they could not have an independent evolutionary history. But that is like saying that humans are part of the evolution of plants, since we could not survive without them. It is true that memes need our minds to exist and evolve, but then so do we require air, water, and photosynthesis, among other things, for our survival. Therefore it does not seem that memes are any more dependent on their environment than we are.

Some purists will object that memes do not reproduce by themselves, and therefore they could not be considered a separate life-form. But this objection depends on a narrow view of what counts as reproduction. We are accustomed to thinking of evolution as involving sexual reproduction, during which half of the genetic information in each parent gets recombined to form a new individual. This, however, is not the only way organisms reproduce. Asexual species do it by replicating the information in the bodies of their members and making new organisms. A colony of bacteria needs only a nutrient medium, and then each individual will split to form two new identical bacteria. And there are many other ways in which

reproduction has been managed: through spores, buds, regenera-
tion, and so on.

Information contained in memes is passed on by different mech-
anisms than those involved in transmitting genetic information.
Memes require only our minds to feed on, and they will replicate
images of themselves in consciousness. A catchy tune I hear on the
radio may colonize my mind for several days, surviving there thanks
to the psychic energy I devote to it. If the tune is good enough,
others who hear me whistle it may take it up, too. Memes are new
players on the evolutionary stage, and we should not expect them
to act exactly as their biological predecessors have. Nevertheless, the
evolution of memes is easier to understand if we compare it to how
genetic information changes and gets transmitted.

For instance, the competition between memes resembles that
between genetic alleles. There will be two or more equivalent
options perceived by people as being alternatives to each other.
Depending on which option is endorsed, the future shape of society
is changed. A simple example of a counterpart to a chromosome
containing mimetic alleles would be the ballot in a political election.
The typical ballot consists of two lists, one for Republican, one for
Democratic candidates. For each office, there will be at least two
names, one in each column. The columns represent alternatives
between two sets of ideas for the future, corresponding to the two
parties' platforms. Voters go through the list, selecting now one,
now another name. At the end of the election, one candidate for
each office will have won out. It is through this competitive process
that the two American political ideologies survive from election to
election. Of course it is possible that if one of the ideologies fails to
impress voters, the party that espouses it will eventually disappear.

Usually there are more than just two alleles involved. When we
are trying to buy a car, or a brand of cereal, or decide on a college
or a cruise, a great many alternatives clamor for our attention. When
we make up our minds, we invest psychic energy in the choice—we
pay if it is a purchase, we vote if it is an election, we dedicate space
in the mind if it is an idea—and in so doing we provide a medium
for the meme to survive and grow. But how does one select between competing alleles? Unfortunately, at this time there is no
simple answer to that question. Choices are generally dictated by

anticipated future advantage. A homeowner will vote for the mayoral candidate who is least likely to raise property taxes. A feminist may vote for the pro-choice candidate. If the alleles involve two otherwise similar car models, the customer is likely to buy the cheaper one because that one needs the least expenditure of psychic energy to accumulate the money involved in the purchase.

Generally memes that do the job with the least demand on psychic energy will survive. An appliance that does more work with less effort will be preferred. The politician who promises the most benefits with the least sacrifices from the electorate will get elected. The most efficient method of production, storage, and transportation is likely to win out against its competitors. The tune easiest to remember will be the hit, and the painting that is easiest to remember and recognize will become the masterpiece influencing the next generation of artists.

Sometimes selection is based on logic or internal consistency. For instance, until a little more than a hundred years ago, each country, and sometimes each region and village, had its own way of measuring weights or distances. A length of fabric could be expressed in ells, feet, inches, cubits, spans, or reaches of the arm, and it took many calculations to convert one measure to another. When a city or country became powerful, it tried to impose its own system on its conquests, but usually without much success, because its way was just as arbitrary and unwieldy as any of the others. Finally in 1875, during the Paris World Fair, the representatives of most European countries agreed to adopt the metric system, which the French had developed almost a century earlier. This was a theoretically justified, consistent, precise, and much easier method than previous ones had been. It won out handily over competing mimetic alleles, because it indeed saves a great deal of mental processing space. At this point only the United States lags behind, confident in its supremacy; but as competitive pressures from rival technologies escalate, even the minds of American schoolchildren may have to be equipped with the more efficient metric system.

Although we might initially adopt memes because they are useful, it is often the case that after a certain point they begin to affect our actions and thoughts in ways that are at best ambiguous and at worst definitely not in our interest. Karl Polanyi and other economic historians have described how the introduction of standard-ized currency as a means of exchange at first helped traders because it simplified and rationalized commerce, but eventually undermined traditional economies and the social systems on which they were based. Previous economies built on kinship obligations, or on re-spect for religious values, for honor, or for ethnic solidarity had to give up their idiosyncratic practices if they wanted to participate in the impersonal logic of monetary transactions. Nobody could fore-see in advance what consequences easier trade would bring; by the time they were recognized, it was too late to do anything about them.

Similarly Max Weber saw the early stages of capitalist competi-tion as an exciting game in which entrepreneurs created new modes of production. The pioneering capitalists wrote their own rules, discovered innovative ways of making things happen. But by the twentieth century, according to Weber, capitalism had become an "iron cage" from which neither producers nor consumers could escape. The markets were saturated, government regulations were instituted to protect the status quo, and entrepreneurs had to obey the rules of the system their ancestors had created. The point is that, once a meme is well established, it tends to generate inertia in the mind, and forces us to pursue its logical consequences to the bitter end.

Weapons provide probably the best-documented history of how memes actually evolve, and their development could thus serve as an example for many others. Among the earliest human artifacts, axes, spears, and arrowheads are the most numerous. The psychic energy invested in their manufacture must have been substantial. Finding the right stones, flaking them to sharp edges, and attaching them to shafts required both time and effort. Our ancestors traveled across great distances to get the best obsidian or other hard stone that would take a sharp point. Some of the earliest trade routes devel-oped to make the traffic of arrowheads possible.

At this point in history, a man who flakes a stone axe simply extends the reach of his arm, making himself more powerful. The axe is a tool to be used at the will of the man who made it. It is nonsense to claim that the axe exists independently of its maker. However, as the man uses his weapon, sometimes against deer, sometimes against other humans, the axe generates in the mind of someone else (hereafter referred to as Man 2) the idea—or meme—for a weapon even better than the axe. Let's suppose Man 2 combines the idea of the axe with the thrusting of sticks he learned playing as a child. So he attaches a sharp stone to a stick, and presto! he has a spear. Now Man 2 can reach farther and slash Man 1, who only has his axe. But it won't take long for the meme of the spear to generate in the mind of Man 3 the idea of something that could prevent the thrust from reaching flesh: perhaps a bundle of interwoven twigs or a skin stretched between branches. So Man 3 invents the first shield.

Of course this scenario is an absurdly foreshortened version of a development that may have lasted many tens of thousands of years. The point is that each new technological advance in weaponry begets either its own negation or an even more powerful version of itself. The sword begets the helmet as a protective device, and then the helmet begets the two-handed axe as a way to slash through the brain despite its protection. Then there is the whole wonderful generation of projectiles, starting with arrows, then bolts, catapulted stones, cannonballs, explosive bombs, nuclear bombs, then incinerating laser rays. . . . In less than ten thousand years, the amount of destructive power a projectile can deliver has increased at an exponential rate. The way this development occurs is always the same: an older, viable meme generates in the mind of a person a new meme that is more attractive and has an even better chance of surviving in the human mind because it is more powerful, more efficient, or cheaper.

Who has benefited from this evolution? The obvious answer is the people who have discovered the new meme. Otherwise, why would they have invented it? But this is exactly the paradox: there is no evidence that a new weapon (to stay with the example) will actually enhance the survival of the people who created it. Let us remember that enhancing survival, in evolutionary terms, means increasing the number of one's own offspring relative to that of other members of one's group. If memes evolved like biological traits, attached to their inventors' bodies, they would have to help the survival of their children and grandchildren. And this seems definitely not to be the case.

The first handguns, or pistols, were developed in the Tuscan city of Pistoia. They were quite an advance on previous weaponry, but they certainly did not lead to any discernible selective advantage for their inventors. Pistols, not Pistoians, spread all over the world. Samuel Colt, who patented the six-shooter in 1836, did not seem to gain any selective advantage from it, whereas his revolvers spread all through the Western Hemisphere. In 1862 Richard J. Gatling patented the six-barrel, revolving machine gun; tens of thousands of Confederate soldiers died because of it a few years later. Brigadier General John Taliaferro Thompson invented the first submachine (or tommy) gun in 1916. Again, this invention did not seem to have enhanced in the slightest the genetic fitness of General Thompson, but it did spawn a long line of vigorous descendants of its own, down to the Kalashnikov and the Uzi.

The history of weapons suggests that these memes evolve independently of the humans who make their existence possible. Sometimes they enable their hosts to prosper at the advantage of their enemies, often they are neutral, and sometimes they may even help exterminate their masters. But there is one thing they *always* do: they force us to react to them by trying to perfect an even better new generation of armaments, thus assuring their own replication and survival. And in doing so they exact a price from those who let their minds be colonized by them, a price reckoned in psychic energy, labor, resources, and money. In this sense weapons clearly conform to the definition of a parasitic species.

MEMES AND ADDICTION

Another clear example of mimetic parasitism is the case of mind-altering drugs. Drugs are consumed because they modify brain chemistry and thus temporarily improve the quality of experience. Alcohol, for instance, has been distilled all over the world, in one form or another. In the West, wine has become a prolific meme: there are poems written about it, and drinking songs; finely wrought silver cups are fashioned to hold it; enology is developed and becomes a form of art; the blood of Christ is symbolized by it; taverns are built to distribute it; and so on and on. In the sixteenth century the Dutch discovered how to distill hard liquor; it would play a devastating role in the genocide of the American natives. In the meantime, alcoholism has become a severe social problem in many of the countries that have adopted it, from Ireland to Yugoslavia. Who benefited from the evolution of alcohol? Certainly many have made money on it, and a great number of drinkers have enjoyed it. But it would be hard to argue that the development of gin and whiskey is a crucial factor in the saga of human evolution, that they are examples of our adaptation to the environment. Whiskey and gin, like viruses, elephants, and whales, evolved simply because they found a fertile medium of growth. It makes little difference that for the whales, that medium of growth is the sea; for bacteria, spoiled food; and for gin, the human brain.

Chemical parasites can invade and destroy entire societies. Archeologists have recently discovered in South America traces of powerful and advanced civilizations that had apparently been wiped out, even before the Spanish conquest, by addiction to drugs. At first, all such relationships between human host and parasitic meme must be symbiotic: The host reproduces the drug because he enjoys it. And he believes that it is he who chooses the drug, and therefore it is he who is in control. Only later does the true nature of the relationship become clear: the human is no more in control of the drug than the trees are in control of the humans whose existence the trees made possible in the first place.

Sometimes we parasitize plants, sometimes plants return the favor and parasitize us. Tobacco is a good example. When the first explorers of the New World discovered that the natives smoked, they thought it was absurd; they sent tobacco leaves to Europe as a hilarious curiosity. But soon enough smoking became the rage in Europe, too; the Vatican had to pass a ban against priests' smoking cigars during the mass when they elevated the host. Sensing a great commercial opportunity, John Rolfe planted the first crop of tobacco in Virginia in 1612; in a few years it was the leading export of the colony. Once there is a demand, someone is always available to provide the supply. A few years later smoking outdoors was forbidden in the colonies, because too many fires were started that way, and in 1647 Connecticut enacted a law against smoking more than once a day, and then it was permitted only if the smoker was alone, for fear that smoking in a group would lead to dissipation.

As tobacco was used ever more widely despite these prohibitions, the plantations required more labor, which meant that slaves had to be imported from Africa. Today we have lung cancer and ghettoes in large cities. In truth, there is no way to argue that tobacco has been a benefit to humans. It is, in fact, the other way around: humans have benefited the spread of tobacco.

But it is not just obviously dangerous goods like weapons and drugs that compete with us for scarce resources. Every product of technology takes up space in the mind, and requires some investment of attention that could have been used for some other purpose. Therefore it is vital to make sure that memes are truly symbiotic— that they contribute to our well-being, rather than become parasitic. The distinction is not always easy to make. For instance, how do we judge airplanes?

The meme for flying came with very high credentials. To soar above the earth was thought to be the privilege of superior beings: angels, dragons, spirits. Practically all religions worshiped airborne gods. Over two thousand years ago, magicians busied themselves building a flying chariot for the Chinese emperors of the Han dynasty (though they never came close to getting it off the ground). There has always been a belief that if we could only fly we would be released from the bondage of terrestrial existence. If we broke the chains of gravity, we would be as gods—or so it must have seemed to the ambitious thinkers of the past who looked longingly at the flight of birds. Well, the dream of flying has come true, but the hoped-for release is still as elusive as ever.

The first successful flyers—men such as Santos-Dumont, the Wrights, Blériot, and Benz—were driven by the exhilaration common to all great pioneers surveying an unexplored land. Reading Lindbergh's account of his solitary flight across the Atlantic, or Beryl Markham's exploits as a safari spotter in Africa, one feels goose bumps as the mythical tropes of their awesome adventures unfold. There is no question that airplanes were first built because they provided a challenge to the imagination. The inventors, and the pilots who tamed the untested contraptions, were not motivated primarily by the needs of commerce or war. The dream that drove them to risk life and fortune was not that of sending passengers or freight across continents ever faster. What they found irresistible was the challenge of breaking through the ancient limitations of human existence.

But it did not take long for the new invention to start making its demands. As soon as viable planes were produced, men began to lose control over their creations. Instead of helping to free humankind from its perceived limitations, the flying machine began to grow on its own (as is too often the case with the fruits of technology), using up resources as it went.

One aspect of this change is well described by the French aviator-novelist Antoine de Saint-Exupéry in one of his semiautobiographical stories of the 1930s, *Night Flight*. The novel is about a pilot on one of the first airmail routes across the Andes of South America, hopping from town to town without radar and with a very primitive radio link to his base. Caught in a night storm between the shark-tooth peaks, the pilot focuses his thoughts on his duty—to deliver the bundles of mail to his next stop. On the ground, his boss worries about the safety of the young pilot, who is his good friend; even more, he worries about whether the airline could survive the loss of one more craft. Regular air transportation is the almost sacred goal; anything that delays it is a deep tragedy, compared to which the death of a good man is trivial. What the story suggests is that as soon as the airplane became useful so much psychic energy began to be invested into it that mere individuals ceased to have the power to resist its claims.

Much has happened since the innocent days of Fabien and Rivière, the protagonists of Saint-Exupéry's novel. Airliners thunder across the globe incessantly, and we could hardly imagine doing business, visiting distant relatives, or having a vacation without planes. But have airplanes really added to our freedom? Let's look at what we have committed ourselves to. From World War II on, the production of war planes has become a matter of life and death. Whether we like it or not, we are now forced to keep up with air technology, or some "other" country (Germany, Russia—or tomorrow, Japan?) will take the upper hand. And we need oil to keep those planes flying; if we run out, we may be forced to go to war against those who hoard their reserves. Once again, what began as a lyrical dream of humankind has turned into an addiction. Instead of making us more free and powerful, the ability to fly adds one more link to the chain that keeps us toiling away in dubious struggle.

The story of aviation is not unique; in fact, it is typical of what happens to the so-called "fruits of technology." The first automobiles were built to allow drivers to experience the thrill of speed, and for years their only use was in enabling rich young men to race each other over cart tracks across continents. The dreamers who chugged away with flying scarves from Paris to Peking in pursuit of a sporting trophy could never imagine that a few generations later the landscape they were crossing, from the sweet orchards of the Rhineland to the vast steppes of the Don, the forests of Siberia, and even the great Gobi Desert would bear a uniform pall of automobile exhaust fumes.

If we added up all the servo-mechanisms we own—from electric mixers to electric razors, VCRs, stereos, talking bathroom scales, exercise equipment, PCs, automatic pencil sharpeners, food processors—the list would be impressive. According to some calculations, in 1953 each adult in the United States had, on the average, 153 electronic appliances at his or her disposal; twenty years later, the estimate had climbed to 400. To a certain extent, appliances make life easier and pleasanter. But how much of life is spent in buying, servicing, using, and thinking about these objects? At what point do we contribute more to their existence than they do to ours?

Isaac Asimov was probably right when he said that the greatest events in the history of mankind are the technological discoveries—the water wheel, the compass, the printing press, the transistor. If by "greatest" we mean those events that most drastically changed the conditions of human life, the claim is justified. But "greatest" does not necessarily mean best. The changes technological inventions have brought about have increased the range of our options, but each has presented a bill that must be paid. The most important challenge that confronts us now is learning how to assess the pros and cons of the fruits of our imagination. If we fail in this task, memes are likely to win out as they compete with our genes.

MEMES AND MEDIA

Technology could not have developed as successfully as it has if it hadn't been for the parallel development of literacy. The great breakthrough in the growth of knowledge was the first recording of information extrasomatically—outside the memory traces of single individuals. When cavemen learned to scratch lines on stones and bones to mark the passing of the seasons, they took the first step toward the great emancipation of the mind from the constraints of the brain. Before that step, everything people learned had to be passed on from one individual to another, either through example or through words. Information could only be stored in the brain, and if the owner of the information died before she could pass it on, it would be lost forever.

After this invention, all a person had to learn was how to decode the symbols, and a potentially infinite amount of information stored in durable materials was available to him. Once people discovered ways to represent information in symbolic form outside the body, it was possible for mimetic evolution to begin.

It took many thousands of years to move from bone scratchings and cave paintings to the development of true literacy, the invention of characters. In its relatively well-documented beginnings in the Middle East, the earliest methods of writing started out as a way to keep track of what kings owned—pigs, bushels of wheat, barrels of oil. Literacy was a very utilitarian venture, a form of rich man's record keeping. The first "books" are very dull reading; they are long lists of transactions, contracts, inventories, and receipts. In China, the first writings were oracles written on the shells of turtles, to help kings make important political decisions.

Another use for writing was to issue commands. The power of a king was greatly enhanced when he could write an order on a piece of papyrus and send it to a general who would execute the order hundreds of miles away, or when he could carve his decisions on a stone, and make them the law of the land. For the first time, the will of a person could be recorded on a substance outside the brain, and be transmitted to many people and over great distances.

After a while, however, the signs used to record what people knew took on a life of their own. Eventually it occurred to someone that it was possible to write down not only what was but what could be. Literacy made literature possible. And with it came books that were used to support one ideology against another. The crusaders went to war with the Bible in hand, the Muslims with the Koran; not so long ago the cultural revolutionaries in China trampled the bourgeoisie while waving Mao's Little Red Book. The invention of literature was certainly a huge step in freeing human imagination from the constraints of actuality. But again, the evolution of literature does not necessarily serve our best purposes. Books spawn more books, as the *Iliad* eventually begot Harlequin Romances.

Nowadays books experience an intense competition for survival. With close to a hundred thousand titles published in the United States every year, the struggle for shelf space in bookstores and libraries is fierce. And how many of these volumes will be remembered, or quoted, ten years from now? One in a thousand? Probably not even that many. Even if the information in all these volumes were important, we just don't have enough memory to recall it all. And it is not only the individual titles that vie with one another, but entire "species" of memes compete with other media for survival. The possibility that books will be eventually replaced by laser discs, audio cassettes, or some even newer technology that directly implants information in the brain no longer seems far-fetched.

A similar situation obtains in the field of the fine arts. It was probably not until the Futurists' manifestos began to proliferate at the beginning of this century that an analogy between the history of art and evolution was first perceived. "Musical evolution is paralleled by the multiplication of machines," wrote Luigi Russolo in 1913, and claimed that the familiarity of the classical musical repertoire bred boredom. "Now, we find far more enjoyment in the combination of the noises of trams, backfiring motors, carriages and bawling crowds than in rehearing, for instance, the *Eroica* and the *Pastoral*."

Colin Martindale, a psychologist of art, has recently developed the same train of thought in his painstaking analysis of artistic styles, claiming that the shock value of literature, painting, and music steadily escalates every few decades. Each generation of poets has to use more vivid images, more sensually arousing words, or nobody will pay attention to them. The few poems that survive among the thousands that are written each year are the ones that deal with more emotionally loaded themes or use the most outlandish word play. The paintings that attract attention are those that the jaded taste of the contemporary audience finds most shocking. To be noticed, new memes must be clearly different from prior ones, and the easiest way to attract attention is to exploit the propensities of our genetic conditioning. Sexuality, aggression, and fear of death provide an inexhaustible supply of artistic themes, but each time one of these subjects is embodied in a work of art, it forces the next artist to be even more graphic and explicit, lest she be ignored.

According to the census bureau, half a million adults in the United States list "artist" as their occupation. But probably not one in a thousand among them can earn a living from painting or sculpting. And how many of their works will survive to the next generation? The point again is that, except for a handful of experts, none of us can dedicate enough psychic energy to appreciate or remember more than a few works of art. How many contemporary artists can you name? It would not be surprising if the average response was less than one. The last artist most people probably remember is Picasso, and they don't feel an overwhelming need to keep up with what has happened in the art world since. After all, there are so many demands on one's mind . . .

It is generally held that the number of great artists is supply driven; that is, if there are few of them, it is because few individuals produce great works of art. But the opposite is more likely to be the case: What gets to be recognized as great art is more a function of demand, or more precisely, of the limits on attention. The average person cannot know and remember more than a few living artists, musicians, writers, and other producers of new memes. Yet these days to be recognized as "great" an artist must be generally known. In the past, if a few powerful princes and clerics appreciated an artist, this was a sufficient guarantee that his work would go down in history. In a democratic culture, a greater consensus is called for— but is very difficult to obtain. The reason there are few great works of art is that we are unwilling or unable to devote enough psychic energy to the appreciation of artistic memes, so few of them survive. In contrast, the enormous amount of attention devoted to rock music—all one has to do is look at the amount of space given to the latest groups in newspapers, especially those directed at youth—guarantees that those memes will have a chance to have a powerful effect on consciousness, at least in the present.

Even though an artist may never become famous, at least he is free to pursue his vision. Isn't that true? Well, not completely. Art follows its own laws to a large extent, regardless of an artist's wishes. A contemporary painter is forced to position her work in relation to the most recent wave of art works. If she wants to be noticed, she will have to use or react to the latest stylistic convention, but bring to it some new twist, an "original" addition. Thirty years ago, when abstract expressionism was the canonical style in American painting, thousands of gifted young artists who were interested in representative art chafed under the ridicule of their teachers, their colleagues, and the critics. Most of them gave up, bewildered. Why was it a sin to draw like Raphael? A few of them persevered, and during the period of hyperrealism that followed in the 1970s found that the memes they produced could now survive. During approximately the same period that abstract expressionism triumphed in America the opposite trend took place in the Soviet Union. There an artist had to paint realistically for his work to be preserved. To say that artists cause the evolution of art reveals an anthropocentric bias; it would be more accurate to say that artists are the medium through which art works evolve.

Scientists are not much freer than artists to decide what project they will work on. Each young scientist enters his or her professional career at a certain point in the evolution of ideas within a particular discipline. If the scientist wants to be taken seriously, and if he wants to find a job, he will have to invest his psychic energy in research that is fashionable, using theories that are *au courant*. The breadth of a scientist's thought is limited by the symbolic system in place at the time. Unless she uses the memes accepted by the community of scientists, her thoughts are likely to be ignored and will disappear.

Only the most independent young psychologists could resist becoming carriers for behavioristic or psychoanalytic ideas in the 1940s or 1950s, just as these days most young people entering the field will spend their professional lives spreading the memes of cognitive psychology. Graduate courses are taught in the most popular subjects, and job announcements specify hiring in those areas. A young person entering the field has very little choice; fortunately, he or she rarely considers how dated this state-of-the-art training will look a decade or so in the future. It is not that the scientific establishment is particularly short-sighted or bigoted. It's just that, as everywhere else, when successful memes take over the minds of a group of individuals, reality becomes peculiarly distorted. There is little that can be done to counter this, but it is important not to delude oneself into believing that we are in control of our actions, and that we are privy to an absolute truth.

These days, the most ubiquitous medium for the exchange of information is television. It is the one that takes up by far the most of our psychic energy. It is also the most powerful in terms of attracting and holding attention, and therefore the one potentially most open to enriching, as well as manipulating and exploiting, the mind. Because this meme excludes so many other alternatives from attention, it is particularly important that we learn to control it.

Television competes with other media, such as reading or music; within the medium itself, different channels and programs struggle to attract the attention of the audience. This distinction is important because most discussions of television are focused on differences between programs. A popular argument is that, if better programs were produced, viewing experience would be improved. While this may be true, research also shows that viewing television has very powerful and distinct effects all its own, regardless of the program that's on. The mere act of watching TV has different consequences for the mind from reading or listening to music, and very different from those that follow on more active forms of leisure.

Television the world over seems to have the following effects on viewers: It makes them feel very relaxed, but also significantly less active, alert, mentally focused, satisfied, or creative compared with almost anything else they could be doing. At the same time, in every culture where TV is accessible, people watch it more than they pursue any other activity in their free time. Television is a dramatic example of a meme that invades the mind and reproduces there without concern for the well-being of its host. Like drugs, watching TV initially provides a positive experience. But after the viewer is hooked, the medium uses consciousness without providing further benefits. In fact, research suggests that heavy viewers enjoy TV less than light viewers, and that the more one watches TV in one sitting the worse one's moods progressively get. Certainly it does not seem reasonable to argue that television is a tool that helps humans adapt to their environment. It does not enhance moods, nor does it improve chances of survival. All television does is replicate itself: screens get bigger, pixels multiply, sitcoms beget other sitcoms, talk shows generate further talk shows, all the while using our psychic energy as their medium of growth.

But we are not entirely helpless confronting the onslaught of the media. It seems that people who are in control of their consciousness derive some benefits from watching television, while those who are less able to channel their attention will succumb to the meme. Their minds become colonized by the vivid images on the screen, and they end up being able to do little else than push buttons and watch. People at risk for TV addiction tend to be less educated, have less desirable jobs, less satisfying family lives. Those who tend to watch TV less do so more critically and with more discrimination. They get out of the medium what they want; they control it instead of being controlled by it. In this respect TV provides an excellent example of what is involved in our relationship with memes in general. If we don't take charge and use them for our own goals, they do have a tendency to take over and use us for their own ends. Of course memes don't *know* what their ends are, but most of the time we don't know what ours are, either.

THE COMPETITION OF IDEAS

More ephemeral ideas also evolve like objects do, and they can affect our survival just as drastically. The idea of equality catalyzed the oppressed classes in France two centuries ago, and justified the execution of at least seventeen thousand noblemen and other "enemies of the people." The notion of Aryan supremacy justified to the Nazis their extermination of Jews, gypsies, and anyone else who did not match that ideal. Russians, Chinese, and Cambodians, among others, killed off with a clear conscience millions of their countrymen who could not be trusted to have internalized Communist memes. From the great persecutions of Christians in the Roman

Empire to our own day, memes have been busy killing genes as well as each other.

Rules written down in political constitutions provide a clear example of how ideas binding on human conduct are passed down from one generation to another. Professors Fausto Massimini and Paolo Caligari from the University of Milan have analyzed all the extant constitutional texts from over one hundred sovereign nations that existed at the time of their study, and found that all these texts addressed a limited number of issues—such as rights, labor, property, the right to spread information, individual values, and so forth. The memes dealing with these issues were arranged in the constitutions somewhat like genes on a chromosome; depending on the hierarchy of the arrangement, different political systems were created. Thus the idea of the rights and responsibilities attached to work tend to take precedence over any other idea in socialist constitutions, whereas personal freedoms and rights to property are the central memes in liberal democracies.

Moreover, all the constitutions could be traced back to a few ancestral prototypes like the Magna Carta, the French Declaration of the Rights of Man, the U.S. Constitution, or the first Soviet Constitution of 1918. Originally constitutional codes are conceived by people; they are the expression of human intentionality. But once they are written down, they acquire a reality of their own, as jurists subsequently try to decode their meanings and apply them to new situations. The laws of the land governing the lives of people are the extensions of those texts. At what point do the written words begin to override the living will of the people?

There are few more glaring examples of how easily ideas can take precedence over people than the history of communism provides. Marx gave shape to a recurring utopian idea that has attracted people in every generation as far back as memory goes: the hope that men and women could live in peace, without conflicts, without exploitation, free to fulfill their individual potentialities. Marx differed from previous thinkers in that he presented his utopian yearnings as scientific deductions derived from studies of past history, and he claimed that the inevitable laws of material determinism could eventually lead to an earthly paradise. The one condition for entering that blissful state was the abolition of private property, and this in turn required passing through a temporary stage of revolution and of proletarian dictatorship—a small enough price to pay for forever abolishing unpleasantness from life.

Marx's ideas were heady stuff in an age when science, even if spurious, was taken so seriously. Engels, and later, Lenin and a host of pseudo-scientific ideologists tried to add even more certainty to the doctrines of dialectical materialism by finding parallels between evolutionary processes and human history. All over the world people who experienced a great deal of entropy in their lives and were unable to find a way to bring back order embraced the memes of communism as their last hope: factory workers without prospects, children of wealthy families without a purpose, ambitious but disenchanted intellectuals, the oppressed farmers of Asia.

What happened to communism was what usually happens when wishful thinking takes over. The institutions based on Marx's ideals were almost immediately infiltrated by mimetic parasites who promptly dispatched their more idealistic comrades. The humanitarian tenets on which communism was originally based eventually justified putting to death millions of farmers who resisted the collectivization of their fields, of artists who chose to tell the truth rather than parrot party directives, of soldiers who did not want to be led by bureaucrats, of scientists who believed that facts took precedence over ideology, and millions more assorted innocent folk. Rarely in human history did so few memes kill off so many genes, and to so little avail.

Nowadays people are most vulnerable to having their minds invaded by economic, political, or scientific memes, because it is economics, politics, and science that have the most credibility in promising to enhance the quality of life. In the past religion served this purpose, and religious memes survived for a long time in human consciousness, sometimes helping, sometimes hindering the evolution to higher levels of complexity. In the Judeo-Christian religion the Ten Commandments are one example of cultural instructions that evolved to try shaping human behavior.

Another example of such instructions is the notion of sin in Christianity. The seven mortal sins are those that will result in eternal damnation. Warnings against them act as a powerful constraint on their believers' psychic energy. Their injunctions try to make sure that we don't pay too much attention to the goals we are naturally inclined to pursue, such as food, money, or sex. Such instructions can be extremely useful in that they liberate psychic energy from instinctual goals, energy that can be invested in pursuing more complex, more uncertain goals. In this sense, the advocacy of moderation in satisfying these instincts is shared by Christianity with practically every other religion or ethical philosophy. The problem arose, as it did with Marxism, when parasites infiltrated the institutions based on the ideals of Christianity. At that point, the keepers of the sacred memes began using the threat of eternal damnation to exploit their flock and build themselves palaces and pleasure gardens.

MEMES AND MATERIALISM

Consumer goods comprise another huge category of memes that reproduce very rapidly. The human species is peculiarly vulnerable to being invaded by material memes not so much because we need the comforts they provide, but because, as was discussed earlier, in Chapter 3, objects and conspicuous consumption provide such obvious symbols for the expansion of the self. As he looks on the objects he possesses, a man is deluded into thinking of himself as a big deal. According to archaeologists, the very first artifacts of metal our ancestors created ten thousand or so years ago—the copper breastplates, the ceremonial bronze daggers, the heavy necklaces— had no utilitarian purpose save to attract attention to their owners, who could feel their egos enlarge under the admiration of their peers. Soon after, however, people realized how easy it is to spend one's whole life accumulating property without end just to feed one's ego.

Partly for this reason, sumptuary laws were eventually passed in almost every culture in an effort to curb runaway spending on luxury objects. In 1675, thirty-eight women were arrested in Connecticut for wearing too extravagant dresses, and thirty men for wearing silk clothes. At about the same time in Hungary, members of the lower classes were not allowed to drink coffee after meals, nor serve a pâté or torte at a wedding. Sumptuary laws, however, cannot really be enforced consistently. As long as people have the means, they can find ways of buying whatever luxury items they can afford—not because this makes them happier, but because minds are easily seduced by rare and expensive objects.

As we all know, automobiles now change in small details every year, yet the essential structure of cars has remained the same since Oliver Evans built a five-horsepower steam engine almost two hundred years ago. At this point it would be extremely difficult to change this basic mode of locomotion. The momentum of the meme is so powerful that it is almost easier to conceive of the destruction of the human race than the abolition of the automobile. Both the extreme rigidity of the underlying form and the rapid succession of individual variations are typical of evolutionary processes in general. And does GM or Toyota have a choice about introducing new models every year, highlighted by the latest panoply of electronic gadgets? Of course not. If they stopped innovating, their products would not sell, and soon they would be out of business. Car manufacturers are simply the means by which the meme of the car reproduces.

As is the case with other forms of addiction, the car at first provides positive feelings. It induces a sensation of freedom and power, of pride at the ownership of an expensive piece of machinery. But the idea of having a car can begin to take up too much space in the mind. Instead of using it we begin to be used by it. We worry about payments, its upkeep, about the insurance, about vandals, accidents, and so forth, and soon part of our control over consciousness is gone. But all along cars keep multiplying because they find a rich medium of propagation in the human mind. The year 2000 models will beget the 2001 models, and so on and so forth, with the inflexible regularity of generations of fruit flies.

Cars are one of the best-adapted technological memes. Another is the "home." Shelters are, of course, necessary for survival, but the houses we live in owe more to the evolution of memes than to our personal comfort and well-being. A drive through any affluent suburb shows the incredible array of the ghosts of former houses transported into present-day America. On the coastal highway between San Diego and Los Angeles one drives by an almost uninterrupted line of housing developments. The first consists of hundreds of identical half-timbered Tudor homes, the next of a hundred

Mission ranches, followed by a hundred Swiss chalets with particle-board shutters pasted to the walls, followed by a hundred southern mansionettes . . . punctuated by, among others, impressive examples of Queen Anne, Federal, modern, and postmodern architecture. Dormer windows that would look good on a six-story Parisian boulevard apartment house dwarf rows of two-story houses, and fake widow's walks crown fake saltbox cottages. It is difficult to understand the power these images have on our minds, and why people would pay enormous sums to make it possible for long-dead houses to have descendants, and why twentieth-century individuals would want to live the rest of their days in them.

The situation indoors is not much healthier. We keep stuffing our houses with artifacts that have no reason for existing except that they have fastened themselves onto our minds, and we have been unable to shake them off. It is true that in every home people keep objects they cherish because they make life easier, or even more importantly, because they enrich life with their symbolic meanings. Old furniture passed on in the family, the quilt sewn by grand-mother, a silver mug inherited from an uncle, a painting purchased during a honeymoon, some favorite books, plants one feels good taking care of—these are things the mind can use to create harmony in experience. But unfortunately much effort and energy are spent trying to purchase objects that use psychic energy but give very little in return. Of course, expensive objects like cars, cameras, stereos, and jewelry can also produce harmony in consciousness. The question is not what kind of objects we cherish, but rather what we get for what we pay. Expensive items have a way of worming them-selves into the unwary mind, not necessarily to make us happier, but simply to reproduce themselves.

Fashion also evolves as other memes do. A way of dressing, a way of grooming or decorating oneself makes an impression on the minds of other people, and then reproduces itself at the expense of the host. In Renaissance Italy, men discovered that if their shoes were unusually long and curved upward, others would notice them. So shoes grew to be an inch or so longer than the foot. Soon, if men wanted to be noticed, they had to wear shoes that were even longer than the now-fashionable ones. Each shoe had a progeny longer than itself; after a while they became so extended that the curvy points had to be secured to the knee with a string, otherwise they couldn't be walked in. Similarly with hair. Every now and again, men start growing their hair longer, and then the length of hair goes through a runaway inflation, limited only by what the scalp can produce. According to the General Court of Massachusetts, Indian attacks on the colony were mainly due to men's wearing their hair too long. The jurists were probably wrong, but they expressed an inchoate frustration that generations of elders would feel for centuries to come.

Memes survive because people first store them in memory, and then reproduce them through their behavior. The idea of democracy, formulated by the early Greeks, has been transmitted through an uninterrupted chain of generations to our own time, and it is still a powerful influence on many cultures—including the former Communist nations that styled themselves "democratic republics." Through the centuries what democracy means has changed considerably—the men who drafted the U.S. Constitution had a very different interpretation of it than we now have. The ancient Greek meme has spawned some strange offspring with time, yet democracy can still be differentiated from other cultural alleles, such as despotism or oligarchy.

But again, in no way can we say that democracy has survived and changed over time because it helped the genetic fitness of the people who first adopted it—let us say, the Athenians. The idea has evolved simply because it has found a receptive medium of growth in the minds of people, to a large extent regardless of whether it helped them to reproduce and multiply. Democratic forms of government have won out in competition with such alleles as sacred rulers—of which only a few, such as the Pope and the Dalai Lama, remain today—and seem to be triumphing over monarchies and perhaps even dictatorships. Are we better off for it? One hopes this is the case, but we can't take even a good idea like democracy for granted. We must remember that memes, once they have claimed our attention, will try to reproduce themselves whether it is good for us or not.

Memes, whether consisting of technological artifacts or abstract concepts, instruct us to act, just as genes do. Much of our psychic energy is devoted to trying to select among them and reproduce them. Generally we feel that this activity represents our own desires. In a sense this is true—we may *want* to buy the latest Cadillac, grow our hair long, or die for democracy—but what choices do we actually have? As long as the mind has been influenced by the memes in question, we inevitably feel that to replicate them is in our interest.

It is not easy to know when we are serving the runaway replication of memes, and when we are doing something because it is best for us. It is impossible to rid ourselves completely of the artifacts and ideas populating the mind. But as with the other sources of illusion—the world created by genes, by the culture, by the ego, by oppressors, parasites, and mimetic exploiters—we can at least take cognizance of our limits, step back and evaluate where our psychic energy is being directed, and why. Even if we stop there and go no further, we will have claimed a certain amount of freedom for our lives, and we will be better prepared to face the new millennium.

FURTHER THOUGHTS
ON "MEMES *VERSUS* GENES"

The Competition of Memes

The world of the future will consist of the ideas and objects to which we choose to pay attention in the present. Have you thought much about the kind of world you are helping to create now? For instance, are you satisfied with your choices in politics at the national level? At the local level? With your choices in religion? With the way you relate to other people?

We are accustomed to the idea of choosing the things we pay for (cars, homes, dresses, politicians), but not the memes that make up our cultural environment. For instance, most people take a fatalistic attitude toward the way moral values change, or artistic styles develop, as if influencing such things were out of their hands. Yet culture changes only if we make it happen, or allow others to change it. And culture will shape the way people in the future will think. Are there some values you would like to see part of tomorrow's culture, such as family values, work values, attitudes toward the environment? What can you do, realistically, to influence this?

Memes and Addiction

Memes are supposed to help improve our lives, but become addictive when they make us act against our interests. It is often difficult to tell, however, when that line is crossed. For instance, the idea of "country" is a necessary and beneficial component of culture. Yet patriotism can easily turn into ethnocentrism and chauvinism, or lead individuals to mindless self-sacrifice. Are there some memes— for example, the flag, "mother," the dollar, health, television—that control your behavior, without your quite knowing why?

Assuming that you wanted to, would it be possible for you to resist the continuous refinement of the following artifacts of technology: cars, exercise machines, athletic shoes, diets, TV sets, personal computers? Or do you feel compelled to select the latest versions of these artifacts, whether you wish to or not?

Memes and Media

The term "media" is short for "information media," that is, forms of communication that are supposed to mediate information. Newspapers, radio, television, and such were supposed to extend people's power by providing useful knowledge. When you read the papers, do you benefit from the information, or do the newspapers benefit from your reading them? And when you watch TV, who is benefiting more from it, you or the sponsors of the programs?

Media generally act as extensions of their owners' power, in that they spread memes in the population that will be advantageous to the owners' interests. For instance, *Pravda* for many decades reinforced in readers' minds the legitimacy of the Communist regime that published it. Television networks carry the commercials their sponsors need to spread their products. How much of your psychic energy is taken up by memes that conflict with your own interests?

The Competition of Ideas

We acquire ideas and beliefs from the climate of opinion pervading the social environment in which we live. For example, our ideas as to what rights people have are largely based on the Constitution that has regulated the behavior of people in this country for two centuries. At the same time, rights have been extended over time to all sorts of groups and behaviors that originally were not covered by the framers of the Constitution. Where did these new ideas about human rights come from? What are your own ideas about what rights individuals should have?

Public opinion is generally split on most important issues. For instance, there are strong pro and con arguments about abortion, about entitlements, about U.S. intervention in foreign wars—even about evolution. In deciding which side of an argument to endorse, are you most influenced by: (a) fundamental moral principles, (b) empirical evidence, (c) rational logic, (d) trust in the source of information?

Memes and Materialism

Most people believe that if they became suddenly rich—for instance, by winning $100 million in a lottery—they would be happy. In reality, those who experience such "good fortune" tend to have all sorts of unexpected problems, and unless they already have a firm sense of control of their lives they often end up worse than before. Suppose your net financial worth increased a hundredfold. Which parts of your life would improve? Which parts would suffer?

When asked how much money they would need to earn in order to be financially comfortable, the average person mentions a sum that is twice as large as their current income. It is extremely rare for someone to believe that an income *smaller* than the current one would make them comfortable. In your case, do you think you could live comfortably on 25 percent less than what you are making now? How about on half of your current earnings? And if not, why?

PART II

THE POWER
OF THE
FUTURE

6

DIRECTING EVOLUTION

As far as we know at present, the way life has evolved up to now has not been the result of any planned effort. Billions of large and small events interacting with one another, generally at random, have woven the chain of causality that now binds us. Asteroids impacting with the earth, volcanoes, ice ages, and even the tiny shrews who developed a taste for dinosaur eggs have all played an unwitting part in shaping this world we live in.

And now we suddenly realize that, unless we take things in hand, this process of change will continue under the sway of relentless chance, a chance entirely blind to human dreams and desires. Like horrified passengers on an airplane who are told that the pilots have mysteriously vanished from the cockpit as the plane is cruising miles above the ground, we know that we must find a way to master the controls or the trip will end in disaster. But will we conquer ignorance and fear before the fuel runs out?

If there is a central task for humankind in the next millennium, it is to start on the right track in its efforts to control the direction of evolution. Much irreparable damage could be done either by ignoring the necessity confronting us, or by a panicked overreaction that could lead to the kind of racist applications of social evolution that the Nazis attempted earlier this century, and the Serbs attempted at the century's end.

To start on this task, we need to reach a better understanding of what evolution entails. The previous chapters have examined how evolutionary processes have affected the ways we think and feel. We have also seen how the successes of cultural memes both support and threaten our own survival. It is now time to bring together the scattered examples from the previous chapters and look more closely at how evolutionary processes actually work. Of course it will be impossible to give a thorough, detailed account. We cannot have certain knowledge even of events that happened a few decades ago—who killed John F. Kennedy? could the Great Depression have been averted?—so it is unrealistic to expect an accurate reconstruction of the millions of years of changes that accumulated to form the present.

But while many of the specific details are lost forever, the overall mechanism of evolution is becoming clearer. It is these general principles that must be comprehended in order to ask the relevant questions about our future, and then to formulate reasonable plans to face it.

SOME PRINCIPLES OF EVOLUTION

Traditionally, evolution described how species of *living organisms* multiplied, changed, and died out. However, it has been realized recently that it is not easy to determine what is alive and what is not. Are viruses alive? How about a quartz crystal? It does reproduce itself, and scientists have been used to thinking that anything that reproduces itself must be alive. Are "vants" (the "virtual ants" crawling across landscapes simulated by computers) alive? The busy little critters on the screen learn all sorts of amazing tricks in order to survive in their environment, and this also has been held to be a sure sign of life.

It seems clear that in order to understand the future of evolution we have to expand our notion of what it is that evolves to account for more than just furry beasts and feathery birds, AIDS viruses and tulip bulbs. Somehow the definition of "organism" must also include crystals and memes—artifacts, symbols, and ideas that exist and reproduce only in our minds. From an evolutionary viewpoint, an "organism" might be defined as *any system of interrelated parts that needs inputs of energy to keep existing*. Plants need the energy of the sun, or they would decay into their component molecules; lions need the energy contained in the protein of their prey; dollars need attention—the confidence and desire of millions of people—in order to continue to exist. If it no longer commanded our attention, money would at best survive only in museum displays, just as extinct dinosaurs do; at worst, dollar bills would all be shredded and their fibers dispersed.

With this expanded definition in mind, we might state the first principle of evolution as follows: *(1) Every organism tends to keep its shape and to reproduce itself.* How this is accomplished varies tremendously, depending on the organism involved. Crystals are held together by molecular bonds. The bodies of mammals are held together by incredibly complex chemical forces, and by inherited, genetically programmed instructions for self-preservation—namely, instincts. A catchy tune continues to be sung because its notes are related to each other by intervals pleasing to our ears. Humans reproduce their biological shape by having sex, and their psychological shape by trying to spread their values and beliefs. Songs reproduce their form by inspiring similar tunes in composers' minds.

Of course this first principle is in part tautological, because if an organism did not keep its shape, it would cease to be an organism. But it is useful to state the obvious in this case: The universe is composed of bundles of information that stand out from the background noise, and are kept together by mysterious forces. Galaxies and atoms, species and individuals, nations and families, civilizations and works of art have unique identities that endure over time. If it were not so, there could be no evolution. *Why* there are organisms in the first place, however, is not a question anyone can even begin to answer. Science can give a perfectly good description of how a bundle of cells combine to create an amoeba or ringworm, but why some cells are attracted to others and what keeps them united in a permanent system is still a mystery, despite our knowledge of atomic bonds, the force of gravity, and electromagnetic phenomena. In any case, since it appears that organisms exist, and likewise that they evolve, it is logical to continue by looking at how organisms behave.

The second principle of evolution is: *(2) In order to survive and to reproduce, organisms require inputs of external energy.* Evolution's first principle—that a rock tends to remain a rock and a song a song—appears to contradict what is perhaps the most fundamental tenet of physics, the famous second law of thermodynamics. According to this law, every system tends to decay into simpler forms. Mountain ranges turn into desert plains, burning stars freeze, great geniuses turn into indifferent ash. To keep itself in an ordered state, a system needs energy. Yet energy cannot be created; it can, however, be dispersed. Thus, with time, every pattern tends to unravel and turn into chaos: Leonardo's great fresco of the "Last Supper" fades into random splotches of color, the Parthenon crumbles to dust, great religious ideas and philosophical insights decay into vulgar ideologies. Entropy—or the dissolution of order into redundant randomness—is one of the most reliable features of the universe as we know it.

It is against this backdrop that the significance of the second principle of evolution emerges. Organisms can exist only if they find ways to forestall entropy, and this self-preservation involves utilizing some outside source of energy to keep themselves intact over time. In a sense, all living things are parasites, in that they live off the energy that keeps some other organism alive. Humans destroy plants and animals, for example, to get the calories our bodies need to keep going. Some species—ours included—are not only parasitic; they also contribute, in a symbiotic way, to the survival of other organisms. For instance, we devote energy to preserving wilderness areas, lawns and ornamental plants, pets and domestic animals. It is true that we do this for our own sake and not for the sake of the organisms preserved, but the fact that we do it at all exonerates our species from being considered purely parasitic.

And, of course, human beings have also invested an enormous amount of energy in the creation and evolution of culture. This is our pride and glory, for if our ancestors had not poured parts of their lives into songs and machines, paintings and theories, our credentials as a species would not be very far above those of the leech as far as parasitism is concerned. The entire world of cultural artifacts, or memes, exists only because we have diverted part of our energies to make their existence possible.

The third principle of evolution follows from the two prior ones: *(3) Each organism will try to take as much energy out of the environment as possible, limited only by threats to its integrity*. If it is true that every organism tries to maintain itself and reproduce, and if it is true that to do so requires energy, this conclusion is inevitable.

What the third principle says, among other things, is that we all tend to eat as much as we can, short of getting ill or fat (if being fat threatens our self-concept); that we all try to get as much money as we can without getting fired or arrested; that we all try to get as much love and respect as possible provided we don't lose face and appear ridiculous. Because memes exist in our minds, the energy they need to survive and reproduce is our attention, and that is what they compete for. Therefore, the tune of a song tends to exclude other songs and gets us to obsess about it. Artifacts also vie for notice and try to capture as much attention as they can. A "seductive software" is a computer program that will entice the user to continuous use. A brand of bicycle that cannot stimulate desire among prospective buyers will soon be discontinued.

Some may object that there is no comparison between a person who wants to survive and prosper, a tune that stays popular, and a bicycle that sells for many years. The person is conscious and struggles against wear and tear, and suffers at the prospect of failure. The tune and the bicycle simply endure, without wishing for anything or trying to compete with other tunes and bicycles. While these differences between humans and artifacts are extremely significant, they are largely irrelevant to the issue of evolution. For in the court of survival, humans, tunes, and bicycles are equal: they all require some form of energy to keep existing, and they all disappear when this energy runs out.

One important difference between us and other organisms is the fact that we try to preserve not only the integrity of our physical bodies but also the integrity of our selves. This means that if the self of a person is built around ownership of material possessions or power, then that person is going to try to control far more energy than his biological system requires for survival. On the other hand, if the self is organized around humanitarian or altruistic goals, the person may require less energy than biological drives would prompt him to acquire.

The three principles considered thus far do not deal directly with evolution. They simply define organisms and specify what they need to survive. They are necessary to prepare the ground for the fourth principle, which finally begins to describe the dynamics of evolution. *(4) Organisms that are successful in finding ways to extract more energy from the environment for their own use will tend to live longer and leave relatively more copies of themselves.* This is the basic scenario for evolution. If a bird is born with a genetic mutation that makes its beak larger, and the larger beak enables the bird to crack seeds more easily, chances are it will live a more comfortable life than birds with smaller beaks, it will have a chance to have more offspring, and its offspring who inherit the stronger beak will in turn have more offspring, and so on until after several generations the former small-beaked species is transformed into a new, improved model.

The same progression holds for the development of weapons, car models, scientific theories, and other species of memes. The new forms may not be "better" than the old ones in any sense except that they leave relatively more numerous progeny, which means that they are more successfully adapted to their environment, which in turn usually implies that they are able to extract more energy from it. Cars or weapons that attract the most attention are likely to be kept in production longest, and will leave the most progeny—that is, later models based on the successful prototype. A scientific theory is successful if it captures the attention of many scientists who will use it in preference to competing ones, and if future theories will be based on its premises. The success of the theory would not be diminished if it led scientists to create an explosive that destroyed all human life on earth—it would still have been the theory that, up to the big bang, prevailed over others.

This consideration leads to another important principle: *(5) When organisms become too successful in extracting energy from their habitat, they may destroy it, and themselves in the process.* Evolution bestows only temporary successes: yesterday's winners can easily become today's losers. Because few organisms have built-in restraints against appropriating as much energy as possible—the general rule seems to be that the more energy obtained, the better—it is easy for an individual or a group to exhaust the resources of its habitat, unless ways to limit its desires are found.

The danger of destroying the life-sustaining environment has never been as acute as it is now. In the first place, no species has ever achieved a fraction of our success in transforming energy, whether turning beef into protein, coal and oil into electricity, forests into lumber, the most basic forces of matter into nuclear energy.

Second, we have no intention of stopping at any point in our consumption—let us say, as soon as we are no longer hungry or cold—but keep using up natural resources to prove that our selves are powerful, or to amuse ourselves (at least seven percent of the energy consumed in the United States is devoted directly to leisure). It seems that fewer and fewer people are able to enjoy life without feeding gasoline and electricity into power boats, snowmobiles, or TV-VCRs.

And finally, technology and democracy have combined to make mass consumption possible to an unprecedented extent. There have always been powerful individuals who indulged in obscene extravagance. In the thirteenth century the emperor Frederick II of Hohenstaufen, who liked hunting, had a spectacular stone castle built on the top of a hill in southern Italy. It became his favorite retreat for practicing falconry. Unfortunately, his hawks kept getting lost in the neighboring forests, so Frederick had all the trees cut down in a circle of about twenty miles around the castle. Even today, Castel del Monte sits in solitary splendor, surrounded by a stony desert. This degree of ecological insensitivity is not unusual for powerful individuals, from the early pharaohs to Joseph Stalin, because they depend on transforming nature into dead monuments to validate their inflated self-images. But now ever larger segments of the population can indulge their egos' artificial needs, and the impact of their numbers more than compensates for the more modest scope of their ambitions.

The principles reviewed so far suggest the next one: *(6) There are two opposite tendencies in evolution: changes that lead toward harmony (i.e., the ability to obtain energy through cooperation, and through the utilization of unused or wasted energy); and those that lead toward entropy (or ways of obtaining energy for one's purposes through exploiting other organisms, thereby causing conflict and disorder)*. It is admittedly difficult in many cases to make judgments with precision about which tendency is dominant in a given situation. Both processes are often present at the same time. Does breeding cattle, for instance, lead to harmony or to entropy? It could be argued that animal husbandry contributes to harmony because it reduces the need for hunting and for raiding other human groups for food; also, by raising the level of human prosperity it makes other cooperative developments possible. But it could also be argued that cattle farming brutally exploits cows, destroys rainforests, and therefore is an evolutionary step that increases conflict rather than harmony. Perhaps the answer is that the value of some practices changes with time. Hunting buffalo was an appropriate adaptation for the Plains Indians, but it became a manifestation of entropy when herds were senselessly destroyed for sport by white settlers.

And what about the Nazis' claim that by exterminating Jews, gypsies, and the unfit they were helping to usher in a better, more harmonious world? It is true that every criminal will defend his actions, no matter how heinous, by trying to ascribe to them a positive motive. But does this mean that we should give up on trying to distinguish between actions that are relatively more or less destructive? We cannot afford to ignore the implications of human actions, even if it means arriving at ambivalent conclusions, such as admiring Frederick II (who was called by his contemporaries *stupor mundi*, "wonder of the world") for having built a castle that enriches our conception of architectural beauty, while at the same time holding him responsible for the wanton destruction of nature. As for the Nazis, it seems obvious that their social program was so thoroughly based on entropy—on violence, conflict, and denial of human rights—that no amount of social order they could have achieved would have compensated for the entropy produced.

The final principle of evolution is: *(7) Harmony is usually achieved by evolutionary changes involving an increase in an organism's complexity, that is, an increase in both differentiation and integration.*

Differentiation refers to the degree to which a system (i.e., an organ such as the brain, or an individual, a family, a corporation, a culture, or humanity as a whole) is composed of parts that differ in structure or function from one another. *Integration* refers to the extent to which the different parts communicate and enhance one another's goals. A system that is more differentiated and integrated than another is said to be more *complex*.

For example, a person is differentiated to the extent that he or she has many different interests, abilities, and goals; he or she is integrated in proportion to the harmony that exists between various goals, and between thought, feelings, and action. A person who is only differentiated might be a genius but is likely to suffer from inner conflicts. One who is only integrated might experience inner peace, but is not likely to make a contribution to culture. Similarly a differentiated family is one in which parents and children are allowed to express their distinct individuality; an integrated family is one in which the members are connected by ties of care and mutual support. A family that is only differentiated will be chaotic, and one that is only integrated will be smothering. Complexity, at any level of analysis, involves the optimal development of both differentiation and integration.

Many thinkers have claimed that complexity is the direction in which evolution proceeds. It is true that, with time, molecules tend to become more complex, that multicellular organisms come after simple cells, that organisms with larger brains follow those with simpler ones, that nation-states and world religions arise from more fragmented and parochial institutions. Yet this is not the only sequence in which events can occur. Simpler forms also develop to take advantage of more differentiated ones. For every complex organism, new parasites are born, and as recent history reminds us, mighty empires predictably disintegrate into smaller units. Complexity is not necessarily the direction in which evolution inevitably progresses, but it is the direction in which it must move to secure us a livable future.

THE NATURE OF COMPLEXITY

It is easy to misunderstand what is meant by complexity in the sense used here. For example, it is often thought to be synonymous with "complicated." But usually when we call something complicated we are reacting to its being hard to figure out, unpredictable, confusing. These are, in fact, traits of something that is differentiated but not well integrated—hence, that lacks complexity. A complex system is not confusing, because its parts, no matter how diverse, are organically related to one another.

The concept of complexity can be applied usefully at many different levels. Originally it was developed to describe living organisms. Because of the specialization of its internal organs, and the sophistication of its functions, a crab could be said to be more complex than a sponge. But the concept can easily be extrapolated to apply across a much broader range, from molecules to machines, from TV programs to political systems.

Sometimes size is considered to be a reflection of complexity: A larger organism appears to be more complex. But again, this is not necessarily the case. An elephant is no more complex biologically than a mouse, and architecturally a gigantic high rise is not necessarily more complex than a Frank Lloyd Wright home. The Soviet Union, however large, was not a complex society primarily because its monolithic central administration and ideology stifled personal initiative and diversity, and hence it imploded because of insufficient differentiation. The United States, in contrast, is highly differentiated; the threat to its complexity comes from the opposite direction: an erosion of common values and norms of conduct that may result in a society that disintegrates for lack of integration.

The reason complexity appears to be such a central principle of evolution is that when two organisms compete for energy, the one with the more complex physiology or behavioral repertoire tends to have the advantage. Suppose you are about to buy a camera. It is likely that you will prefer a model that, compared to others available, has more unusual features (differentiation) that work together well (integration) and thus is easier to use. Other customers will presumably have the same preferences. Thus the competition among cameras will slowly eliminate the simpler devices, and result in a population of models that have progressively more features and that are easier to use. In this sense, complexity is selected out over time; one could even say that it is forced on us.

Yet, as has been observed earlier, complexity does not win out every time. The course of evolution appears to be exceedingly erratic, full of false starts and temporary reversals. During an ice age, for instance, many otherwise complex species will die out, while simpler organisms with a tolerance for cold will flourish. In human history such reversals are even more common. Short periods in which people are free to develop their individuality, and yet are bound together by common goals and values, are usually followed by "dark ages" in which chaos and turmoil predominate. Given a choice of living either in the Athens of the 5th century B.C. or the

5th century A.D., few would choose the later date; just as few would prefer to live in Florence in the year 1000 or 1800 if they could live there in the year 1400. It is precisely because complexity does not prevail automatically and inevitably that we bear such a responsibility for the shape of the future. With every passing decade, our actions are becoming increasingly more influential in determining whether harmony or chaos will prevail.

Complexity provides a benchmark for evaluating the direction of evolution. But we have few guidelines to teach us how to enhance complexity in everyday life. Competing choices clamor for attention, each claiming to benefit us the most. Which one of the four candidates running for the Senate appears to have the most complex platform? Which TV program is likely to deliver the most complex information? Which newspaper article? Some car models are more complex than others because they have more unique components, and the components perform well together. Some restaurants are more complex than others because they offer distinctive dishes that are smoothly blended, or because they present an interesting, but not too jarring, decor. It is a challenge to recognize complexity in everyday life, because it trains us to make the kinds of distinctions that will be useful when our choices will actually have a chance to alter the course of evolution.

MORALITY AND EVOLUTION

Choosing the more complex car or restaurant involves trivial consequences compared to the kind of choices that involve judgments of "right" versus "wrong." Yet moral choices also usually involve complexity. What we consider right brings about harmony, while the wrong choice causes chaos and confusion.

In every human group ever known, notions about what is right and what is wrong have been among the central defining concerns of the culture. Moral codes have become necessary because evolution, in liberating humankind from complete dependence on instincts, has also made it possible for us to act with a malice that no organism ruled by instincts alone could possess. Therefore, every social system must develop memes to keep the intergroup harmony that genes no longer can provide. These memes constitute the moral system, and generally they have been the most successful attempts humans have developed to give a desirable direction to evolution.

But ever since the social sciences began to "debunk" human institutions a little over a century ago, it has been fashionable—at least in intellectual circles—to believe that the different moral systems every culture develops are entirely relative, arbitrary constructions. They are interpreted as the result of historical accidents at best, at worst the outcome of willful mystifications invented by those in power with the purpose of keeping everyone else in line.

It is true that every culture has notions of right and wrong that, from another culture's viewpoint, seem bizarre. For instance, why would men in central India believe that eating chicken the day after their fathers' deaths is a worse offense than striking their wives? Why would it be a sin for Catholics to eat meat on Fridays? Yet behind such idiosyncratic beliefs there is often a rationale easily comprehensible to anyone, regardless of culture. For instance, Catholics don't eat meat on Friday in order to commemorate the death of God's Son on that day. In fact, what is so remarkable is how similar the world's major moral systems are in considering "good" to be the achievement of the kind of harmony within consciousness and between people that we have called negentropy, and which in turn leads to higher levels of complexity.

For example, Buddhists teach that every individual can experience one or more of "Ten Worlds" in the course of his or her lifetime. These worlds are hierarchically ordered, so that the more instinctive, genetically programmed ones are at the bottom, and the ones that depend on progressively greater control of consciousness are at the top. A person who chooses to lead his entire life in the six bottom worlds ruled by desire never develops the potential of existence, and is condemned to a continued dependency on external forces. Only the "Four Noble Worlds" lead to a fulfillment of the human condition. These are, in order, Learning, Realization, Bodhisattva (characterized by compassionate and altruistic behavior), and finally Buddhahood, a state of absolute freedom and understanding of ultimate truth. This Buddhist hierarchy is built on the assumption that the ideal direction for human development involves differentiation (i.e., the ability to free oneself from genetic and social determinism by developing control over one's impulses and desires) and integration (i.e., compassion, altruism, and finally a blending of one's hard-won individuality with the harmony underlying the cosmos).

Despite huge differences in emphasis, and striking variations in the metaphors used to explain why some things are right and others wrong, the great moral systems across the world are congruent with Buddhism in essential respects. Zoroastrians of Persia, Hindu yogis, Christians, and Muslims could all recognize and sympathize with the concept of a progression toward complexity—if they were only able to see beyond the veil of Maya spun by the historical accidents that account for the superficial differences between their creeds. Unfortunately, most religious individuals are so caught up in the illusions of culture that they believe their morality is the right one not because it actually reflects universal harmony, but because it is specifically the Christian, or Muslim, or Hindu morality. In other words, caught in the lower worlds of the Buddhist metaphor, they mistake the accidental elements of their belief for the essential one.

Contemporary psychology has not progressed far beyond these insights from traditional religions. Models of human development still stress the importance of emancipation from instinctual responses, from selfishness, then from conformity to societal standards, then from excessive individuality, until at the most advanced levels the autonomous individual ends up blending his or her interests with those of ever larger groups. This general pattern fits Abraham Maslow's "hierarchy of needs," Jane Loevinger's theory of "ego development," Lawrence Kohlberg's theory of "moral development," George Vaillant's "hierarchy of defenses," and most other accounts of how people can cultivate a more complex self. In each case, progress means freeing oneself from genetic commands, then from cultural constraints, and finally from the desires of the self.

All ethical systems—religious or psychological—are efforts to direct evolution by channeling thought and behavior away from the past and into the future. The past—represented by the determinism of the instincts, the weight of tradition, the desires of the self—is always stronger. The future—represented by the ideals of a life that is freer, more compassionate, more in tune with the reality that transcends our needs—is by necessity weaker, for it is an abstraction, a vision of what *might* be. Anything that is hopeful, new, and creative must be more ephemeral than what is tried and true. The realist can easily scoff at the impractical idealist who is willing to invest psychic energy in the insubstantial stuff of a blue-sky world, for the realist knows that he deals with what is concrete, what is here and now. Without him we could not survive. But without investing life energy in more challenging goals, we could not evolve.

If we are to direct evolution toward greater complexity, we have to find an appropriate moral code to guide our choices. It should be a code that takes into account the wisdom of tradition, yet is inspired by the future rather than the past; it should specify right as being the unfolding of the maximum individual potential joined with the achievement of the greatest social and environmental harmony. The development of this code is no easy task, as the next section will clearly illustrate.

THE CONTROL OF POPULATION

Perhaps the most urgent moral choice confronting our species—now as in the past—involves matching people with resources. One aspect of this problem currently is overpopulation, another involves the growing disparity between the rich and the poor, still another the destruction of our natural habitat. At the very center of all these issues is the question of whether and how to regulate the number and quality of future organisms. When confronted with a dilemma of this magnitude, the application of a moral code based on the maximization of personal freedom and social harmony becomes very difficult.

Most people are understandably leery at the thought of direct intervention in the balance of nature, when human beings arrogate the role of natural selection, phasing out the progeny of some organisms while helping others to become more numerous. As far as animals and plants are concerned, we have of course practiced such intervention since the dawn of time through farming and breeding, and the pace of human control in determining the fabric of life keeps accelerating every year. Genetic engineering is barely a few decades old, but we can begin to imagine what powers it will place in our hands when its technology matures. The more frightening prospect, however, is the thought of eugenics applied to humans—of some individuals deciding what sort of people should survive and reproduce, and what sort should not.

In a dim, half-conscious way, human eugenics has also been practiced throughout history. It is easy to discern it in its negative form, when one tribe or nation did its best to exterminate another. Genocide is not a modern invention. Historical instances may have lacked the ideological trappings of our own century's Nazism or communism, but they were based on equally robust stereotypes and superstitions. The troops of Tamerlane and Genghis Khan had no compunction about disemboweling non-Mongols by the hundreds of thousands, because they could not bring themselves to believe that those who did not share the same mares' milk were really also people. The European invaders of North America could justify shooting the natives because they had not been baptized. The Maoris, who only a few hundred years ago sailed to New Zealand and exterminated the native population, are now asking to be protected from the ravages of white colonialism. Similarly in the southwestern United States, the descendants of the Spaniards who conquered Central America have become "natives" themselves, asserting all sorts of priority rights with respect to the Anglo invaders.

But genocide is not the only form of eugenics that has been practiced historically. The rape of the Sabine women is a dramatic but by no means unusual example of the other side of the coin of eugenics: the relatively greater reproduction of some individuals at the expense of others. Legend has it that when the city of Rome began to emerge as a strong and prosperous settlement, it attracted many adventurous young men from neighboring tribes to the seven hills around the ford on the Tiber. But women were scarce, so at one point the Romans threw a big party, to which they invited trading partners from the Sabine mountains to the east. After the orgy the Romans took off with the Sabine women, who eventually bore them half-Roman, instead of all-Sabine children. The details may vary, but the substance of this story must have been repeated thousands of times in human history.

At a more immediate level, eugenics concerns the right to procreate. Who should be allowed the right to reproduce the information in his or her chromosomes, and transmit that information down through time? The popular consensus today is that everyone has a right to have children. Just recently we have seen girlfriends of death-row inmates protesting the infringement of their rights to have babies with convicted murderers, and class-action suits threatened on behalf of severely retarded persons whose procreative chances have been limited. But what is this supposed "right" based on? Is it a natural right—that is, a necessary condition of existence, like breathing—or is it a socially constituted agreement that results from a social contract involving responsibilities as well as rights?

The belief that in nature every mature individual is guaranteed the freedom to bear offspring is certainly contradicted by the facts. What determines whether an individual will or will not reproduce is not simply parental desire, or parental "rights," but the carrying capacity of the ecosystem—and, in gregarious species, the requirements of the group. Few fish, reptiles, or birds see their eggs hatch into maturity. Among many mammals, mating is reserved for those at the top of the dominance hierarchy. Among primates, males are often relegated to a life of enforced bachelorhood. Although most females do bear children, the babies of subdominant mothers die young in disproportionate numbers, often at the hands of other females. This behavior is not due to "bestial" callousness, but to the need of the group to find a way to ensure its survival in a precarious environment.

For the same reason, every human group that we know of has developed de facto ways to limit the right of procreation to those adults who are expected to have the resources and ability to provide for their offspring. Usually this limitation has been enforced by restricting marriage. The various customs that throughout the world required relatively huge capital investments in dowries and bride-wealth before a person could marry were not quaint and arbitrary traditions, but the best solution these people were able to come up with for addressing the problem of how to take care of children. *No cattle, no children,* was the implicit rule for the majority of human societies. A couple could not marry without the backing of an extended family, which acted as social insurance in case the parents were unable to provide for their children on their own. Young couples generally could not afford the necessary dowry or bride-wealth; it had to be placed in escrow for them by their older kin as a guarantee that the offspring of the union would not become a burden on the community.

Polygamy, which has been by far the most widely practiced form of marriage around the world, further restricted procreation to those males who could draw on sufficient resources to support their offspring, and to the women who lived with them. Until recently men without property had a lesser chance to leave descendants even in Europe and in America; younger sons without land often did not marry, and women who could not find a husband to support them remained spinster aunts helping in their sisters' households.

Nowadays spokespersons for the disadvantaged bridle at any suggestion of restricting the procreation of the poor, and accuse the more affluent classes of attempted genocide if they try to do so. Such critics blame the racist, capitalist nature of our society for even allowing such an idea to be proposed. Attempts to restrict procreation, however, have been practiced by every culture, on every continent, as far as human memory extends. It is difficult to imagine how any society could have survived without making provisions that children be raised by parents who could take responsibility for them.

It is problems of this magnitude that will test a moral code based on complexity. Clearly, property, race, and even health can no longer be seen as criteria for increasing or reducing reproductive chances. Yet some form of control seems necessary. How can personal rights and social harmony both be best served in this case? A specific answer might be beyond our wisdom at this time. However, if enough people become aware that the direction of evolution is in their hands and develop a commitment to complexity, a suitable answer—a next step in the history of the future—will surely be found.

EUMEMICS: LIMITING THE REPRODUCTION OF MEMES

If we wish to begin directing evolution, it is not only genes that we need to be concerned about. Technology, lifestyles, ideas, and beliefs all take up energy, and therefore have an impact on human survival. Of course, contesting the spread of ideas is in large part what history has been all about. Struggles between different religions, political systems, ethnic groups, values, and philosophies are all examples of how memes compete with one another for space in our minds. So it could be said that without realizing it people have been engaged all along in *eumemics* (admittedly an awkward coinage combining the Greek for "good" and for "imitation").

If we practiced eumemics consistently, we would first of all realize that the objects we use and the ideas we think do not come without a cost. Objects require energy to make—both physical and psychic—and once we begin to use them, they start shaping our minds and actions. For example, nuclear reactors are powerful tools, but they mortgage future generations to the expensive chore of finding ways to dispose safely of radioactive waste; they also make us vulnerable to terrorist blackmail, as when the Serbian militia threatened to wreak havoc in their nuclear installations should the Western European nations intervene in the Bosnian civil war. Realizing how easily things and thoughts can take over one's life energy is the initial step toward controlling the evolution of memes.

The next step consists of trying to evaluate the complexity of the memes in question—and the complexity that they are likely to add to one's life. Learning how to do this takes time, and it is best to start with the most simple and trivial situations. Let's suppose that while sitting in a doctor's waiting room you look around and see two magazines on the table, one a typical celebrity rag, the other a nature magazine. Since you can't think of anything better to do, and you have a few minutes to spare before the doctor is ready to see you, you reach out to get one. Which will you take? You may just choose at random, or pick the one closest, or the one that lies on the top of the other. Or you may pick the one with the most colorful cover, or the one that seems most titillating.

But it is good practice, before making such a choice, to ask yourself: Is one of these two magazines going to give me a more complex experience than the other? In other words, will I be more likely to learn something new (differentiation) that will add meaning to my experience (integration), from one magazine than from the other? The gossip magazine may report juicy bits about rock stars and starlets, and knowing about their romantic tangles may help you understand better your own emotional life, but on the other hand the facts that you will learn are just redundant repetitions of the same few basic soap-opera elements, so that neither learning nor meaning are likely to be very intense. The nature magazine may tell you about the habits of spiders and whales, but here perhaps you will have the chance to learn something worth remembering. You may also feel the deeper experience of understanding from the information you got. So which magazine is likely to provide the more complex experience? For most people the answer would be the second, but the question cannot be answered conclusively in the abstract—it depends on the momentary needs, the long-term goals, and the interests of the person involved. The important thing is to develop the habit, when confronted by the typical choices of everyday experience, to evaluate which alternative promises to bring more harmony into one's life.

If one does not do so in small matters, it will be difficult to learn how to give a consistent direction to the evolution of memes when the stakes are higher. All too often we make even important decisions—such as which person to marry, what job to take—for reasons that are dictated by unexamined genetic instructions or social conventions. These choices are occasionally the best ones, but often they are found wanting. If we let our actions be dictated by the vector of external forces, our contribution to evolution will be at best erratic. When the veils of Maya disguise reality, actions are more likely to increase entropy than harmony.

So the third step in helping to direct the evolution of memes involves taking action on one's assessment of the relative complexity of various choices. By reading the more complex magazine, having the more complex conversation, voting for the candidate with the more complex platform, learning the more complex skills on one's job, choosing the more complex leisure activity, taking on the more complex religious beliefs, a person can contribute to a more complex future, adding to a harmonious human destiny while keeping entropy to a minimum.

It is essential to remember that every time we invest attention in an idea, a written word, a spectacle; every time we purchase a product; every time we act on a belief; the texture of the future is changed, even if in microscopic ways. The world in which our children and their children will live is built, minute by minute, through the choices we endorse with our psychic energy. It is not only the legislation we help pass, the wars we help wage, the great inventions and works of art that will shape the future, but also our small habits of mind and behavior: the way we talk to our children, how we spend our free time, whether we always increase the consumption of finite resources or whether we find ways to live within less wasteful limits. These small choices, these trivial decisions, have as much weight in the long run as all of Napoleon's wars.

But why should you be concerned with helping the future be more harmonious when there are already so many demands on your psychic energy? The temptation to just worry about Number One, and let the future take care of itself, is indeed strong. After all, our genetic program, laid down before our ancestors achieved consciousness, dictates that we place all our efforts into what it takes to replicate our own genes. This is by no means a trivial concern, and for many it may be a satisfying program by which to live. Yet there are also many people for whom the goals of survival and reproduction are not sufficient. It is for these individuals that the possibility of contributing consciously to evolution might be a very attractive proposition.

It may seem that having to calculate how complex the outcomes of one's choices are will turn everything into a tiresome bookkeeping chore. Where does it leave spontaneity, the joyful abandon to the whim of the moment that adds so much zest to living? Learning to direct evolution need not turn us into dour accountants, humorless clerics who weigh each action against an endless balance sheet. Just the opposite is likely to happen. It is true that at first learning to estimate the impact of each choice on global harmony may indeed be a difficult and halting process. But once acquired, it becomes a liberating skill. Within the guidelines for action it provides, one can act with greater resolution, free of doubts and regrets.

Like the challenging discipline of the martial arts, which must be slowly practiced until the technique is so well mastered that one can act without thinking yet with immediate precision as soon as the need arises, so commitment to complexity provides a discipline that allows a person to cut through the chaos of life with ease and without soul-searching. This old Italian proverb applies to directing evolution, as it does to every other difficult practice: *Impara l'arte, e mettila da parte.* Very loosely translated: "Learn how to do it, and forget that you know it." After the principles for discerning choices that lead to harmony are understood and become second nature, one can act again with a spontaneity that is now much more deeply informed.

Here is, for instance, how the early Confucians expressed the idea that a strict dedication to disciplined habits of mind could eventually result in complete freedom of action:

> The Sage gives free rein to his desires, embraces his spontaneous dispositions, and all he controls is perfectly ruled. . . . Thus the *jen* person walks along the Way without purposive effort; the Sage walks along the Way without striving. (*Hsün Tzu:* 21.66–67)

But to become a "*jen* person" (roughly, a person who fulfills his or her humanity) or a sage requires a long period of training, of understanding how to choose the most harmonious alternative—which corresponds to the Chinese metaphor of "walking along the Way." It is only because sages disciplined their consciousness to recognize complexity that they could eventually reach the point of dispensing with plans, since their unpremeditated actions could not fail to be moral, and suitable for every contingency.

COMPLEXITY OF CONSCIOUSNESS

The Confucian sages may not have been as wise as they claimed to be, and with time Confucianism—like most great cultural movements, East and West—lost its creative spark and became a highly routinized institution. When coopted by oppressive rulers, it helped to legitimize their power and to exploit the poor. It is for this reason that Communists and feminists alike abhor Confucius and his historical role in China. Yet the early Confucians understood something extremely important about human well-being: that the best way to live is by learning to control consciousness, and that to control consciousness one must cultivate certain skills, acquiring a discipline that at first may seem like mindless ritual, but eventually sets us free to be in harmony with the universal order. But Confucianism was certainly not alone in coming to this conclusion. All major world religions, all synthesizing philosophies, despite the great superficial differences due to accidental historical developments, agree that unless a person learns to control consciousness, he or she cannot achieve harmony with the cosmos, but will forever remain prey to the random forces of biology and society.

Nor will we know how to direct evolution in the direction of greater complexity unless our consciousness becomes more complex. What makes us different from other animal species is the variety and mutual dependence of our psychic processes. Being able to remember, to abstract, to reason, to control attention are some of the most important functions that set people apart from their primate cousins. It is these functions that made it possible for humankind to build the cultural systems—such as language, religion, science, and the various arts—that mark the evolutionary divide between us and other species. Although each infant inherits the genetic potential for remembering, reasoning, and so forth, these abilities do not become effective unless developed through appropriate, socially constructed activities—that is, through patterned, voluntary investments of attention that result in learned skills. Complex skills are built up by complex activities.

Evolution is the history of the complexification of living matter. From protozoans swimming in a primeval soup we see, through time, the appearance of organisms fit for all kinds of different niches, developing all sorts of specialized skills—amphibians, reptiles, birds, mammals—or at least, this is as we understand the process at this point in history. It might be that the real story of evolution will turn out to be the survival of viruses or of robots—especially if we fail to develop integration between ourselves and the rest of the planet at the same rate as we are differentiating. But wherever evolution is heading, given that we are humans living at the threshold of the third millennium A.D., we cannot easily abdicate a certain preference for complexity, or relinquish our responsibility for helping it along.

The opposite of complexity at the level of psychological development is a form of *psychic entropy*. This concept describes disorder within human consciousness that leads to impaired functioning. Psychic entropy manifests itself by an inability to use energy effectively, either because of ignorance or because of conflicting emotions—such as fear, rage, depression, or simply lack of motivation.

Usually it takes psychic energy from outside the individual—encouragement, support, teaching—to reduce entropy and restore the order in consciousness necessary for complex functioning.

To avoid psychic entropy from taking over consciousness, to maintain the gains our ancestors have made, while increasing psychic complexity for the use of our descendants, it is necessary to take part in activities that are themselves differentiated and integrated. Education is the main institution charged with providing young people with complex experiences: from the earliest curricula such as the trivium (grammar, rhetoric, and logic) and the quadrivium (arithmetic, geometry, astronomy, and music) to the bewildering variety of choices offered by modern universities, cultures have tried to package what they deemed to be important to know for transmission to the following generation. But formal schooling at its best tends to provide only complex *information;* it offers few experiences that help the growth of emotions, character, sensitivity—and often does a poor job of integrating even the knowledge it does provide. Not so long ago, a chancellor of the California higher educational system proudly announced that he was no longer presiding over a *uni*versity, but a *multi*versity. Compare his views on education with this brief dialogue from Confucius's *Analects* (15.3):

> The master said: "Ssu, do you take me for one who studies much and remembers it all?"
> "Yes," was the reply. "Is it not so?"
> "No. I link all upon a single thread."

Nowadays, "studying much and remembering it all" is too often the goal of education, even if the various bits of knowledge one absorbs are not sensibly related to one another.

But a community concerned about the survival of its skills and its values needs to invest in more than schools if it wants to preserve, let alone advance, the complexity its former members have so painfully acquired. If families fail to both support and challenge, if the community fails to offer diverse experiences, children are unlikely to grow into complex adults. Boring jobs, oppressive or excessively bland political arrangements, lack of a common moral code and trustworthy leadership, leisure opportunities that cater to the lowest common denominator, all contribute to an environment in which it is difficult to learn complex skills, with the result that psychic entropy is bound to increase everywhere.

Yet it is by no means foreordained that entropy will win out in the end. Fortunately we are not programmed to be only ruthless brutes. What makes the evolution of complexity possible is the fact that we also have a built-in predilection for learning new skills, for doing difficult things that stretch our abilities, for creating order in our consciousness and in our environment. It is this propensity for ever more complex behavior that will be explored in the following chapter, and Chapter 8 will describe how this propensity can be used to create the kind of self that might contribute to a harmonious future.

FURTHER THOUGHTS
ON "DIRECTING EVOLUTION"

Some Principles of Evolution

Have you thought about which other organisms you are competing against, whether consciously or not? Is this competition unavoidable?

Besides food and the other obvious material necessities, what keeps you alive? What do you mean by "living"?

The Nature of Complexity

Do you think that the family in which you grew up was a complex one, i.e., was it differentiated (did it give you freedom and stimulation) and integrated (was it supportive and harmonious)? If you had to make some changes in your own family, what would they be?

What external changes in your job or your daily schedule could make your experiences more complex?

Morality and Evolution

What rules do you follow now that you would never break under any condition? Do these rules make you feel constrained, or more free?

What do you think is the most important advance in morality that humanity has made in the last thousand years? What is the most important advance to be made in the next thousand? How can you help bring it about?

The Control of Population

Are there some limitations on reproduction that you would favor? How could they be implemented?

Does the community have the right to impose minimum requirements for parenting? If yes, what should they be, and how could they be enforced?

Eumemics: Limiting the Reproduction of Memes

Are there limits to how much energy you are willing to use for yourself?

How could society assess the price of such activities as (a) producing toxic wastes; (b) attracting children's psychic energy to wasteful entertainment; (c) depriving the elderly of their savings through unethical speculations; in such a way that the eventual price the community will have to pay is charged as a current business expense to those engaged in such activities?

Complexity and Consciousness

Is differentiation more of a problem for you, or is integration? Which is more difficult: to stand out and assert your own goals and ways of being, or to relate to other people and work toward joint goals?

What kind of discipline do you think might increase the complexity of your self? For instance: learning to be patient with your relatives or co-workers; clarifying your goals and priorities; learning a new skill; taking up a new hobby; keeping a diary; or finding time for reflection or meditation.

7

EVOLUTION AND
FLOW

Helping to shape a more harmonious future is a noble ideal, but, one may ask, what's in it for me? None of us is going to live long enough to see the long-term results of his or her actions, even assuming that they have any visible impact on history at all. So should we expect virtue to be its own and only reward, without any tangible benefits for those who sacrifice satisfaction in the present in order to build complexity in the long run?

In fact, when we struggle against entropy, we do get an immediate and very concrete reward from our actions: we enjoy whatever we are doing, moment by moment. The self is flooded with a sense of exhilaration when we undertake a task that requires complex skills, that leads to a challenging goal. In those moments we feel that, instead of suffering through events over which we have no control, we are creating our own lives.

In order to ensure their own continuation, evolutionary processes seem to have built into our nervous systems a preference for complexity. Just as we experience pleasure when we do things that are necessary for survival, as we do when we eat or have sex, so, too, do we experience enjoyment when we take on a project that stretches our skills in new directions, when we recognize and master new challenges. Every human being has this creative urge as his or her birthright. It can be squelched and corrupted, but it cannot be completely extinguished. This enjoyment that comes from surpassing ourselves, from mastering new obstacles, is the positive counter-part of the eternal dissatisfaction discussed in Chapter 2, and so well expressed by Goethe's *Faust*.

Depending on the skills a person was born with, or has cultivated during a lifetime, different activities will provide enjoyment and lead to complexity. For instance, everywhere around the world women (and, fortunately, many men, as well) enjoy bringing up their children. There are few things that are both so gratifying and at the same time so necessary for creating a more harmonious future. Here is a mother in one of the flow studies answering a question about what she considers the most satisfying experiences in her life:

> Oh yes, when I'm working with my daughter; when she's discover-ing something new. A new cookie recipe that she has accomplished, that she has made herself, an artistic work that she has done that she's proud of. Her reading is one thing that she's really into, and we read together. She reads to me, and I read to her, and that's a time when I sort of lose touch with the rest of the world, I'm totally absorbed in what I'm doing.

Here we see the joy of creativity at two levels: the daughter's fascination with discovery is itself a discovery for the mother, whose creation she is. Another woman describes the same feeling of ex-treme involvement and pleasure as she shares her skills and experi-ences of success with her older children:

> I try to involve my children in my work, especially my older daugh-ter who's been coming [to the office] and working with me. There are frequently times when we are home or driving around and talking about my work or something like that . . . sort of a sense of joy and accomplishment in what I am doing and able to bring them into it also.

Such feelings—which include concentration, absorption, deep in-volvement, joy, a sense of accomplishment—are what people de-scribe as the best moments in their lives. They can occur almost anywhere, at any time, provided one is using psychic energy in a harmonious pattern. It is typically present when one is singing or dancing, engaged in religious ritual or in sports, when one is engrossed in reading a good book or watching a great performance. It is what the lover feels talking to her beloved, the sculptor chiseling marble, the scientist engrossed in her experiment. I have called these feelings *flow* experiences, because many respondents in our studies have said that during these memorable moments they were acting spontaneously, as if carried away by the tides of a current.

Flow can occur in almost any activity. Although the nature of those pursuits may be as dissimilar as playing with one's child is different from hang-gliding, the quality of the inner experience in each case is described in often astonishingly similar words. Flow appears to be a phenomenon everyone feels the same way, regardless of age or gender, cultural background or social class. One of the most often mentioned features of this experience is the sense of discovery, the excitement of finding out something new about oneself, or about the possibilities of interacting with the many opportunities for action that the environment offers.

A rock climber describes flow in his sport: "It's exhilarating to come closer and closer to self-discipline. You make your body go and everything hurts; then you look back in awe of the self, of what you have done, it just blows your mind. It leads to ecstasy, to self-fulfillment." On a more sober note, a surgeon describes why operating is so enjoyable: "The personal rewards are greatest in challenging cases where you extend the self and think more." And a chess master: "It is exhilarating, like I'm succeeding at putting a very hard puzzle together." In each of these very different activities, joy comes from going beyond what one has already achieved, from mastering new skills and new knowledge.

To experience flow one must begin with a certain level of skill, training, and discipline. Here is how a professional ballerina describes her flow experience; note the importance of disciplined preparation, and of having a harmonious consciousness in order to perform well physically, a point repeatedly mentioned by most athletes, as well:

> This type of feeling begins roughly after one hour of warmups and stretching, when one has achieved a fine-tuning of muscle strength and psychological security. I feel happy, satisfied, light. Training

helps to make it come about, but I must be very serene and mentally relaxed to get into it. What makes it go on is fitness, willpower, and enthusiasm.

A teacher of dance, in contrast, derives the most profound enjoyment from passing on the complex skills of her craft, and thus contributing to evolution by enabling others to experience the joyful expression of bodily harmony:

> I get an immense amount of pleasure from dancing and I'm quite sure that I communicate it to my students. In fact I think it is very important to pass this on because one can only dance if one enjoys it. It should not be a hassle but pure joy.

Over and over again, as people describe how it feels when they thoroughly enjoy themselves, they mention eight distinct dimensions of experience. These same aspects are reported by Hindu yogis and Japanese teenagers who race motorcycles, by American surgeons and basketball players, by Australian sailors and Navajo shepherds, by champion figure skaters and by chess masters. These are the characteristic dimensions of the flow experience:

1. Clear goals: an objective is distinctly defined; immediate feedback: one knows instantly how well one is doing.

2. The opportunities for acting decisively are relatively high, and they are matched by one's perceived ability to act. In other words, personal skills are well suited to given challenges.

3. Action and awareness merge; one-pointedness of mind.

4. Concentration on the task at hand; irrelevant stimuli disappear from consciousness, worries and concerns are temporarily suspended.

5. A sense of potential control.

6. Loss of self-consciousness, transcendence of ego boundaries, a sense of growth and of being part of some greater entity.

7. Altered sense of time, which usually seems to pass faster.

8. Experience becomes autotelic: If several of the previous conditions are present, what one does becomes autotelic, or worth doing for its own sake.

Reviewing them in closer detail should help explain why the struggle to achieve complexity can be so enjoyable.

THE ELEMENTS OF FLOW

Intense flow experiences may be relatively rare in everyday life, but almost everything—play and work, study and religious ritual—is able to produce it, provided the conditions spelled out above are present.

In the first place, flow usually occurs when there are *clear goals* a person tries to reach, and when there is *unambiguous feedback* as to how well he or she is doing. Most games, sports, artistic performances, and religious ceremonies have well-specified goals and rules, so that at any moment participants know whether their actions are appropriate or not. Such activities provide flow readily and are intrinsically motivating. Some jobs, like surgery or computer programming, are also especially rewarding because one usually knows what needs to be done at every step of the process, and one gets immediate visual feedback along the way. In everyday life, and all too often on the job or in classrooms, people don't really know what the purpose of their activities is, and it takes them a long time to find out how well they are doing.

Sometimes the feedback in flow is immediate, as in a game of tennis, in which information about how well one did is there the moment after one hits the ball. But it can also take time, as in the accounts of these two women interviewed by Professor Fausto Massimini's team in Italy. The first is from a seventy-five-year-old farmer, the second from a fifty-year-old seamstress:

> To work in the fields is the healthiest thing: You get tired, but you feel great. Being with the animals, hoeing, planting, harvesting, taking care of potatoes, vegetables, flowers. . . . When I look at the field and it looks good I am happy, satisfied. I feel relieved.

Of course sewing is my work, but when I stop thinking of it as just a source of income it becomes something more. This is why sewing and working are not exactly the same thing as far as I am concerned. I begin to enjoy it when I see that the dress has no defects. I try to use all my skills. I see the well-made dress and think, "I did that!"

In these cases the feedback—the field that "looks good," the dress that has "no defects"—is relatively slow to appear, yet it is clear and meaningful to the skilled artisan. What is so intriguing about this process is that almost any goal, if sufficiently clear, can serve to focus attention long enough for one to achieve a flow experience. The value of the goal is simply that it offers an opportunity to use and refine one's abilities. It does not have to have any monetary or social value. For instance, the goal of a climber—to reach the top of a mountain—is simply an excuse for climbing. There is really no reason to get to the tops of mountains otherwise, especially not with all the pain and danger involved, when one might as well use a helicopter and be comfortable. In the words of a young climber who is also a poet:

The mystique of climbing is climbing; you get to the top of a rock glad it's over but really wish it could go on forever. The justification of climbing is climbing, like the justification of poetry is writing; you don't conquer anything except things in yourself. . . . The act of writing justifies poetry. Climbing is the same: recognizing that you are a flow. The purpose of the flow is to keep on flowing, not looking for a peak or utopia but staying in the flow. It is not a moving up but a continuous flowing; you move up only to keep the flow going. There is no possible reason for climbing except the climbing itself; it is a self-communication.

What is true of rock climbing is true for many other things we do in life, whether it's work, study, or taking care of children. When we enjoy it, it is because we think of it as something that allows us to express our potential, to learn about our limits, to stretch our being—the very process implied in the "self-communication" of the climber's quote. It is for this reason that flow is such an important force in evolution. Without it, our genetic programs would instruct us to continue pursuing what has been "good for us" in the past; but flow makes us receptive to the entire world as a source of new challenges, as an arena for creativity.

A second condition that makes flow experiences possible is the *balance between the opportunities for action* in a given situation and *a person's ability to act*. When challenges and skills are relatively high and well matched, as in a close game of tennis or a satisfying musical performance, all of the person's attention needs to be focused on the task at hand. Here is a musician describing flow while playing the piano; note the emphasis on mastering technique as a prerequisite for achieving this state:

> It is really great. I no longer notice my fingers, the score, the keys, the room; only my emotions exist, and they come out through my fingers. You become one with the music, because the music is exactly what you are feeling, too. That's why I prefer playing without a score, because then this process comes much easier. I don't look at my fingers, except when the passage is technically very difficult. I don't look at anything. Perhaps I look inside myself. One needs years and years of practice to achieve the technical mastery that allows your fingers to produce the sounds you like.

An ophthalmological surgeon describes the challenges that make his profession so rewarding: "Everything is important—if you don't close it the right way, the cornea will be twisted and vision impaired. . . . It all rests on how precisely and artistically you do the operation." And an orthopedic surgeon: "It's very satisfying and if it is somewhat difficult it is also exciting. It's very nice to make things work again, to put things in their right place so that it looks like it should, and fits neatly."

The challenges can be as varied as the goals of the activity. In chess they are mainly intellectual; in surgery they involve restoring a patient's health; for an ocean sailor they include keeping a fragile boat afloat in a hurricane; for someone reading a good novel the challenge may consist of translating the words on the page into mental pictures, guessing the motivation of the fictional characters, anticipating turns of the plot, and so on.

If challenges and skills are in balance, it is possible for a person to experience a *sense of control*. In everyday life there are so many

imponderables that can affect us, events over which we are powerless. The boss may take an irrational dislike to us; as we cross the
street a cab may run us down when we least expect it. In flow,
however, we feel up to any eventuality. For instance, a dancer
describes this feeling: "A strong relaxation and calmness comes over
me. I have no worries of failure. What a powerful and warm feeling
it is! I want to expand, to hug the world. I feel an enormous power
to effect something of grace and beauty." And a chess master explains: "[The best things about chess are] being in control of a
situation and having all the evidence right there. . . . In chess
everything is in front of you to see. No other variables . . . [you can]
control it." And another: "Although I am not aware of specific
things, I have a general feeling of well-being, and that I am in
complete control of my world." Here is how a world-class figure
skater describes a typical flow experience:

> I knew every single moment; in fact I even remember going down
> into a jump and this is awful, but thinking, "Oh gosh, this is so real!
> I'm so clear in my thoughts." There was just a real clarity to it all
> . . . I felt in such control of everything, of every little movement, I
> was very aware, you know, like what was on my hand, I could feel
> my rings, I could feel everything, and I felt I had control of any-
> thing.

Actually, in a flow state one is not, in fact, in complete control.
If one were, the tenuous balance between challenges and skills
would tilt in favor of the skills, and the intensity of the experience
would decrease. Rather, what happens is that one knows that control is possible *in principle*. In daily life, there are too many things
happening for anyone to feel that control is possible. In contrast, a
climber hanging from his fingertips three thousand feet above the
valley floor is not securely in control of his destiny, either, but he
knows that if he does his best and concentrates, the probability of
success is extremely high.

Because in flow the challenges are high enough to absorb all of
a person's skills, one needs to pay complete attention to the task at
hand, and there is no attention left over to process any irrelevant
information. For instance, if a violinist begins to think about some-

thing else while playing a difficult piece, she is likely to play a wrong note. A tennis player who gets distracted during a game is likely to make mistakes and lose. Therefore, another element of the flow experience is the effective *merging of action and awareness*. One becomes so concentrated and involved that the usual dualism between actor and action disappears; one does what needs to be done spontaneously, without conscious effort. This unified consciousness is perhaps the most telling aspect of the flow experience. A well-known composer of music describes how he feels when his work is going well:

> You are in an ecstatic state to such a point that you feel as though you almost don't exist. I have experienced this time and time again. My hand seems devoid of myself, and I have nothing to do with what is happening. I just sit there watching it in a state of awe and wonderment. And [the music] just flows out by itself.

Here is how another skater describes the utter absorption when one feels that a performance is going well:

> It was just one of those programs that clicked. I mean everything went right, everything felt good . . . it's just such a rush, like you feel it could go on and on and on, like you don't want it to stop because it's going so well. It's almost as though you don't have to think, it's like everything goes automatically without thinking . . . it's like you're on automatic pilot, so you don't have any thoughts. You hear the music but you're not aware that you're hearing it, because it's a part of it all.

When one is immersed in flow, interruptions are very frustrating because they break the spell and force us to return to the everyday state of consciousness. A schoolteacher from Bangalore in India, who mentions teaching as her favorite flow experience, has this to say:

> I am generally immersed in my work. I try hard to concentrate on it and dislike disturbances. Frequent disturbances upset my concen-

tration and I find it difficult to revert to my work. [But when work is enjoyable] it is a very absorbing feeling. I get very involved in my work and once it's started I like to complete it without interruptions.

Such deep concentration, in turn, results in a *focusing on the present,* so that problems and worries that in everyday life are a drain on psychic energy tend to disappear. People report forgetting their troubles because the intensity of the experience precludes ruminating on the past or the future. This condition is described in almost identical terms in a great variety of activities.

[In chess] When the game is exciting, I don't seem to hear nothing— the world seems to be cut off from me and all there is to think about is my game.

[In rock climbing] When I start on a climb, it's as if my memory input had been cut off. All I can remember is the last thirty seconds, and all I can think ahead is the next five minutes. . . . With tremendous concentration, the normal world is forgotten.

[In basketball] Sometimes on the court I think of a problem, like fighting with my steady girl, and I think that's nothing compared to the game. You can think about a problem all day but as soon as you get in the game, the hell with it!

[In figure skating] The focus was so narrow, because my partner was in the same focus, and it was just she and I skating. . . . Everything else goes away, it almost happens in slow motion—even though you're doing things at the correct time with the music and everything. Nothing else matters, it's just such an eerie, eerie feeling.

[In rock climbing] When you are climbing, you're not aware of other problematic situations. It becomes a world unto its own, significant only to itself. . . . Once you are into the situation, it becomes incredibly real, and you're very much in charge of it. It becomes your total world.

By creating a temporary world where one can act with total commitment, flow provides an escape from the chaos of the quotidian. But this escape does not represent a descent into entropy, as when one dulls one's senses with drugs or simple pleasure; it is an escape *forward* into higher complexity, where one hones one's potential by confronting new challenges.

Because the fine balance between challenge and skill makes it necessary to concentrate on the task at hand, people in flow report a *loss of self-consciousness*. In flow a person cannot afford to worry about how good he or she looks, or whether others like her or not. In daily life, these are the sort of preoccupations that most often cause entropy in consciousness. But when we are deeply involved in what we do, concerns about the self drift out of the focus of attention.

Quite often people mention experiencing self-transcendence in flow, as when a musician playing a particularly beautiful melody feels at one with the order of the cosmos, or a dancer feels his body moving to a rhythm beyond that which any individual person could have conceived. An engineer from Bangalore in India, whose flow comes from computer programming, describes his absorption in that work: "It leads me into an imaginative world of program variables, operations, and algorithms. I feel as if I am an inside part of a computer—or another computer."

Rock climbers are particularly eloquent on this score: "It's a pleasant feeling of total involvement. You become like a robot . . . no, more like an animal . . . getting lost in kinesthetic sensation . . . a panther powering up the rock." D. Robinson, a climber who has written much on this subject, tries to describe how one achieves the "oceanic feelings of clarity, distance, union, and oneness" while climbing, and in the process captures the eerie strangeness of this state of mind, which seems full of internal contradictions when compared to the simple confusion of everyday consciousness:

> You could get so immersed in the rock, the moves, the proper position of the body, that you'd lose consciousness of your identity and melt into the rock and the others you're climbing with . . . you are not quite sure whether you are moving or the rock is. . . . You are climbing yourself as much as the rock. . . . If you're flowing with something, it's totally still. . . . Lack of self-awareness is totally self-aware to me.

This last sentence raises an important paradox: This "lack of self-awareness" is sometimes interpreted to mean that people in flow simply tune out, that they are less conscious or focused. In fact, the opposite is true. Being less aware of oneself leaves more psychic energy to concentrate on what one is doing. The unselfconscious climber can focus more intensely on the rock, on the moves he has to make, on the conditions of the weather. The unselfconscious skater skates better because she pays more attention to her body and its motion; the unselfconscious composer writes better because all her concentration is devoted to following the notes flowing in her mind.

Another component mentioned in connection with the flow experience is a *distortion of the sense of time,* so that often hours seem to pass by in minutes. As a surgeon reports: "Time goes very fast; but afterwards, if it was a difficult operation, it may feel as if I had been working one hundred hours." And a chess master: "Time passes a hundred times faster. In this sense, it resembles a dream state. A whole story can unfold in seconds, it seems." Or in the poetic words of the climber Robinson: "It is said to be only a moment, yet by virtue of total absorption he is lost in it, and the winds of eternity blow through it."

The mechanical division of time that rules our daily schedules is one obstacle that interferes with flow. For instance, students in school often report that just as they are starting to get involved with a subject that is interesting to them, such as an art project or a science experiment, the bell signals the end of the fifty-minute period, and they have to change classes. Similarly the spontaneous, organic work patterns of craftsmen and artisans were disrupted two centuries ago by the requirements of factory production and replaced by rigid schedules. But in flow, the sense of time again becomes a natural feature of one's total experience, rather than an arbitrary restraint that ignores what we do and how we feel about it.

When most of these seven dimensions are present in consciousness, the activity being undertaken tends to become *autotelic,* that is, worth doing for its own sake. Because the experience is so pleasurable, one wants to repeat whatever helped to make it happen. If one experiences flow in scuba diving, then one will want to go back diving so as to have a similar experience again. If one gets into the flow state by solving a mathematical problem, then one will keep seeking out more problems to solve. Sometimes a flow experience in a particular activity is so satisfying that a person will devote his entire life to it. Jim Macbeth, an Australian researcher, describes people who have left their jobs to sail in their own tiny boats across the southern seas because they were tired of working in windowless buildings, or of having three-martini lunches. As one man who did make such a break explained: "[I wanted to] cast off a humdrum life, be a bit adventurous. I had to do something with life beside vegetate. . . . It was a chance to do one really big thing with my life; big and memorable." A climber we interviewed reports:

> I would have made a great deal of money in corporate life, but I realized one day that I wasn't enjoying it. I wasn't having the kind of experiences that make life rewarding. I saw my priorities were mixed up, spending most of my hours in the office. . . . The years were slipping by. I enjoy being a carpenter. I live where it's quiet and beautiful, and I climb most every night. I figure that my own relaxation and availability will mean more to my family than the material things I can no longer give them.

Of course, if a person learned to enjoy working in an office, he or she would not need to sail the Pacific or turn into a nocturnal climber. But what is relevant here is that whenever an activity produces flow, a strong attraction to repeat that activity begins to operate. It is for this reason that it becomes so important to learn to enjoy activities that lead to harmonious complexity rather than chaos. Some of the most frightening glimpses of a possible future, like the movie *A Clockwork Orange,* show societies in which the only joy in life comes from vandalism, obsessive sexuality, and aggression. Unfortunately, this scenario is not one we can confidently rule out as a vision of our own future; when people lack the skills to recognize more interesting opportunities, they tend to regress to simple and brutal choices.

WHY IS FLOW REWARDING?

Defining these aspects of the flow experience doesn't quite explain why people can experience flow in such diverse activities. Why would one person enjoy tending her potato patch, while another one is hooked on figure skating? In the past, one popular explanation has been that the enjoyment derived from apparently self-rewarding activities is really due to the fact that they serve as a disguised release for repressed desires. For example, people play chess as a substitute for the expression of aggressive impulses, especially those of an Oedipal nature. The mating of the opponent's king with the help of one's queen stands for castrating daddy with mommy's help. Another explanation holds that those who engage in dangerous sports like hang-gliding or rock climbing have peculiar personality traits that drive them to seek extreme sensations. Such accounts that offer "deep" reasons in the personality makeup of the agent are often on the mark in explaining why a person chooses a certain activity rather than another to experience flow, but they tend to be shortsighted, in that they fail to recognize the common subjective state that underlies the various activities, and that accounts for the fact that they are rewarding.

Another explanation of why some individuals are drawn to rock climbing and others to chess is provided by the concept of interest. One becomes interested in an activity either because it was satisfying in the past, because one is talented at it, or because somehow one has attributed value to it. Certainly there are strong differences between people in terms of initial interest in different activities. Some love to garden, others can't stand to putter around in the dirt. But whatever the original motivation was for playing chess, or for playing the stock market, or for going out with a friend, people will not continue to pursue activities unless they enjoy them—or unless they receive extrinsic rewards for them. Castration anxieties, the need for taking risks and seeking sensation, interest, and other similar reasons could be the initial motivations for taking on a certain type of challenge. But ordinarily people would not continue undertaking a certain activity unless it provided flow—or unless external rewards or punishments prompted them to undertake it.

Other explanations for why people keep doing things for their own sake cite the addiction that results when certain activities—such as jogging, or gambling, or playing music—release endorphins that stimulate the pleasure centers of the brain. According to this theory, the intrinsic rewards of flow can be reduced to a chemical dependence on certain stimuli. The argument, however, begs the question in that it fails to explain why these particular activities resulted in the release of endorphins in the first place. It has become clear by now that endocrinal and other physiological changes in the nervous system are not always—or even usually—what cause mental processes. Just as often it's the other way around: how we think about something causes changes in brain physiology. The fact that psychic rewards must be mediated by neurophysiological processes is beyond question; this does not mean, however, that flow can be explained by resorting to neurophysiological accounts alone, without considering the state of a person's consciousness.

Almost every activity has the potential to produce flow. Some—such as games, sports, artistic performances, and religious rituals—are designed expressly to facilitate the experience. But in everyday life flow experiences are reported more frequently in the context of work, family interaction, and driving a car than in leisure activities, provided that these supply the necessary conditions, such as a balance of challenges and skills.

The phenomenology of flow further suggests that the reason we enjoy a particular activity is not because such pleasure has been previously *programmed* in our nervous system, but because of something *discovered* as a result of interaction. It is reportedly quite common, for instance, for a person to be at first indifferent to or bored by a certain activity—such as listening to classical music or using a computer. Then, when the opportunities for action in the context of the activity become clearer, or the individual's skills improve, the activity starts to be interesting and finally gratifying. For example, if a person begins to understand the design underlying a symphony, or if a person's ability to recognize and remember musical passages increases, then he or she will genuinely begin to enjoy the act of listening. It is for this reason that the rewards of flow lead to relatively more complex evolutionary changes. Whenever we discover new challenges, whenever we use new skills, we feel a deep sense of enjoyment. To repeat this desirable feeling, we must find ever higher challenges, build more sophisticated skills; in doing so, we help the evolution of complexity move along one more step.

The dimensions of experience reported when an activity is pleasing suggest why flow is intrinsically rewarding. The sensation of being fully involved, of performing at the limits of one's potential, is apparently a highly desirable state. It contrasts markedly with much of everyday life, in which we cannot act with total involvement because the opportunities for action are either too few or too many, unclear, confusing, or contradictory. Because many jobs, for instance, consist of repetitive actions that require little concentration, the attention of a worker is likely to begin to wander. In this state of split attention the worker begins to wish for more satisfying things to do, or begins to ruminate on unpleasant subjects. In either case the situation in which he is involved is devalued, and the person experiences boredom or frustration. In comparison with this all-too-frequent condition, the total involvement of flow is experienced as rewarding.

As mentioned in Chapter 2, our studies over the years suggest that when attention is not focused on a goal, the mind typically begins to be filled by disjointed and depressing thoughts. The normal condition of the mind is chaos. Only when involved in a goal-directed activity does it acquire order and positive moods. It is not surprising that one of the worst forms of punishment is to place a person in solitary confinement, where only those survive who can discipline their attention without depending on external props. The rest of us need either an involving activity or a ready-made package of stimuli, such as a book or a TV program, to keep the mind from unraveling.

But the question remains: Why should full immersion in a challenging activity be so rewarding? Apparently humans who experience a positive state of consciousness when they use their skills to the utmost in meeting an environmental challenge improve their chances of survival. The connection between flow and enjoyment may have been at first a fortunate genetic accident, but once it occurred, it made those who experienced it much more likely to be curious, to explore, to take on new tasks and develop new skills. And this creative approach, motivated by the enjoyment of facing challenges, might have conferred so many advantages that with time it spread to the majority of the human population.

Conversely, the negative feelings of boredom and frustration we experience when not totally involved seem to function like the settings on a thermostat that trigger a furnace to resume functioning. Boredom directs us to seek new challenges, while anxiety urges us to develop new skills; the net result is that, in order to avoid such negative feelings, a person is forced to grow in complexity.

In any case, when the conditions of flow are present, people tend to report an optimal state of inner harmony that they desire to experience again. Aristotle was among the first to recognize that enjoyment was the result of achieving excellence in any activity, as did the great poet Dante Alighieri well over six hundred years ago:

> [I]n every action . . . the main intention of the agent is to express his own image; thus it is that every agent, whenever he acts, enjoys the action. Because everything that exists desires to be, and by acting the agent unfolds his being, action is naturally enjoyable . . .

It is not difficult to find evidence for Dante's assertion. For instance, we have a cocker spaniel by the name of Cedric whose genes have been selected through many generations for the ability to retrieve birds in tall grass. Cedric has never been out hunting, but his instincts for retrieving are so strong that he has spontaneously applied them to the similar task of chasing and finding tennis balls. The harder they are to track down, the better. His notion of heaven is taking a walk next to tennis courts in Vail, Colorado, where stray lobs often fly far away and get lost in overgrown ravines. Cedric slaloms down the slopes at full speed, frantically searching through brambles and bushes, never stopping to look, but sniffing all the time. His whole demeanor changes when he gets a whiff of a ball in tall grass; he starts loping like a gazelle, then zooms in to where the ball lies, and won't rest until he digs it out of its hiding place and gets it into his mouth. Then he climbs back to the path and walks with his head held high, prancing like a Lippizaner stallion on parade, as proud as can be. There is no question that Cedric "unfolds his being" when chasing tennis balls, and that he greatly enjoys this unfolding. As Dante says, we all desire to be what we are, but are all too often prevented from acting out our being.

Children—provided they are healthy and not too severely abused—seem to be in flow constantly; they enjoy "unfolding their being" as they learn to touch, throw, walk, talk, read, and grow up. Unfortunately they soon have to stop "unfolding," as school starts to force their growth into patterns over which they have no control. When that occurs, flow begins to become rarer, and many young people end up experiencing it only in games, sports, and other leisure activities with peers.

THE CONSEQUENCES OF FLOW

There are many reasons why experiencing flow is beneficial. Perhaps the most important is also the most obvious: the quality of life depends on it. People are happier after having had a chance to experience flow, and as we have known ever since Aristotle, happiness is the true foundation of existence. Every other desire—for health, wealth, or success—is sought after only because we expect that it will make us happier. But few people ever become genuinely happy by winning two or twenty million dollars at the lottery. What appears on the surface to be the most ephemeral and subjective condition is actually the most concrete and objective: whereas money or possessions cannot bring about happiness, control over subjective experiences can.

But for those who have not yet learned to trust the value of inner experience, there is quite a bit of evidence that flow also has more directly measurable—although not necessarily more significant—effects as well. What follow, very briefly, are some of the most interesting ones.

Creativity

People who have made creative contributions to the arts and the sciences are usually very eloquent in ascribing their success primarily to the fact that they enjoyed their work. Paolo Uccello, the great Renaissance painter who was one of the discoverers of how to represent three-dimensional objects on flat surfaces, used to wake up at night in his cold garret in Florence and walk back and forth, crying out loud: *"Che bella cosa é questa perspettiva!"*—"What a lovely thing is perspective!"—meanwhile annoying his sleepy wife no end. Albert Michelson, the first American to win a Nobel Prize in physics, spent his entire adult life devising more and more precise ways of measuring the speed of light. When he was asked in his old age why he had done so, he answered, "It was so much fun!" What these anecdotes suggest is that a person would not invest psychic energy in the usually frustrating goal of breaking new ground unless he or she derived profound satisfaction from the activity. The expectation of money and fame will keep one motivated to a certain extent, but the chances of success in a creative endeavor are usually too slim to warrant continuing dedication if the only rewards are extrinsic.

Peak Performance

Great athletes, musicians, and performers in general must also derive some flow from their activity, otherwise they would not push themselves to the limit. Research shows that flow occurs during peak performance, and that athletes are motivated to do their best in order to experience flow again and again. Of course it is not only top performers who experience flow, and are helped by it; anyone can enter this state while doing his or her "personal best." For instance, in a Japanese study it was shown that among the hundreds of students who took a course to learn swimming, those who experienced flow in training made the most progress by the end of the course.

Talent Development

In another study, conducted by my team at the University of Chicago, we followed over two hundred teenagers who at age thirteen had been identified as talented in either math, science, music, art, or athletics. What we wanted to investigate was whether teens who enjoyed working in their talent area were more likely to continue through high school in the difficult task of cultivating their gifts. As expected, math-talented students who reported flow while doing math ended up taking much harder courses in that subject and were much more committed to advancing their training in college than those who did not. The same was true of the other four groups. The frequency of flow, more than objective measures of cognitive ability (such as the Scholastic Aptitude Test), and more than personality traits or parental status and income, was the best predictor of the development of talent.

These results suggest that flow has important implications for teaching students in our schools. The general attitude toward education—especially in math and the sciences—is that learning is a hard and unpleasant task. Hard it may be, but why should it be unpleasant? Since we know that creative individuals, peak performers, and talented young people all enjoy what they are doing, and it is enjoyment that makes them want to learn more, it should be possible to translate this knowledge into the ways we deal with students.

Productivity

Similarly, it stands to reason that workers who enjoy their jobs will be more dedicated than those who are either anxious or bored. Hard research data on this topic is still lacking, however. The most relevant evidence comes from one of our early studies, where we found that those workers whose frequency of reported flow experience was above average were in general happier and more motivated, especially when working. They also worked half an hour a day more on the job (as opposed to daydreaming, doing their shopping lists, or talking on the phone about personal matters) than their peers who reported less flow. Half an hour a day adds up to about fifteen extra working days per year, or three extra weeks of work each year per worker. This, multiplied by the millions of workers in the United States, would make quite a difference in the GNP, as any economist would readily admit. It is true that we do not know whether the workers who work longer actually accomplish more; but lacking evidence either way, we are safe to assume that this is so.

Self-Esteem

People who spend more time in flow generally report higher self-esteem. In addition, directly after a person has been in flow, his or her self-esteem is higher than at other times. After being in flow people report being more successful, they feel better about themselves, and they feel that they are living up more to their own and others' expectations. This finding has been replicated in several studies focused on working mothers, average teenagers, and talented teens. At first, this result seems to contradict the assertion that in flow self-awareness disappears. Indeed, while in flow one does forget the self, and so self-esteem is for all intents and purposes suspended. But afterward, in recollection, one is led to say that the experience made one feel successful. It is in this way that flow builds self-esteem.

Stress Reduction

There is also some evidence that business executives who experience flow when they are challenged by stressful events report fewer health problems than executives who feel anxious under the same amount of stress. In a study of managers, it was found that the men who reported flow more often were also happier, more motivated, and felt stronger, in control, and less tense, both at work and at home. Those executives who reported more stressful life events—such as family problems, job changes, or financial or emotional losses—also reported more physical illnesses. But if they experienced flow in their work, stress resulted in fewer health problems. Apparently the ability to match the challenges of the job with personal skills—or at least the *perception* of doing so—acts as a buffer between entropic conditions and their usual negative psychic consequences.

Clinical Applications

One practical domain where flow seems to have much promise is psychotherapy. It can help psychotherapists identify those situations in a patient's life that, if expanded, would promote a greatly improved quality of experience, and hence a possible healing of the patient. So far I have verbal descriptions of treatments based on flow from only a handful of psychiatrists and clinicians involving perhaps fifty patients; so it would be premature to claim miraculous cures. But the cases seem convincing, and the potential enormous. One of the few published case histories, reported by the team of Professor Massimini in Milan, might give an example of the kind of treatment involved.

Caterina, a twenty-five-year-old single woman, had been suffering for years from acute anxiety attacks, usually of an agoraphobic type. Whenever she found herself in a public place, on the streets or on a bus, she would become breathless, and her heart would start racing. For the past three years she had been taking 1.5 mg of alprazolam and attending group therapy, without any noticeable improvement. When she came to Professor Massimini's clinic for individual psychotherapy, she was asked to provide a week of Experience Sampling Method data, in order to find out which activities and experiences she felt most positive about. The ESM revealed that Caterina spent most of her time with her family, and was very rarely outdoors or with others. A full 45 percent of her waking hours were spent watching television. Her moods were consistently negative; most of the time she was in a state of apathy, very seldom achieving anything like a flow state.

The therapy was based on the following principles:

> The application of optimal experience theory in psychotherapy is centered on reinforcing both the patient's personal search for challenging possibilities for action in daily life, and his/her effort to develop personal skills in order to meet these challenges and not avoid them. Optimal experience is related to the subjective perception of environmental challenges: each individual will selectively pursue the activities that best meet his or her own intrinsic motivation and spontaneous interests. Such a therapeutic approach is therefore individualized, focusing on the personal motivation and tendencies of the subject.

To accomplish these goals, Caterina took walks with the therapist on the crowded streets of Milan, so as to become desensitized of her fear of people; she was helped to become involved with group activities she enjoyed, such as volunteer work and dancing: "The therapeutic approach was therefore centered on supporting Caterina's involvement in these intrinsically motivating and challenging activities." The goal was not simply to reduce the symptoms of anxiety and agoraphobia, but to expand the narrow limits of her daily routine, and replace her apathy with something akin to enthusiasm and flow.

After a year and a half of this intervention, Caterina's life had substantially changed for the better. Instead of spending half the day with her family, she now spent only between 10 and 20 percent. She reduced the time spent watching TV from 45 percent to 15 percent. Instead, she spent more time in public or alone, and she was involved in a host of new activities. The quality of Caterina's experience had also improved dramatically in every area. Apathy decreased from 60.6 percent of all her responses to 34.5 percent. In contrast, responses that had some of the elements of flow increased from 15 to 51 percent. At that point she stopped medication and ended therapy. This and similar cases point to the close connection between flow and a consciousness that is harmonious, capable of developing a self that is in control of its inner energy.

WHAT HAPPENS WHEN FLOW IS ABSENT?

All the evidence agrees that when people in flow act at the peak of their capacity, it both improves subjective well-being and has the potential for socially positive consequences. In each case, flow seems to be the engine of evolution propelling us to higher levels of complexity. But what happens when people aren't able to operate at full capacity, when their opportunities are either too few or too daunting for them to experience flow?

What typically occurs under such conditions is that people are drawn to activities that are wasteful or destructive, and in such cases, the result of seeking enjoyment is entropy, rather than harmony. A striking example is the juvenile delinquency that has grown so rapidly in the affluent suburbs of the United States. It is generally due to the boredom endemic to so many teenagers, who feel they have nothing to do in their sterile neighborhoods. "Show me something that's as much fun as breaking into a house and stealing the jewelry while the owners sleep," says a young man from a wealthy family who was arrested for a burglary, "and I'll do it. But here there's nothing else to do." Of course there would be plenty of other things to do if the young man were able to recognize the challenges available to him. For instance, he could play tennis, read, do volunteer work, go camping, learn to draw, or learn a foreign language—but to get interested in such activities one needs role models, among other things, and all too often there are no adults in the community who can induct a young person into complex activities.

It is no exaggeration to say that a great many of our social problems are due to the lack of flow in everyday life. Addiction to various chemicals is obviously an attempt to recapture some of the qualities of optimal experience by artificial means. Alcohol, cocaine, and heroin change our perception of challenges, or of our skills, and make us feel for a while as if we have achieved a balance between opportunities and abilities. But artificially induced flow is dangerous on two counts: first, it does not stretch skills and hence does not lead to complexity; and second, when it becomes physiologically addict-ive, it causes enormous amounts of entropy to the individual and to the group.

Another sign that everyday life is providing little flow is that the culture becomes too dependent on passive, redundant entertain-ment. In an ideal society each person would carve, weave, program computers, paint, tell stories, sing, and dance, and there would be little need for professional performers to take people's minds off the monotony of what they do day in, day out. There are examples that come close to this ideal, in places like Bali or some isolated villages in Europe, where a variety of traditional crafts are still practiced at a high level of skill by every member of the community. Examples of the opposite pattern are unfortunately more obvious: the circuses of ancient Rome come readily to mind, or the chariot-racing of Byzantium in its period of decline. Our culture, too, has been parasitized by memes that mimic the appearance of flow but do not produce its benefits. Recorded music, videos, TV, movies, pulp fiction, and sleazy magazines soak up an enormous amount of atten-tion. They produce a semblance of excitement in the mind, but to the extent that they do not require skills of any kind they take up energy without increasing complexity.

One might say that, as a species, we are addicted to flow. It is that condition that has enabled us to evolve to the point at which we are now, and it is why we may change into even more complex beings in the future. Ideally, we can derive such deeply satisfying experi-ences from the real challenges of everyday life, from work, from creative expression, from family relationships, and from friendship. If we can't, then we will continue to invent substitutes such as chemicals or rituals that will project phantasms of flow onto our consciousness. Because, however, some of these substitutes can be very dangerous, it is worth considering what opportunities for flow are present in our daily existence.

FLOW IN EVERYDAY LIFE

There is no objective way to measure whether a person is in flow or not, comparable, let us say, to the way we measure whether he or she has a temperature or a high cholesterol level. But there are two indicators that in the past have proven to be both reliable and valid measures of the frequency and intensity of flow. The first relies on interviews or structured questionnaires asking respondents to indicate whether they have ever experienced occasions of deep concentration, complete involvement, and so on—and if yes, how often. The results obtained with this method indicate that about 87 percent of American adults report having experienced flow, while the remaining 13 percent claim never to have had it. The frequency of flow varies greatly among those who do recognize the experience; some say it happens to them less than once a year, others that it occurs several times every day.

People who report infrequent flow experiences get little pleasure from their work and their relationships, and depend on various forms of entertainment for amusement. In contrast, those who say that flow is a daily occurrence are people for whom work and family life are fulfilling. Here is an example of a forty-eight-year-old man and his seventeen-year-old son, both of whom work on the mechanical looms their family has owned for many generations, and who were interviewed by Massimini's team in northern Italy. Both listed weaving as the activity that brought them closest to flow. First the father describes the challenge of keeping a dozen looms working at the same time, without running out of thread or stopping:

> It is hard to concentrate on a single thing. I try to keep everything under control, as I am fixing one loom I am already thinking about the next one that needs to be loaded, one thing or the other. It seldom happens that I run out of thread. I always try to anticipate . . . in any case, when I work I am concentrated.

The teenage son listed as his most enjoyable experience "to see a loom that wasn't working starting to run, and to know that it's you who made it go." When asked to list his favorite activities, he wrote down two: to work during the week; to have a good time with friends on Saturday. Here is how he describes his feelings while working:

> I feel that concentration when I work on the looms; I am there and that's it. Because if your head is somewhere else and you get distracted you make a mistake; you must keep following a logical thread or you mess up. But even when all the looms are running you must keep paying attention; it's three years now that I have been watching them alone, that's why I can keep up with them . . . some things are automatic because you always do them the same way; others may be new—because here you are always learning—so you must pay attention to what you are doing.

This type of work, in which entire families can pursue a productive and gratifying common activity, is of course becoming more and more rare. Yet the results obtained with the Flow Questionnaire suggest that there are still many opportunities to find such creative challenges in everyday life, whether in work, in play, in prayer, or in relationships.

A second way to estimate flow is by using the Experience Sampling Method, or ESM. This technique, which I developed at the University of Chicago in the early 1970s, requires respondents to wear an electronic pager or a programmable stopwatch for a week, and to respond by filling out two pages of a booklet every time the pager signals. The pagers are activated by signals sent at random times during the day, so that most respondents fill out about fifty responses during the week, providing a running record of what they do and how they feel in typical situations of everyday life.

The way we measure flow with the ESM is by looking at the ratio of two responses: the challenge the person is facing at the moment of the signal, and the skills the person perceives himself to have at the same moment—each rated on a ten-point scale. When both challenge and skills are rated above the person's average for the week, we say that the person is in *flow*. If both variables are below average, the person is considered to be in a state of *apathy*. If challenge is rated above average while skill is rated below, the situation is one of *anxiety*. In the reverse situation, low challenge and high skill, the corresponding state of consciousness is labeled *boredom*. Many studies have shown that the ratio of challenges and skills does indeed reflect the expected states of consciousness.

It should be noted that this method for measuring flow is extremely liberal, relying on the same sort of generalizations one would use if one were to say that everyone above five feet in stature is "tall." With that in mind, using the criteria of this method, one would expect one-fourth of all experiences to be in flow. In actuality, for some individuals, only 5 percent of responses indicated that both challenges and skills were above average at the same time, while others had as many as 60 percent. (Caterina, in our example above, started her therapy with 15.2 percent of her responses in flow by this definition, and ended up by having 50.9 percent in flow.) Of course one could also stipulate that only the most intense experiences, occurring once in a thousand, or once in a million times, should be considered flow, but to do so would not record the more modest events that make everyday life meaningful. For instance, if we had adopted such a stringent measure, we would have concluded that Caterina was never in flow, and thus the therapists would not have known which activities were relatively more enjoyable, and thus how she could be helped to improve her life.

Using this "above average challenges/above average skills" definition for measuring flow, one gets the surprising result that typical working adults in the United States experience flow on the job three times as often as in free time. In a representative sample of urban Americans of both genders, including assembly-line and clerical as well as managerial workers, above-average levels of both challenges and skills were reported 54 percent of the time during actual periods of work, versus only 17 percent of the time in leisure. But perhaps this finding should not surprise us. If it is true that what we enjoy most is the "unfolding of our being," then it makes sense that this should occur more often at work than in free time. Just as Cedric the cocker spaniel is most himself when he hunts tennis balls, we tend to be most ourselves at work, when our peculiar skills are in use. In an ESM study of adolescents, we found a similar pattern:

40 percent of teenagers' responses as they were studying or doing homework were in flow, against only 8 percent of the responses given while watching TV.

Whenever they were in flow, adults and teenagers reported being very significantly more happy, strong, satisfied, creative, and concentrated. There is, however, one disturbing exception. Motivation is affected more by whether one works or is at leisure than by the presence of flow. People in general preferred leisure to working, regardless of whether they experienced flow or not. Thus, paradoxically, in our culture the aversion to work is so ingrained that even though it provides the bulk of the most complex and gratifying experiences, people still prefer having more free time, although a great deal of free time is in fact relatively boring and depressing.

The kind of activities that provide flow at work differ depending on the type of job and the worker's skills. For some managers, solving difficult problems and writing reports tends to produce the most flow; others, who have not developed a facility for expressing ideas, dread having to write. Generally clerical workers enjoy typing and keypunching; blue-collar workers enjoy fixing equipment and working with computers. The least flowlike work activities include paperwork for managers, filing for clericals, and assembly-line work for the blue-collar employees. As one would expect, novelty, variety, and excitement tend to provide flow on the job. But then, some individuals do find flow on the same assembly line where the other workers find only boredom, proving again that it is not the objective, external conditions that determine the quality of experience, but how we respond to them.

In terms of what produces flow in free time, the three occupational groups are very similar to each other. Surprisingly, across all occupations, driving a car is the most consistent source of flow experiences, followed by conversations with friends and family. The least flowlike activities in free time are watching TV and maintenance functions, such as cleaning the house or trying to sleep. Reading for pleasure is generally a more positive experience than watching TV, but most of the time it falls short of providing a flow experience. On the rare occasions that people are involved in active leisure—singing, bowling, biking, building a cabinet in the base-ment—they report some of the highest levels of flow, but such activities seem to occur so infrequently in the life of the average person that they leave hardly a trace.

One of the most intriguing mysteries revealed by these studies is the question why people spend so much time in passive leisure, such as watching television—which is by far the most time-consuming leisure activity in the modern world—when they enjoy it so little. Television viewing is universally reported as involving practically no challenges and requiring no skills.

The fact that people prefer this low-complexity activity to others that provide greater potential for growth is another example of the paradox of why attaining flow at work does not appear to be a stronger motivation. There are two reasons why this occurs with reference to television. One is that when choosing where to invest attention during free time, people seek to balance the energy they have to expend with the anticipated benefits. Television viewing provides little enjoyment, but it requires also very little effort. Play-ing the piano or taking a bike ride are much more enjoyable but require greater expenditures of psychic and physical energy. So we save a small amount of energy up front by watching television, but we forfeit the opportunity to experience flow and to grow in complexity as we do so.

The other explanation is that, while children can spontaneously enjoy flow, in most societies the mismatch between opportunities and abilities leads to a progressive atrophy of the desire for complex-ity during the course of a lifetime. With few adults who can serve as models for how to enjoy complex activities, with little encour-agement to become interested in challenges for their own sake, with living environments that are too boring or too unsafe to explore and to learn from, many children gradually lose their ability to find flow in everything they do. Having learned that boredom and worry are the norm in the family, in the school, and in the community at large, children give up curiosity, interest, the desire to explore new possi-bilities, and become used to passive entertainment. Parasitic memes take over their minds, mimicking enjoyment without providing substance. By the time they reach their teens, they have become adolescents who no longer perceive opportunities for action around them, who no longer feel that they have skills they can use. Even though passive leisure provides little joy, they see it as the only way within their means to occupy their minds in free time.

Yet flow does not just improve the quality of experience momentarily for young people, since it also has important long-term effects. As we have seen, people who are often in flow have higher self-esteem than those who experience flow rarely. Teenagers who report more flow tend to be happier, and they develop academic talents further than teens who are in flow less often. Adults who spend more time in flow work longer, yet are less prone to stress-related illness.

So the question is, how can we learn to enjoy complexity, instead of being forced to find pleasure in activities that provide only a semblance of harmony to consciousness? Individuals who cannot experience flow, or who enjoy only passive and simple activities, end up developing selves that are often in turmoil, riven by frustrations and disappointment. Those, on the other hand, who master enough skills to find flow in more complex activities tend to develop selves that can transform everyday events, even when these threaten to bring chaos and entropy in their wake, into meaningful experiences. In so doing they not only enjoy their own lives, but they contribute to the evolution of complexity for humanity as a whole.

FURTHER THOUGHTS ON "EVOLUTION AND FLOW"

The Elements of Flow

When do you feel that you are truly "unfolding your being"? How often does this happen?

What opportunities for action are you most attracted to? Sports, meditation, other people, reading, work, art, the outdoors? Which ones are you missing out on?

Why Is Flow Rewarding?

Knowing the kind of person you are, the interests and skills you have, what would be the most rewarding flow activity for you?

Can there be too much flow in a person's life? Could flow become addictive? Under what conditions could this be so?

The Consequences of Flow

How differently do you feel after being involved in a complex flow activity (e.g., skiing, reading a good book, having a stimulating conversation) and after a passive leisure activity like watching television?

Think of the last time you really felt good about yourself. What made you feel that way?

What Happens When Flow Is Absent?

Which elements of flow (i.e., balancing challenges and skills, setting clear goals, getting feedback, not fearing to lose control, concentrating fully, losing consciousness of self, feeling at one with what you are doing, losing the sense of time) are the hardest for you to achieve? How could you change this situation?

Which aspects of your life are affected most adversely by lack of flow?

Flow in Everyday Life

What experiences provide flow in your life, and why aren't you having more of them?

What could you do to make your job more flow-like? What about your family life?

8
THE
TRANSCENDENT
SELF

It is said that the Emperor Nero was ecstatic at the sight of Rome burning; he is known to have loved watching gladiators kill each other in the arena and lions tear apart innocent Christians. Many of the physicists who were involved with the Manhattan Project recall the exhilaration of working on the enormously challenging problem of how to build a nuclear bomb. Thousands of people fly every week to Las Vegas and to the rapidly proliferating casinos across the country, unable to resist the addiction of gambling. Unfortunately, as these examples suggest, flow can be experienced in activities that are destructive rather than constructive, that lead to entropy instead of to harmony.

To help guide the progress of evolution it is not sufficient for a person to enjoy merely any kind of life, but a life that increases order instead of disorder. To contribute to greater harmony, a person's consciousness has to become complex. Complexity of consciousness is not a function of only intelligence or knowledge, and is not just a cognitive trait—it includes a person's feelings and actions as well. It involves becoming aware of and in control of one's unique potentials, and being able to create harmony between goals and desires, sensations and experiences, both for oneself and for others.

People who achieve this are not only going to have a more fulfilling life, but they are almost certainly more likely to contribute to a better future. Personal happiness and a positive contribution to evolution go hand in hand.

Many cultures have honored with special names people who find flow in complex activities. The Confucians called them sages, the Mahayana Buddhists called a person who attained the Ninth World a Bodhisattva, while the one who attained the final stage of Buddhahood (or *butsu* in Japanese) was given no fewer than ten titles, including Teacher of Gods and Humans. In the Christian tradition, those who are called saints share many similar characteristics, such as freedom from the dictates of the genes, freedom from social controls, and a compassionate attitude toward others. They may have suffered and even died for their beliefs, but by all accounts, despite whatever hardships they had to endure, sages, saints, and Bodhisattvas led a serenely joyful existence.

Nowadays we don't have official names for complex persons, but what is more regrettable is our inability to distinguish them from others who do not contribute anything to the future, or who actually increase entropy with their actions. By not recognizing individuals who nurture harmony, we make it more difficult to learn from their example. To help alleviate this state of affairs, it might be useful to call a person whose psychic energy is joyfully invested in complex goals a *transcender,* or a T-person.

What Transcenders Are Like

There are many individuals whose actions demonstrate what a life dedicated to complexity could be like. But they cannot be reduced to a type, for there cannot be a single path for reaching personal harmony. Because differentiation is one-half of a complex consciousness, each person must follow his or her own bent, find ways to realize his or her unique individuality. And because we are all born with a different combination of temperamental strengths and weaknesses, and with different gifts, and grow up in different family contexts, communities, and historical periods, each of us displays a characteristic pattern of potentials. Therefore, there is no such thing as a typical T-person, nor a best way to achieve complexity.

But fortunately there are many examples of transcendent lives that one can cite. For instance, a good illustration is that of the poet György Faludy. I happened to meet him for the first time a few days after his eightieth birthday, in Budapest, where he had recently returned to receive official recognition for a complete edition of his works. He has a halo of silvery hair and a quietly self-mocking smile; while his features resemble the furrows on a drying apple, his eyes brim with the curiosity and enthusiasm of a ten-year-old. I had often been moved by his terse, sinewy, yet touchingly gentle verse. In his long life Faludy has experienced more tragedy than one would suppose any man could endure, yet has contributed more to the complexity of the future than most.

At nine years of age, Faludy remembers, he had decided to become a poet, for playing with language was the only thing he could do well. But why a poet, I asked. "Because I was afraid of dying," he answered. Lying in bed at night, in terror of not waking up in the morning, he resolved to create with words a world where he could feel safe, a world of his creation that would live on after he himself disappeared. As he grew up, Faludy kept writing as one possessed; he enjoyed it more than anything else, and most people who read his work were deeply moved.

But there was an obstacle: Faludy was Jewish, and he was too well read to restrain his imagination within the staid boundaries of pre–World War II bourgeois sensibilities. He was blacklisted and his poetry banned from print, so he resorted to the expedient of translating, especially the verse of Villon and Verlaine. This the censors reluctantly allowed, not wanting to seem opposed to what was, after all, classic French poetry. Emboldened by this success, Faludy began to publish his own poems, pretending that they were Villon translations. The Budapest intelligentsia were on to the ruse, and appreciated the bold verses even more because of the risks their author was running.

As World War II advanced, and German troops invaded Hungary, the local fascist collaborators rounded Faludy up with other Jews and threw him into a deportation camp. From there he somehow escaped, and succeeded in crossing half of warring Europe to end up in North Africa, where the French who collaborated with the Nazis promptly put him back into a camp that had just been vacated because all the inmates had died of cholera. Faludy barely survived this imprisonment until the Allied troops liberated North Africa and he had a chance to emigrate to Canada and then the United States.

By then he had translated several volumes of some of the greatest of the world's poetry: from the Chinese, from Sanskrit, from Greek, Latin, Italian, German, French, English, and several other languages. These poems were as fresh and brilliant in translation as if they had been written originally in Hungarian, yet they also preserved the particular flavor of the culture and the time in which they had actually been composed. But this linguistic genius was not very useful to Faludy in North America. Although he was offered visiting professorships at various East Coast colleges, he could never feel as comfortable with an adopted language as he did with his native one. This, of course, is true for every writer who must choose exile, even for Nobel Prize winners like Solzhenitsyn or Czeslaw Milosz, but being in such good company did not really help Faludy to come to terms with the fact that his skills were almost useless in an alien land.

So a few years after the end of World War II he decided to return to Hungary, where, in a socialist republic, his brand of revolutionary poetry should have been welcome. Of course the opposite turned out to be the case. The new regime was even less receptive to truth than the old one had been. Faludy got in trouble early by writing a haunting allegorical attack on Stalin. The upshot was predictable: Faludy was arrested, tortured in the cellars of the secret police, and then sent to Recsk, one of the Communist "punitive" camps from which few ever returned. Somehow he survived this ordeal for more than three years, until, after Stalin's death, the camp was abolished and he was allowed to return home.

Yet it was precisely in this dreadful environment, where inmates were whipped to labor from dawn to dusk, with slops to eat and rags to wear, that Faludy's muse really started to sing. His prison verses are among the most lyrical ever written in that genre. (Hungarian is an excellent language to translate into, but very difficult to translate from; hence it is unfortunately almost impossible to get a feeling for the original in an English translation.) They deal with the most concrete, realistic, and painful aspects of life in a concentration camp: hunger, frostbite, the brutality of ignorant and frightened men. Yet these clinical accounts of entropy are narrated so concisely and elegantly that their tragic content is transformed into a thing of beauty.

In fact, this was precisely Faludy's intent. In order to maintain his own sanity, and that of his fellow prisoners, he tried to give meaning to an otherwise intolerable existence. In one of his last poems before being released Faludy wrote:

> *What was the best thing I learned?*
> *That after need*
> *left my ravaged body*
> *love did not leave.*
> *Susy[1] became a light, silvery mist; shimmering always*
> *before my eyes*
> *even when shut*
> *in pain, in gnawing hunger, as senses left,*
> *love stayed,*
> *love, the eternal fire, burning without harming,*
> *not born of scalding desire,*
> *no dreg of glands,*
> *no juice of sex organs,*
> *Dante, not Boccaccio,*
> *Apollo, not the world of the dead.*
>
> *Let Ziggy Freud go soak his head.[2]*

In the extremity of a life-threatening situation, the former rebel sought sustenance from the most hopeful aspects of the past, from

[1]The name of the author's wife.
[2]Tanulságnak mi volt a legszebb?
 Ahogy érzéki vágyaim
 elhagyták a kifosztot testet
 s nem hagyott el a szerelem.
 Zsuzsából könnyü, ezüst köd lett; ott lebegett folyton elöttem,
 ha be is hunytam a szemem,
 hajszában, kínok közt, kegyetlen éhségben s már önkívületben,
 velem marad a szerelem,
 a szerelem, az örökmécses, a láng, mely ég, de meg nem éget,
 nem párzó vágyunk származéka, nem a mirigyek hanyadéka,
 nem nemi szervek váladéka,
 nem Boccaccio, de Dante,
 Apollo, s nem az alvilág.

 Menesd a búsba Freud Zsigát.

the most meaningful memes of his civilization—and from the love for his wife. Perhaps one of the most touching aspects of Faludy's oeuvre is that originally it was not written down, for the simple reason that pencil and paper were not available in the camp. At first Faludy memorized each of his poems. Then, to avoid losing them through death or forgetfulness, he had fellow prisoners learn them by heart as well. In one case, toward the end of his captivity, he composed a long elegy for his wife, and each part of it was memorized by different inmates. Some of these prisoners were freed before Faludy, and went to visit his wife, to bring news of her husband and to recite the part of the poem they had memorized. At the end of the recitation, they would typically announce: "That's all I learned. But in a few days Jim Egri should be released, and he will come and tell you the next twenty verses."

When Faludy was finally allowed to return to civilization, and then escaped once more to the West during the Hungarian Revolution of 1956, he published his prison verses, relying on his memory aided by various mnemonic devices. (For instance, he had made certain that the first poem he composed began with the letter "A," the second with "B," and so on). Soon after, he started to receive letters from all over the world, from Brazil to New Zealand, containing corrections to his poems. They were written by former inmates, now scattered across the globe, who had committed to memory the harmoniously transformed accounts of their deadly experiences. Most of these corrections were incorporated in later editions of Faludy's work.

Faludy's life serves as such a valuable example for two complementary reasons: In the first place, it is so idiosyncratic in its specifics as to be obviously inapplicable to the lives of most people. How many of us have such a gift for language, have suffered so much persecution, and triumphed over so many obstacles? Yet despite—or rather, because of—its uniqueness, Faludy's story is typical of those individuals who have been able to fulfill the potential complexity of their selves. He is certainly not a saint, and he may not qualify as a Confucian sage or a Bodhisattva, either. But he learned to find flow in complexity; he learned to transform entropy into memes that create order in the consciousness of those who attend to them, and so because of him the world is a little more harmonious than it would have been otherwise.

Other representative individuals would be very easy to find. We all know people who fit this profile, without having a name or a category to describe them. We can measure IQ quite accurately, and can calculate a person's net worth down to the last dollar, indicators we take very seriously. But when it comes to the much more meaningful issue of whether a person's life increases harmony or chaos, we become very tentative and tongue-tied.

In their recent book, the psychologists Ann Colby and William Damon describe the lives of deeply committed moral leaders, and profile five exemplars in great detail. One of these could serve as a model for many others. Suzie Valdez is a Hispanic woman from California who, after a very deprived and disappointing youth, moved to Ciudad Juárez in Mexico, where she became the "Queen of the Dumps." She established her own mission house, and devoted her life to teaching the homeless, who were forced to scavenge in the mountains of refuse around town, some basic principles of hygiene, as well as trying "to show the children that there's a better life than they're living now." Although poor and uneducated herself, she managed the transition from being a welfare recipient to providing welfare to hundreds of families, simply through her initiative and dedication.

"For Suzie," write the authors, "her work is her life. . . . As she sees it, the work with the poor of Juárez is what she is here for, what she most wants to do. This kind of wholehearted desire to pursue one's moral goal is what we mean by unity of self and morality. In Suzie, this unity is the key to her stamina, her certainty, and her joy." When a person learns to enjoy this kind of complex experience, the self that results is bound to be internally harmonious, and contribute to the harmony of others.

But a transcendent self need not be one that, like Faludy and Valdez, has stepped out of the confines of normality to assume a burden few shoulders could support. Most people add to complexity in more modest, less spectacular ways. For instance, consider a fifteen-year-old in one of our recent studies of adolescents; I call him Ben. Ben is only remarkable in that, despite his young age, he knows what he wants to do for the rest of his life, he is good at it and enjoys doing it, and even though his own goals are clear and pressing, he is also concerned with helping others realize theirs. The only thing truly extraordinary about these qualities is that they occur so seldom in young persons.

Ben had the first glimmers of becoming an artist in eighth grade, when he designed and built out of balsa wood, a Viking ship, complete with oars and shields. "I started working with balsa wood and saw that I could create things, not just draw them. I had so much fun doing that. . . . That was about the best year because that was when I coordinated not only drawing but also construction into one. That is when it *all came together*." As he hones his skills, Ben acquires confidence and develops long-range goals that might sustain him for the rest of his life. He hopes to become an architect, or perhaps a car designer. He already has fairly clear ideas about what success would mean to him: "I'm competitive in what I do, and I like to see myself succeed; when I don't succeed at what I do I get pretty angry at myself. . . . To me being my own boss would be successful, to others making a lot of money would be successful. Just knowing that you have accomplished this yourself . . . that's successful."

Ben's sense of autonomy and self-confidence indicate that his self is becoming differentiated. At the same time, he is sensitive to the people around him, and knows that he is linked to them by indispensable ties. In other words, integration is also a strong component of his self; this is revealed in what he says about his parents: "I love my parents very much and I like to see them happy in what I do. Pretty much anything I do I consult them, even if I don't need to." And he tries to learn from the best traits of his grandfather:

> We were real close and it's hard to say why. He was always very calm in situations. I'd never seen him get angry. . . . He could work with his hands like you couldn't believe and do intricate things at the age of 75. . . . When certain situations come up . . . I look back and see that I could be subtle and it would complement the situation more, looking at him as an example.

Isn't this what being an adolescent should be like? But how many parents of teenagers are fortunate to recognize their own children in

Ben's sketch? Perhaps if we took more seriously what it requires to build a complex self—as seriously, perhaps, as developing a strong backhand or a high IQ, as earning a basketball letter or a good college admission—Ben's case would not seem exceptional at all.

To go to the other extreme in the life cycle, there is the example of another person we interviewed for one of our studies—the physicist Linus Pauling. When we talked to Pauling he was over ninety years of age. Straight as a pine sapling, sharp as a tack, he sat for two hours reminiscing about his life and work. He could remember the dates on which he wrote various papers over sixty years ago, and the circumstances that led up to them; he recalled with a smile the boys he used to play with in Portland, Oregon, over eighty years ago, and the street addresses at which they lived. More than any single impression, what was so striking in Pauling's account is how much he seemed to have enjoyed every day of those ninety years, and how much of a piece his entire life was.

Pauling's biography is a textbook case of complexity. In his youth he was able to visualize the relationship between quantum mechanics at the subatomic level and the molecular structure of chemical elements; having been able to demonstrate the nature of that relationship, he earned a Nobel Prize in chemistry. In a sense, this part of his life was dedicated primarily to a process of highly specialized intellectual differentiation. Later Pauling turned his energies toward integration. He became concerned with the responsibility of scientists toward society and toward nature. He put his body as well as his reputation on the line to protest against heedless nuclear development, organized scientists against nuclear armament, and for a while became involved in national politics. For these activities he earned the Nobel Peace Prize.

What is common to the stories of Faludy, Valdez, Ben, and Pauling? They are the kind of people who have learned to derive spontaneous joy and deep satisfaction from living their lives. Not from gaining riches or honors, but from the very process of living, from developing skills and overcoming challenges—from being a part of the evolutionary process that leads to higher levels of harmonious complexity. Before going further to see how such lives can be cultivated, it will be useful to review briefly what we have already learned about the self, and how it works.

WHAT IS THE SELF?

Standing on a beach along the Atlantic or the Pacific, and looking out at the tremendous expanse of water, one cannot help but think something along the lines of "Ah, the mighty ocean!" Yet what we call the "ocean" is actually a mental construction, because all there is in front of us is just a great number of hydrogen and oxygen atoms dancing together to form what we call "water molecules." We don't see the molecules, only the sum of their effects, which we then imagine as a single entity: the Atlantic, the Pacific, the Mediterranean.

In order to make sense of the stimuli that bombard our senses, our nervous system has learned to bundle up information in manageable chunks, so that we are not overwhelmed by a mass of discrete details. Therefore, we see the particles of water as a single substance, we see the particles of air as the "sky," the mineral surface of the planet as the "earth," and so forth. Our minds, in reflecting on what we see, endow these images with separate identities, identities they have only in our imagination. This is the process of *reification,* by which we attribute reality to mental constructions.

The self is such a reification, and certainly one of the most significant ones. We usually think of it as a force, a spark, an inner flame with an indivisible integrity. Yet, from what we know now, the self is more in the nature of a figment of the imagination, something we create to account for the multiplicity of impressions, emotions, thoughts, and feelings that the brain records in consciousness. In simpler organisms, the nervous system consists of more or less closed circuits. Only a few sensory channels are open, and these are connected to single, discrete motor responses. The organism doesn't have to make complex decisions, but reacts instinctively and piecemeal. But because the human brain has become so complex over time, there is too much information coming into it; a great variety of sensory data clamors for attention, and priorities have to be set. Eventually, a "traffic cop" function develops among the neurons of the brain to monitor and control what otherwise would be buzzing confusion. Without a centralized director, the competing sensory inputs would jostle one another in a senseless chaos. But as soon as we begin to use this executive capability that has emerged in recent evolutionary history, it, too, becomes one of the items of information in consciousness. And as we reflect on our ability to control what is happening in the mind, we come to think of it as a concrete entity—the "self"—to which we attribute all sorts of qualities. Many imagine the self as a homunculus, a manikin, a tiny individual sitting in the middle of the brain directing our lives.

While this is not literally true, there *is* something in our mind that is more than the sum of the individual neurons that make up the brain. This something is the self, the brain's awareness of its own form of organizing information. Just as we apprehend the millions of water molecules as a single ocean, we experience the coming together of information in consciousness as the self. And just as the sea has many properties that cannot be imagined from mere knowledge of the discrete molecules of water—such as tides, waves, whales, icebergs, gulls, boats, and beautiful sunsets—so the self has its own features that cannot be predicted from the discrete bits of information that make it up.

Perhaps the most fateful consequence of the self's emergence is the power it eventually acquires over our psychic energy. After the self develops, its primary goal becomes that of every other organism: to defend itself, to aggrandize itself. If we don't control it, it soon takes over all our energy for its own purposes, and we end up being ruled by a figment of the imagination. Of course, it may be better to be ruled by the self and its needs than by external forces, genes and memes, which is the other alternative. But then the question becomes, what sort of a self will we create to rule us?

If the self includes everything that passes in consciousness, it follows that what we pay attention to over time will shape that self. For instance, the Nuer people of East Africa raise cattle and spend most of their time watching their herds. They know each animal intimately, they know its habits and ancestors for many generations. They believe that the calves born to their herd come from the same water wells from which their own babies came, and to which their souls will return after death. Because of the mythical kinship they feel with their cattle, the Nuer very rarely slaughter their animals; having a large herd is an end in itself, an accomplishment that makes them feel proud and contented. It is not just a figure of speech to say that the self of a Nuer is made up, in part, by the cows and the bulls he or she spends so much time attending to.

For a male Nuer, there is another center to the self. Before becoming pastoralists, the Nuer were a warring and hunting tribe, and a man lived by his spear. Even after they turned to cattle raising, however, Nuer men retained their spears. In fact, early anthropologists reported that a Nuer man always kept a spear in his hand, feeling its weight, caressing its blade, balancing its shaft on his shoulder. By constantly attending to his weapon, as he was guarding his cattle or while sitting in front of his hut, the Nuer knew that he was a warlike, powerfully dangerous being; hence, this information became an integral part of his self. It was a similar insight that moved the anthropologist Ruth Benedict to entitle her book about Japan *The Chrysanthemum and the Sword,* because she saw in these two objects a key to the Japanese character, at the same time delicate and fierce.

There is nothing mysterious, or mystical, about the way objects become part of ourselves. The man who spends most of his time polishing his car, tuning up its engine, and talking about it to his friends will gradually end up including the car in his conception of his self. When the chrome shines he feels proud, a rust spot on the fender is almost as distressing as a bald spot on the scalp, and a newer car in the neighbor's driveway can cause gut-wrenching jealousy. Therefore, what we pay attention to is no trivial matter; we are what we attend to.

But it is not just *what* we pay attention to that will constitute the self; it matters also *how* we do so. The way data is organized in consciousness also becomes a defining aspect of the self. For instance, a person who is drawn to other people and pays more attention to social events than to inner feelings or thoughts becomes an extrovert, while a person who always believes others want to harm him becomes neurotic. An optimist turns events around until he sees their bright side; a materialist is someone who always looks for a concrete advantage.

We have said earlier that the self comes into being because consciousness, to avoid being overwhelmed by information clamoring for attention, needs a mechanism to sort out and prioritize the diverse demands. The means by which attention becomes prioritized we call goals. A goal is a channel into which psychic energy flows. Therefore, the self can be considered a hierarchy of goals, because the goals define what we pay attention to, and how. If you know what goal takes precedence for a given person, you can generally anticipate where that person will invest psychic energy, and therefore predict his or her behavior.

Each person's goals are to a large extent similar to those of everyone else. Being human we all want, first of all, to survive, to be comfortable, to be accepted, loved, and respected. After these goals are reasonably satisfied—or blocked beyond hope—we then turn our energy to develop our own unique potential, to achieve what the psychologist Abraham Maslow has called "self-actualization." Then some people shift their priorities again, and envision the goal of transcendence. They attempt to move beyond the boundaries of their personal limitations by integrating individual goals with larger ones, such as the welfare of the family, the community, humanity, the planet, or the cosmos. For a scientist who has invested a great deal of thought into trying to figure out superconductivity, any breakthrough in that field will be as worthy of his attention as hunger or a headache originating in his body. For a transcender like Mother Teresa, what happens to the orphans of Calcutta is as important as what happens to herself.

It is these two last stages in the formation of the self that lead to complexity. Individual uniqueness, or self-actualization, represents the differentiation component; transcendence involves a higher level of integration. Both are necessary for the kind of self that leads to a complex and harmonious evolution, the kind of self exemplified by Faludy, Valdez, Pauling, and Ben. If the third millennium is to be an improvement over its predecessor, more of us will have to build selves around transcendent goals.

EVOLVING IMAGES OF THE IDEAL SELF

An intriguing question to raise here is whether the complexity of the human self has evolved through history. Is the average person today more differentiated and integrated than our ancestors were three or thirty thousand years ago? Of course, there is no reliable evidence on which to base an answer. It is difficult enough to evaluate the inner lives and motivations of our contemporaries, let alone to determine what people in Egypt or Sumeria thought and felt. The best we can do is to consider the way ideal men and women have been represented in paintings and sculptures across time. These images will not tell us precisely what kind of people our ancestors were, but they might at least give us a clue as to what kind of personhood was valued in the past.

As has been noted several times in this book, the great advance that culture contributed to evolution was that it enabled information to be represented extrasomatically. With the advent of pictographs and then writing, it was no longer necessary to keep all of an individual's or a culture's knowledge within the organism, stored in the memory pathways of the nervous system. It was now possible to externalize it in pictures and books, and to transmit images of experience from person to person by means of symbols. Extrasomatic coding and storage of information allowed an accumulation of knowledge many orders of magnitude beyond what could be previously stored in the brain. Perhaps as a result of this advance, humankind became able to give imagination a new meaning. Once people could make copies of events on external media, they must have realized that they could also create images of events that they had not directly witnessed. Thus they could conceive of representations of gods no one had seen, and depict events that never happened. Imagination emancipated itself from its former task as faithful recorder of reality, and was on its way as a reality sui generis, now leading humans to unexpected triumphs, now luring them into illusion.

Of course, images are unable to present a "true" picture of reality. Cartesian coordinates, X-rays, or colored maps of the brain are ways we happen to have learned to mediate visually certain aspects of reality we think are important, in ways the mind can grasp them. These images are just as bounded by the limitations of our nervous system, and of our survival needs, as the images a bee has of its environment are limited by the bee's representational abilities.

One of the most important aspects of experience that humans have tried to represent through images is their own self. As the self began to depend more and more on learning as opposed to relying simply on genetically programmed behavior, its representations began to refer not just to the visible features of the physical body but included psychological qualities, the spiritual essences that people either experienced in themselves, or wished to attain. If human evolution is to continue, it will be because of our trying to live up to increasingly complex images of our selves.

More often than not, the images of the self people created in the past were not intended to represent the self as it *is,* but rather as it *ought to be.* In cave paintings the hunter is usually depicted as successful in the hunt, the early fertility figurines show fat females with enormous breasts and buttocks, the Egyptian pharaohs are invariably represented triumphing over the enemy. Such distortions of reality are of course entirely functional, in that they potentially serve the purpose of propelling the individual toward more desirable states of being.

Personal Objects

Images of the ideal self are often embedded in objects that people wear on their bodies, or are actually carved on the body itself. These images are not always literal depictions of individuals; often they consist of objects symbolizing qualities important to the self. One universal category of objects that represents important aspects of the self includes those a person carries on himself or herself. These tend to be items that are worn in order to enhance the power of the owner, and communicate the person's ability to control energy, to defeat opponents, to command loyalty, to attract attention and envy. Perhaps the simplest forms of this type are body decorations, the paints and tattoos that preliterate people apply directly to their flesh, transforming it from a natural substance into a cultural entity. "The face paintings," writes Lévi-Strauss about the Caduevo Indians of Brazil, "confer upon the individual his dignity as a human being: they help him cross the frontier from Nature to culture, and from the 'mindless' animal to the civilized Man. Furthermore, they differ in style and composition according to social status, and thus have a social function." There are many messages that such decorations convey, one of the most typical being the person's position in a kinship network. Thus a tattoo serves as a badge of identity, and signals the fact that its bearer is not a solitary human being but a member of a social network. In other words, if you attack this man, you are attacking his entire group.

Next in complexity are the various adornments made of feathers, cloth, or metal, which attest both to the social position of the wearer and also to his or her individual accomplishments. Some archeologists now believe that the first use of metals was not to forge weapons or useful tools, but to fashion body ornaments:

> In several areas of the world it has been noted, in the case of metallurgical innovations in particular, that the development of bronze and other metals as useful commodities was a much later phenomenon than their first utilization as new and attractive materials, employed in contexts of display. . . . In most cases early metallurgy appears to have been practiced primarily because its products have novel properties that made them attractive as symbols and as personal adornment and ornaments, in a manner that, by focusing attention, could attract and enhance prestige.

Currently, the use of adornment to enhance one's image is no less obvious. The red "power tie" indicates that its wearer is ambitious; tinted hair, plastic surgery, cosmetics, jewelry, and fashion clothing are ways to make the self appear more desirable or prestigious than it actually is. Historically the body ornaments of males have tended to represent power as physical strength or control over other people and goods; the power of women was traditionally represented by their ability to attract men because of outstanding sexual attributes, the promise of fertility, or intimations of good housekeeping. All of these attempts are quite clearly a cultural extension of the biological markers that so many insects, birds, and mammals possess in order to make themselves appear larger, fiercer, or more attractive— depending on the function the markings are supposed to advertise.

In different cultures, specialized objects may be adopted for representing different dimensions of the self. Among many Native American tribes, adults wore "medicine bundles" around their necks, in which were stored the objects that symbolized the owner's special knowledge or accomplishments: some powerful medicinal herbs, the teeth and claws of a bear defeated in hand-to-hand struggle.

In our own time, people carry a great variety of objects to symbolize the desired quality of their selves. Most men's wallets and women's purses contain the equivalent of a Cheyenne medicine bundle. In addition we tote watches, pens, pocket calculators, pagers, cellular phones, and other paraphernalia calculated to reassure ourselves and impress others about our powers. More than any other single item, the car one drives has become in our culture a representation and extension of the ideal self. With its blatantly totemic symbolism and purely cosmetic appearance, it makes a statement that is hard to ignore about who we think we are and want to be known as. Personal objects thus serve partly as a psychological crutch, reminding the owner of his or her ability to cope with the world; partly they serve to create an image that will give the owner an advantage in interactions with others.

Household Objects

While personal objects worn on the body appear to have primarily defensive purposes, creating as it were a symbolic armor against the dangers of the outside world, the objects one collects in the home seem to serve a different function. As they are more private, their function seems to be to create inner order and clarity in the owner's conception of self, rather than making an external impression.

The most important part of the home in Rome, China, and many other cultures was the corner reserved for ancestral images. The living person acquired identity and meaning in relation to the departed kin whose past lives were memorialized by masks, statuettes, or other symbols to be seen and revered each day. The individual meant little outside the stream of life represented by the eternally renewed kinship group. Wherever Christianity substituted the idea of a universal family ruled by God the Father, holy images took precedence over those portraying earthly relations. The icons of Christ, his mother, and his saints became the symbolic center of the household, to which people could turn to clarify and reaffirm their identities.

In contemporary homes, most people construct a symbolic environment filled with images that help them to remember who they were, to confirm who they are, and to foreshadow the kind of persons they would like to be in the future. But instead of using ready-made and culturally validated icons of the kind so prevalent in past cultures, today we must construct our own vision of self, to a large extent from our own personal experiences. True, visual references to ancestors and kinship roots are still astonishingly important, even in the most modern households, but their significance must be personally validated, rather than simply borrowed from a generally shared and accepted cultural script.

In a study of over three hundred members of eighty-two families living in the Chicago metropolitan area, we found a very wide spectrum of objects that served to represent salient aspects of the owner's self. For example, furniture, stereo sets, books, and musical instruments were among the things owners mentioned most often as standing for important dimensions of the self. A chair in the living room was very special for a man because its practical and economical design expressed perfectly his own values. His wife cherished an old recliner because it was in that chair that she nursed her children when they were babies. Their son favored a third chair because it was like a trampoline, and he could bounce on it and feel free. Each of these chairs was a concrete reminder of an important aspect of the self for a different member of the family.

As in the oldest cultures, modern Americans' relation to kinfolk remains one of the central dimensions of the self objectified in household symbols. Ancestors and parents are remembered primarily via inherited plateware and furniture; in addition, paintings tend to remind people more of their fathers, and sculptures more of their mothers. In contrast to previous cultures, however, things that symbolize children and other descendants were just as much in evidence as objects symbolizing ancestors. Photographs were the objects most often mentioned as being special because they reminded their owners of their children, grandchildren, or the family as a whole. For grandparents photographs were the most valued objects in the home, mentioned by 37 percent; for parents they were the sixth most often mentioned object (22 percent); only 10 percent of the youngest generation mentioned photos, making them the fifteenth most frequent category. For this youngest generation stereo sets were the premier household objects, mentioned by 45 percent of the teenage respondents.

Another aspect of the self that the symbolic environment of the home represents is the owners' ideals. These are most often revealed by books (in 27 percent of the cases), by plants (12 percent), and by musical instruments (7 percent). But occasionally an old pair of rock-climbing boots, a trophy, or the diary one kept in high school can serve this purpose. Values, beliefs, and even the sense of who one is are constantly buffeted, challenged, and corroded through trafficking with the outside world. By returning home each day people not only restore themselves physically, but they also renew and reaffirm their identity by interacting with objects that contain desired images of the self.

Collective Representations

Another set of images is invoked when individuals meet in a public arena to invent or to reaffirm their collective identity. From the first lumbering dances our hominid ancestors performed around the campfire, to the extravagant opening and closing ceremonies of the latest Olympics broadcast around the world on television, we try to find symbolic expressions for our relationships with people who are not bound to us by kinship ties, and with the mysterious forces immanent in the cosmos. Often the images are auditory or kinesthetic rather than visual, as in the rhythm of tribal dances; or the bullroarer *(churinga)* that Australian aborigines rattle to create the impression of an all-powerful spiritual force and that, as Durkheim said, "is counted among the eminently sacred things; there are none that surpass it in religious dignity"; or the *molimo* trumpets that the pygmies of the Ituri forest in Africa use to wake up the sacred trees in the forest when a misfortune threatens the tribe. In each of these cases—as in the rock concerts that are such an important part of our youth's experience—the sound envelops the discrete individuals and creates in them a sense of joint participation in a powerful group entity. Presumably without such collective experiences we would feel even more isolated and helpless than we already are.

A very ancient tool for linking individuals visually with supernatural forces are the masks worn on ceremonial occasions, usually representing gods, heroes, or ancestral spirits central to a group's identity. For the Hopi as well as the New Guinea tribesman, wearing a mask is one of the most widespread means for transforming oneself from a puny mortal into the image of a powerful, meaningful entity. A good account of the transcendent function of masks is given by Monti:

> From a psychological point of view the origin of the mask can also be explained by the more atavistic aspiration of the human being to escape from himself in order to be enriched by the experience of different existences—a desire which obviously cannot be fulfilled on the physical level—and in order to increase its own power by identifying with universal, divine, or demonic forces, whichever they may be. It is a desire to break out of the human constriction of individuals shaped in a specific and immutable mould and closed in a birth–death cycle which leaves no possibility of consciously chosen existential adventures.

Preliterate cultures have also developed more abstract images for representing the collective forces to which they lay claim. In Australia, among the sacred objects of the Arunta that symbolized the essential force of the clan was the *nurturya,* a bundle of sticks or spears assembled at the center of the village on ritual occasions. This same symbol was used by the Romans to represent the authority of the state to punish trespassers of the law. Public officials in ancient Rome were surrounded by lictors who carried bundles of elm or birch rods tied together with red thongs; wherever these *fasces* appeared, any disturbance or unrest quieted down in awe of this symbol of collective power. In 1919 Mussolini's Fascist Party took its name from the *fasces,* which also signified the motto *L'unione fa la forza:* while each rod can be broken one at a time, when joined together the bundle is unbreakable. The universal readability of this image of the force to be found in unity is demonstrated by the fact that it appears conspicuously even on the speaker's stand in the U.S. House of Representatives.

Religious symbols of the collective also represent power, albeit of a sacred rather than a secular kind. As Henry Adams noted, the great medieval cathedrals acted as giant storehouses of psychic energy, equivalent to the large electric turbines of a hundred years ago. Modern-day analogies might be nuclear reactors, supercolliders, and space centers. They transform the physical manpower required to build them into awesome images of a mysterious force, which in turn enhances the self-image of those who identify with them.

Collective power, especially of the religious variety, is not necessarily equivalent to physical force or material control. A great number of the Gothic cathedrals were dedicated to the Virgin Mary, and the images of meekness, suffering, and gentleness associated with her are much more typical of Christian iconography than the representation of naked force. But within the Christian worldview the meek inherited the earth; the Virgin's gentle intercession swayed the might of God the Father. Power is a much subtler concept than Joseph Stalin imagined when he asked derisively how many divisions the Pope commanded.

Nevertheless, most of the images people create of themselves, whether at the personal or collective level, are in some respect an expression of power, whether that power involves influencing others, controlling the course of events, or simply having one's way. Of course, from an evolutionary point of view, this is an important function that images of the self should provide. It could be argued that they supply the goals, they foreshadow possibilities of being, that pull us toward the future. But are some images more useful than others in steering us forward on this journey?

Images of the Ideal Self

Where is one to find the images that humankind has created to give itself a direction, a goal toward which to aspire? The task of choosing relevant examples is made difficult by the very richness of human imagination. There are so many depictions of gods, angels, demons, and anthropomorphic animals that are tempting to use as models, but that ultimately must be rejected as irrelevant. How gods and demons are represented tells us something about a culture's view of the superhuman forces surrounding it, but it is within the more narrow range of representations of actual men and women that we should seek that culture's aspirations.

In the Western tradition, the ideal for human perfection was set almost three thousand years ago by the sculptors of Greece. Different but still very recognizable models were developed more or less independently in Egypt, China, and India. Outside the perimeters of what used to be called the great civilizations, however, it is more difficult to recognize representations of individualized human be-ings—figures of men or women who may have actually existed. The typical style of the complex cultures of Melanesia, Africa, and the New World could be best characterized as expressionistic. Bod-ies tend to be distorted in ways that emphasize desired or magically significant features—huge eyes, enormous genitals. The positions of the body are formalized, arranged according to ritually prescribed lines.

Of course, the difference between the carvings on a Maori war canoe and a frieze on an early Egyptian or Greek temple may be only a matter of degree, and non-Western imagery may be an accurate gauge of ideal personhood for its time. A rigid, ritually prescribed posture may have signified that a person was disciplined, in control of his or her body, in harmony with the laws of the gods and the tribe. A priapic phallus was clearly desirable—what better model for a man than a sexually superendowed being? Even the pharaohs surrounded themselves with outsized phallic obelisks, and Roman busts stood on plinths decorated with erect penises.

We are on slightly more secure ground when trying to interpret the message of the human images sculpted in the classic period of Greek culture. Here, for example, is how Arnold Hauser interprets the iconography of the archaic *kouroi* of the seventh century B.C., and the later statues of the time of Polyclitus:

> It is now that the foundations of the ethics of the nobility are laid: the conception of *areté* with its dominant traits of physical fitness and military discipline, built up on a tradition, birth and race; of *kaloka-gathia,* the ideal of the right balance between bodily and spiritual, physical and moral qualities; of *sophrosyne,* the ideal of self-restraint, discipline, and moderation.

Hauser argues that, toward the end of the aristocratic age of Greece, when the warring nobles were starting to lose political control to the increasingly affluent merchants, they sought to have carved in marble the virtues claimed by their own class. Fitness, moderation, and self-discipline were supposedly the traits that justified the rule of the warrior nobility. The statues that displayed these qualities were intended as a bulwark against the pretensions of the ambitious merchants intent on usurping that rule. Hauser further argues that the statues carved a few hundred years later, in the era of Praxiteles and Lysippus, reveal the changes in values that the victory of the merchant classes had brought to Athens. The human figures now show a humanistic enlightenment, which emphasized beauty rather than strength, alert intelligence instead of resolute character, and spontaneity over discipline.

Many of the ideals suggested by the earliest Greek sculptures are also implied by the typical human representations of Oriental art, especially in the figures of sages and of the Bodhisattvas, the enlightened ones. The trancelike smile, the compressed energy, the serenity of the Greek *kouros,* held in check by some inner discipline, are duplicated in thousands of Buddha images distributed all across East Asia. Despite vast cultural differences, all the great civilizations, from Egypt to Japan, have envisioned a similar state of consciousness as the highest expression of the self. It has to do with a calm power, a restrained energy at peace with itself and with the world.

Some of this inner serenity survived the destruction of the classical civilizations. The otherwise lugubrious figures of Byzantine art retained in their haunting eyes a semblance of that peace, and it continued to imbue medieval countenances. The great cycles of frescoes upon the walls of cathedrals portrayed in an ever more colorful and lifelike manner what the ideal life of a Christian should be, for the edification of the faithful. Martyrs and virgins were represented in the full bloom of their moral superiority, the rewards of the just were visually catalogued, and the sufferings of those who did not live up to the expectations of the Church were depicted with excruciating detail.

Christian educators believed that exposing young children to the images of saints was an effective way of illustrating desirable virtues—and perhaps actually inculcating them into the viewer. Thus at the end of the fourteenth century Giovanni Dominici recommends that one should have:

> paintings in the house, of holy boys, or young virgins, in which your
> child when still in swaddling clothes may delight as being like him-

self. . . . I would like them to see Agnes with the fat lamb, Cecilia crowned with roses, Elisabeth with many roses, Catherine on the wheel, with other figures that would give them love of virginity with their mother's milk, desire for Christ, hatred of sins, disgust at vanity, shrinking from bad companions, and a beginning . . . of contemplating the supreme Saint of saints.

The Renaissance, like the time of Praxiteles in Greece, was a period in which the human form almost exploded out of its defensive carapace and gained a rare spontaneity and freedom. Inebriated by possibility, figures now take on every shape and try every adventure; there are no limits to what humankind can be. The power of the ideal self no longer derives from obedience to divine authority but from the individual's determination to achieve the greatest potential from his or her being. A well-executed painting could even help in the procreation of beautiful children, as Giulio Mancini suggested at the start of the seventeenth century:

Lascivious things are to be placed in private rooms, and the father of the family is to keep them covered, and only uncover them when he goes there with his wife, or an intimate who is not too fastidious. And similar lascivious pictures are appropriate for the room where one has to do with one's spouse; because once seen they serve to arouse one and to make beautiful, healthy, and charming children . . . because each parent, through seeing the picture, imprints in their seed a similar constitution which has been seen in the object or figure.

It took several centuries for the optimism of the Renaissance to fade. By the end of World War I, few artists in the West could sustain belief in the ideal of human perfectability. In the last few generations the human form has been represented in shapes not seen in Europe since before the great civilizations began their difficult journey toward a hopeful future. The great artists of this century have given up idealizing men and women, and borrowed instead distorted images from tribal art, the scribbles of children, and the art of the insane. It is probably erroneous to think that the Africans who originally carved the masks that later inspired Picasso or Klee were expressing a basic existential dread, as some art critics have claimed.

But it is quite clear that the Western artists who replicated their work were portraying their despair at the human condition through the distorted features of their paintings.

For many years now mainstream art seems to have relinquished hope of being able to provide a viable model of the self. In our century, there have been only three currents of idealized images of humankind. Two were political, and the utopias they advocated through their art have both turned out to be horrible failures. The fascist regimes presented a muscular, crude version of the Greek ideal of *areté* as the model for the Aryan race destined to inherit the earth. The statuary around Mussolini's *Foro Italico,* or Hitler's ministries in Berlin provided a concrete representation of the intimidating, merciless, robotlike individual that best fit the ruling ideology. The other human ideal inspired by political ideology was the one depicted by Socialist Realism. For half a century the experiment with communism generated an enormous number of paintings and statues representing rosy-cheeked youth involved in innumerable useful projects, from harvesting to fishing to repairing tractors and feeding children. Less monumental than fascist art, the Soviet variety was perhaps more vacuous. The self it represented was too obviously a creature of propaganda with almost no connection to the social reality it purported to represent. And what is much worse, neither did it bear any relevance to a foreseeable future.

The third set of images representing an ideal self is the one provided by the Western media, usually in the service of commercial advertising. From the flapper girls of the 1920s, used to promote cosmetics or cigarettes, to the Pepsi generation and TV spots selling beer, a form of frankly exploitive representation of what it means to be human has taken over our visual environment. Its purpose is to attract attention to a specific product, and to associate that product with desirable thoughts and feelings, inducing us to a purchase and thus increasing its market share. In order to achieve this, the products are typically associated with healthy young people who appear to be having the time of their lives.

The ideal of selfhood that emerges from these commercial images lacks any hint of the balanced self-discipline of early Greek heroes, of the spiritual ecstasies of the Christian saints, of the ideological fanaticism of fascist nudes, or of the collectivist delusion of the

Soviet workers. What they display is good animal health, sensual contentment, and a lack of worries or responsibilities that could interfere with enjoying the latest fashion in consumption or sensory stimulation. The iconography of modern advertising often seems a return to the fetishism and totemism of our distant ancestors. According to Martin Esslin, who sees TV commercials as a religious drama, the moral universe of the TV commercial

> is essentially that of a polytheistic religion. It is a world dominated by a sheer pantheon of powerful forces, which literally reside in every article of use or consumption. . . . If the wind and the waters, the trees and brooks of ancient Greece were inhabited by a host of nymphs, dryads, satyrs, and other local and specific deities, so is the universe of the TV commercial. The polytheism that confronts us here is thus a fairly primitive one, closely akin to animistic and fetishistic beliefs.

Other commentators have compared advertising to a gospel, "an ultimate source of reference wherein we find ourselves revealed. . . . Each form, moreover, provides a controlling image for our consciousness in apprehending our selves and our world." The world we apprehend by these means is filled with semianimate things that clamor for attention and money, and the selves we apprehend are those of consumers trying to validate their identity through the possession of things.

The message of these images is that the highest goal is to live a life of carefree pleasure. Of course this is not a particularly novel or original theme: As Sorokin has attempted to prove, sensate cultures have alternated with cultures inclined to value ideas more than pleasure for as long as historical records have been kept. Perhaps the liberated figures of Renaissance art come closest to conveying an image of the self that is similar to the one surrounding us in the environment of commercial art. But contemporary observers are likely to find that human representations from the Renaissance are more interesting, more suggestive of complex thoughts and emotions, than their contemporary counterparts obsessed by narcissism and the fetishism of commodities.

It seems, then, that within living memory neither artists nor the two great political movements of the century, nor the commercial energies of the age have succeeded in providing viable representations of the self on which to model feasible ways of being for the future. Does this mean that we have run out of ideas for the millennium that faces us, and artists are justified in representing the human form as the stick figure of a child or the scrawls of a schizophrenic? Is their implicit analysis of what we have come to be correct, and there is no way to imagine a positive way to be human? Or is it that our imagination has been only temporarily stymied, and with time we may hope for a new representation of the ideal self to emerge?

The Self of the Future

I will assume that the last alternative is the correct one. It is by definition impossible, however, to guess what form that representation will take. But because the issue is by no means trivial, it may be worthwhile to speculate on the kind of images that could stand for the qualities to which we might aspire.

The most obvious possibility is that the future image of the self will recapitulate some of the features of the past—the physical dynamism of the classical Greek goddess or athlete combined with the serene inner focus of the *kouroi* or the Bodhisattvas. It is in this *coincidentia oppositorum* that the peaks of human complexity are combined. But is there a viable contemporary visual expression of this state of being? Perhaps we should turn to the movies for our inspiration: Gary Cooper in *High Noon,* or the *Seven Samurai,* or even the image of the astronaut in the person of the fearless Princess Leia, or the earnest Luke Skywalker.

A more radical possibility is that external features—beauty, character, the mask of personality—will grow less and less important. Serious artists have already abandoned the attempt to represent the outer appearance of individuals. But what will take its place? Perhaps the focus will shift toward the depiction of inner complexity. The computer may become the metaphor for the self: the organism as an immensely complex machine. Perhaps it will be something like HAL, the master computer aboard the starship in Stanley Kubrick's *2001;* or the computer world of *Tron.*

Finally there is what for lack of a better term we might call the cosmic self. One example of it is Kevin Costner's character in the film *Dances with Wolves*. This model points to an integration of the individual with larger and more complex units: with other cultures, with humanity as a whole, with other animals, with the natural landscape. The most extreme destination along this trajectory is the "quantum self," which defines itself through union with the totality of existence—with the energy that pulses through the cosmos.

Clearly artists will have an enormous challenge in visualizing and representing these more radical possibilities for being. But then, that is the task that the true artist has always faced. As Karl Jaspers wrote: "The human being is an open possibility, incomplete and incompletable. Hence it is always more and other than what he has brought to realisation in himself." Nevertheless, it is our responsibility to try imagining what that human being could be at the next stage of its history. If we do not, evolution will continue to proceed blindly. Yet we have advanced too deeply into the future to simply let things work out as they will. And we cannot chart a hopeful course without meaningful models, without realistic images of what we can become.

THE DEVELOPMENT OF THE SELF THROUGH THE LIFE SPAN

Psychologists who study human development tend to agree that different sets of goals are typical at different points in the life cycle. In other words, the priorities around which people order their psychic energy change with time. Children generally start with valuing their immediate physical needs, like safety, food, and comfort, and their selves are organized to take care of them. There are people who never progress beyond this phase, however, and continue to invest all their life energy in attending solely to the body and its needs. While these needs remain essential, for most people a new set of values will slowly emerge, and even take precedence, based on the need to be accepted, loved, and respected by others. At this stage a person will begin to follow the rules of his community even if they are not to his immediate advantage, and try to be a reliable, responsible citizen. But if these are the only values one recognizes, the danger is that life will be reduced to thoughtless conformity. With time, such social values will in turn generate for some individuals new, antithetical goals: the drive to be independent and autonomous. People who reach this stage are fully individualized, unique, interesting. At the final level the person who has differentiated herself returns to invest attention in broader goals, and derives satisfaction from helping a cause greater than the self—not because of coercion or conformity, but because of reasoned conviction.

These same patterns have been described, more or less independently, by many scholars who have studied how people change through the life cycle. Some examples are the psychologists Abraham Maslow, who studied how basic needs develop into values; Larry Kohlberg, who investigated the development of morality; Jane Loevinger, who studied ego development; and James Fowler, who was interested in learning how faith developed. In each case, these social scientists describe a dialectical motion between differentiation and integration, between turning attention inward and then outward, between valuing the self and then the larger community. It is not a circular motion that returns to where one started, but rather, it resembles an ascending spiral, where concern for the self becomes steadily qualified by less selfish goals, and concern for others becomes more individualistic and personally meaningful. At its best, this process of spiraling growth results in someone like Albert Schweitzer, the philosopher who played Bach superbly on the organ, and spent most of his life running a free hospital in Gabon, in the former French Equatorial Africa, or someone like the poet Faludy, or Suzie Valdez.

This line of development is not limited to just the American or the Western life cycle. The same spiral ascending between the alternating poles of personal and community values is found in other cultures, as well. The ideal career of a Brahmin male, for instance, is expected to oscillate between these same poles: first he is supposed to be a dutiful son, then a religious scholar, in middle age a successful farmer and family man, and finally in old age a monk who withdraws from active life to meditate in the wilderness. What is perhaps even more interesting is that this pattern of how individuals learn to value different goals as they mature may actually mirror the evolution of the self in the history of the human race.

Those who study human biological development like to point out that the process by which individual organisms mature from conception to full growth resembles the way the entire species evolved over millions of years. The statement that "ontogeny recapitulates phylogeny" refers to the fact that, for instance, human embryos in the womb pass through phases in which they first resemble fish, then frogs, then pigs, and other mammalian embryos—as if the mind-bogglingly slow process of the evolution of the human race was repeated, in fast forward, in the course of a few months, by each baby.

Perhaps the same principle holds true for the development of self. It could be that the need for survival and security were the only meaningful goals during the first stages of human evolution, during which the ideal self consisted in fertility for women and bravery for men. Then presumably came long millennia when the highest values were those that bound the community together, usually based on religious beliefs. We might be now approaching the end of this phase. But because the majority of people, even in such a highly individualistic culture as the United States, apparently still value conformity above all else, the future may hold even stricter social controls of the kind Huxley, Orwell, and Koestler imagined in their novels, in which constant surveillance and drugs kept the majority of people thoughtless and docile. It is conceivable that we still have millennia of increasing conformity in store.

Yet at least since the Greeks began to value independent action and personal vision, more and more people have aspired to a selfhood based on the development of individual potential. Secular humanism, with its roots in the conception of the autonomous individual envisioned by the thinkers of the Renaissance, has moved the center of values from respect for the collective will to the creative strivings of the individual responsible for his or her own priorities. And a few of these individuals have even found ways to use their finely honed uniqueness for the common good—achieving what we have called here a transcendent selfhood. It might be that other millions of years must pass before such values will inform the consciousness of the majority. But time seems to be getting short, and perhaps there are ways to accelerate this process. Selfishness, conformity, and even the development of unique individuality are no longer sufficient to give life a meaningful purpose, at a time when we are capable of destroying ourselves and the environment with increasing ease.

FLOW AND THE GROWTH OF THE SELF

Children learn to talk because they enjoy being able to ask questions, and to walk in order to move to where they want to be. Learning is fun; the exhilaration of a child who is suddenly able to stay on a wobbly bike without falling, or of the young delinquent who for the first time succeeds at picking a pocket, are typical examples of what flow is all about.

And every flow experience contributes to the growth of the self. To be in flow, one has to formulate intentions, and have a way to assess how well one is doing. The self is made up mainly of information about goals and feedback. Therefore after every episode involving flow, we are a little different from what we were before. Our consciousness contains fresh information about what our selves are. For example, the child who learned to ride the bike goes to sleep that night with the proud knowledge that she is now closer to being an adult because she has mastered a two-wheeler; the young pickpocket goes to sleep feeling that he has finally become a professional.

It is useful to return to the concept of complexity in order to understand more clearly how flow affects the self. As we have said before, the complexity of an organism depends on the degree of its differentiation and integration. This is as true of a mollusk as it is of a computer—or of the self. And flow experiences involve both of these dimensions of the self.

To experience flow, we first must recognize some opportunity for action, or challenge. This involves mainly a process of differentiation. To recognize a challenge, one has to know how to let go of the tried and true, be open to possibilities, seek out novelty, be curious, be willing to take risks, and be experimental. Generally we find challenges that are in tune with our temperaments or innate skills. The athletic child will gravitate to physical challenges and competition, the one with a special sensitivity to sound will be attracted to musical instruments. As each person becomes involved with a slightly different set of opportunities for action, he or she discovers more about the limits and the potentials of the self, and becomes more nearly unique.

The second dimension of complexity is related to the acquisition of skills. As one learns to master a challenge, the skills involved in the activity become part of one's repertoire of abilities; this involves a process of integration. To master a skill one needs discipline and endurance, and to accommodate the new skill among the other attributes and priorities of the self a certain amount of wisdom, or self-knowledge, is required. Almost all children are attracted to music at one time or another; most of them would like to learn how to play an instrument. But relatively few will acquire enough skill so as not to be ashamed when playing in front of an audience, and some of those who do acquire it become so carried away that their entire life becomes subordinated to the flow of sounds. Family, friends, all the other potential joys of life are neglected and eventually forgotten. In such cases, a failure to integrate music with other goals inhibits the complexity of the self.

It is the T-person who combines harmoniously these opposite tendencies: he or she is original yet systematic, independent yet responsible, bold yet disciplined, intuitive yet rational. He balances a healthy pride in his uniqueness with a deep interest and concern for others. It is easy to be at one or the other pole of these pairs, and much more difficult to be at both ends at once. Yet only when the apparent antinomy of these two processes is resolved can a self fully participate in the flow of evolution.

THE SKILLS OF SPIRITUALITY AND WISDOM

If one tries to become a transcender, should one first concentrate on building skills or on the ability to recognize challenges? The answer is that an organism must develop on all fronts at the same time. One cannot grow a skeleton of bones first, and then start growing muscles; nor can one part of the body be completed independently of the rest. In our case, a person without skills cannot recognize a challenge; but without confronting a challenge one cannot realize one's skills. In real life, the two develop simultaneously, but since writing is a linear process, we must examine them one at a time. We will begin with a consideration of the kind of skills that lead to transcendence.

In most cultures that have attained the complexity of civilization, the qualities held in highest esteem are those involved in mental processes of a particular character, which for the lack of a better term might be called "spiritual." Spiritual skills involve the ability to control experience directly, by manipulating memes that increase harmony among people's thoughts, emotions, and wills. Those who practice these skills are called shamans, priests, philosophers, artists, and wise men and women of various kinds. They are respected and remembered, and even though they may not be awarded power or money, their advice is sought out, and their very existence is cherished by the community in which they live.

At first glance, it is difficult to understand why spiritual contributions are held to be so important by most societies. From an evolutionary viewpoint, it would seem that they have no practical survival value. The efforts of farmers, builders, traders, statesmen, scientists, and workers produce obvious concrete benefits; what does spiritual activity accomplish?

What is common to all forms of spirituality is the attempt to reduce entropy in consciousness. Spiritual activity aims at producing harmony among conflicting desires, it tries to find meaning among the chance events of life, and it tries to reconcile human goals with the natural forces that impinge on them from the environment. It increases complexity by clarifying the components of individual experience such as good and bad, love and hate, pleasure and pain. It tries to express these processes in memes that are accessible to all, and it helps integrate them with one another, and with the external world.

These efforts to bring harmony to the mind are often, but not always, based on a belief in supernatural powers. Many Eastern "religions," or the Stoic philosophies of antiquity, attempted to develop a complex consciousness without recourse to a Supreme Being. Some spiritual traditions, such as the Hindu Yoga or Taoism, focus exclusively on achieving harmony and control of the mind without any interest in reducing social entropy; others, like the late Confucian tradition, aim primarily at achieving social order. In any case, if the significance attached to such endeavors is any indication, the reduction of conflict and disorder through spiritual means appears to be very adaptive. Without them, it is likely that people would grow discouraged and confused, and that the Hobbesian "war of all against all" would become an even more prominent feature of the social landscape than it already is.

Currently spirituality is at an ebb in the more advanced technological societies. This is in part because memes that validate spiritual order tend to lose their credibility with time, and need to be recast in new forms again and again. At present we are living in an era when many of the basic tenets of Christianity, which has supported Western spiritual values for almost two thousand years, have come into conflict with the conclusions of science and philosophy. While religions have lost much of their power, science and technology have not been able to generate convincing value systems to replace them.

It seems clear that neither the liberal humanism of the West nor the historical materialism that has so spectacularly failed in Eastern Europe and the U.S.S.R. has been able to provide sustenance for the spiritual needs of their respective societies. The United States, in the midst of unprecedented material affluence, is suffering from symptoms of increasing individual and societal entropy: rising rates of suicide, violent crime, sexually transmitted disease, unwanted pregnancy—not to mention a growing economic instability fueled by the irresponsibly selfish behavior of many politicians and businessmen. The problem is well illustrated when our leaders, such as former President Bush, at election time try to appeal to family values or patriotism, using old clichés without connection to what most people in this society know or believe. At a gut level we know that he means well, and we may agree with much of what he says, yet there is no intellectual conviction behind his words.

In the former Communist countries, a half century or more of materialist ideology has left people confused and cynical, thirsting for something credible to believe in—even to the point of embracing again formerly discredited religious and nationalist ideas. A new synthesis on which to base a feasible set of values, one that will unify the best wisdom of past religions with current knowledge, has not yet taken place.

In all cultures, the essence of spirituality seems to consist in an effort to free consciousness from the thrall of genetic instructions. The Ten Commandments, like the disciplines of yoga, like Buddhist rituals, or the practices of practically all known religions, try to guarantee that attention will not be invested exclusively in its "natural" channels. For instance, the traditional Christian catalogue of the seven deadly sins contains memes that attempt to counteract excessive indulgence in behavior that, while biologically speaking, is "good for us," may not be so good if we want to continue evolving.

One of the problems of our time is that there are few effective memes for self-restraint left. For most people the notion of sin is hopelessly old-fashioned, and secular attempts to channel energy into complex goals—such as the concept of good citizenship, of professional pride, of law and order, of disciplined responsibility—have also lost much of their grip on human consciousness. Yet the need to help individuals see the necessity for self-discipline is as urgent as ever. Perhaps if we understood that to determine the course of the future we require all our attention, every last spark of psychic energy, we would be more willing to restrain the natural greed of the self, and heed the call of complexity. After all, it's not a bad bargain. In exchange for the redundant rewards of pleasure, we gain the always exciting joys of spiritual growth.

Related to spirituality is the concept of wisdom. This is the quality perhaps most closely associated with what here we have called a T-person; it is the chief characteristic of a complex self. As the Bible enjoins, "Wisdom is the principal thing; therefore get wisdom" (Proverbs 4:7). But what is wisdom? Compelling as this concept has been through history, and in every known civilization, the contemporary sciences have had almost nothing to say about it. For many centuries knowledge in the West has pursued increasingly specialized goals in a headlong attempt to control the external behavior of things and of people. Little interest was left over for dealing with elusive processes like spirituality and wisdom. Only recently have psychologists again felt the obligation to pay attention to them.

Wisdom has three different aspects. In the first place, it is a way of knowing, or *cognitive skill*. Second, it is a special way of acting that is socially desirable, or a *virtue*. And finally it is a *personal good*, because the practice of wisdom leads to inner serenity and enjoyment.

Three characteristics distinguish wisdom from other cognitive processes we might call "intelligence," "scientific knowledge," or "genius." The first is that wisdom deals not with the variable, superficial appearance of experience but tries to grasp the enduring, universal truths that lie below it. In the past, the basis of all knowledge was assumed to be God, so that Thomas Aquinas could write: "He who considers absolutely the highest cause of the whole universe, namely God, is most of all called wise." When they reach a certain age many scientists feel the need to be "wise," abandoning the narrow pursuits of their specialty as they begin to ask broader questions about the nature of the cosmos. It was during such a period in Einstein's life that he rejected quantum mechanics because he believed that God did not play dice with the universe. Unfortunately, the scientist who tries to parlay his specialty for wisdom quickly loses credibility with his colleagues.

But the quest for universal truth is certainly not the exclusive preserve of great scientists or philosophers. Anyone who is not taken in by the veils of Maya, who looks beyond appearances and does not automatically follow the dictates of instincts and society, has attained a degree of wisdom. The first step to wisdom is to realize that we cannot trust implicitly our senses and our beliefs, yet to still be eager to understand the reality that lies behind our partial perceptions of it. Such an attitude is not limited to those who went to college; on the contrary, the saying that a little knowledge is a dangerous thing applies to many individuals who, having mastered a small field, are now so self-satisfied and contented with their knowledge that they lose all interest in advancing beyond it. But intellectual smugness does not lead to evolutionary advances; it takes someone like Socrates, who kept claiming ignorance all through his illustrious career, to bring new knowledge to light.

These days the quest for truth may not lead one to a contemplation of God, as it did Aquinas, but rather to the comprehension of the underlying causes of reality, of the organic relationship between the various forces and processes in the universe, including the minds of men and women. Some may still prefer to give the mysterious power that binds all these processes into a fabric of incredible complexity the name of God. Whatever one's faith, it is urgent that we grow to appreciate how actions impact on this tapestry that changes with time; and it is the attempt to do so that constitutes the first part of wisdom.

The second aspect is virtue. This word derives from the Latin *vir*, meaning "man"; in their sexist conception of the world the Romans believed that socially valued behavior was the expression of the best masculine traits. For them virtue meant physical courage, a sense of civic responsibility, a stoical acceptance of fate. While these traits are generally considered virtuous in every culture, a society may emphasize others—such as generosity or religious piety—depending upon its needs. In general these are spiritual values, in that they stress internal and interpersonal harmony. The common element among them is the belief that a wise person not only thinks deeply but acts on knowledge. This is why Plato wrote: "First among the virtues found in the state, wisdom comes into view." As Aristotle, Aquinas, and Kant all agreed, wisdom is the most necessary prerequisite of judges and rulers.

Specialists who lack wisdom may also act on their knowledge, but their actions would presumably be skewed by their limited perspective. This is why the actions of a wise person are likely to be more harmonious; instead of being based on a narrow view, they are directed by a broader understanding of the common good. In this sense wisdom is directly proportional to the size of the group whose well-being it takes into account. A person who decides on a course of action simply in terms of momentary consequences is less wise than one who tries to take the future into account; someone who is only interested in maximizing his or her own well-being is less wise than one who takes into account the welfare of his family, and of others. And a person who aspires to a single goal, such as making money, being healthy, or improving the safety of the community, is less wise than someone who understands that money, health, and safety are all related, and that they are only some of the conditions one must consider to ensure human contentment.

The third aspect of wisdom is that, simply stated, it feels good. It was not just the ancient Greeks who believed that, in Sophocles's words, "Wisdom is the supreme part of happiness." Two thousand years later Montaigne wrote: "The most manifest sign of wisdom is a continual cheerfulness." In every culture the sage has been re-garded as a person who is in the enviable position of being serenely happy. When people invest their psychic energy in the most univer-sal goals—as do sages—and instead of striving only for personal gain they aim for a broader harmony, their selves begin to expand beyond the ego-centered mechanism that we inherit as part of our evolutionary heritage. Such a self grows to include goals beyond the limited, mortal frame of the body; therefore, it is less vulnerable to the threats that make others unhappy.

The wise enjoy being part of the powerful forces that blow through the universe, and that manifest themselves temporarily in the reality we know, in the body we own for a few short years. Being aware that the self is an illusion, they know not to take it too seriously. They relish being alive, but they perceive that there is more to life than the small part that is revealed to us, and that most men cling to so desperately. Flow is the usual condition of their existence; no wonder the rest of humankind envies their happiness.

But the envy is usually tempered with contempt. Ever since the Greek milkmaid laughed at the philosopher who, absorbed in his study of the stars, fell into the courtyard well because he failed to notice what was right in front of his nose, the wise have been ridiculed for their concerns with the reality that lies behind appear-ances, while overlooking the obvious and the concrete. True, there is a price to pay for wisdom. The rewards and comforts of ordinary life are neglected, and in terms of the reality shrouded in Maya's veils, the life of the sage is wasted. Thus, paradoxically, it takes a great deal of self-assurance to relinquish the yoke of the self. But those who succeed in doing so seldom regret it.

THE CHALLENGES OF THE FUTURE

It is impossible to recognize a challenge without having already acquired some relevant skills. Looking at a string of mathematical symbols means nothing to the uninitiated, but may present an exciting intellectual puzzle to someone who has a grasp of the basic concepts. The sheer walls of El Capitan in Yosemite National Park are impressive formations of gray rock to most visitors, but to expert rock climbers they promise years of enjoyable occupation. In the very same situation, one person will be bored because he can find nothing to do, another will be paralyzed by excessive demands, while a third one will have fun seeking a task that matches his interests and abilities.

Whether an opportunity for action exists or not, and whether it is a daunting obstacle or a stimulating challenge, depends more on the mental preparation of the person confronting it than on objective material conditions. For instance, when Suzie Valdez encountered the starving urchins of Ciudad Juárez, she did not try to ignore or deny what she saw, nor did she let the misery overwhelm her. Instead she asked herself what she could do in that situation, and found a way to use initially very meager resources to alleviate, at first by only an infinitesimal amount, the conditions of the poor. After that first step, her self-confidence and knowledge increased, and she took on a slightly more ambitious task. Step by step, involvement became more complex, as the flow got deeper.

The kind of challenges a person chooses to recognize depends on what aspect of the environment he or she is particularly sensitive to. There are children who notice every change in light, every shift in the shades of color, or who can't help counting the number of intersecting corners of bricks on every wall they see; for such individuals the visual arts provide the most obvious opportunities for action. Others are sensitive to sounds and will be attracted to music, whereas those whose bodies move with great coordination may turn to the challenges of sport or dance. Faludy became a poet because he had an unusual ear for language. When he was five years old Linus Pauling helped mix drugs in the back of his father's pharmacy, and developed the ambition to understand why the properties of matter change when different substances are combined—a childhood curiosity that led him to the Nobel Prize and still sustains him in his nineties. Vera Rubin, who is now one of the most prominent astronomers in this country, was first intrigued by the stars when as a child she saw the constellations every night from her attic window. "I just couldn't imagine," she says, "how one wouldn't want to be an astronomer." Of course the stars are up there for everyone to see, yet so few people respond to their challenge the way Rubin has.

Unfortunately, it is easier to develop selves around goals that lead to stagnation rather than to growth. Fear of losing control over one's psychic energy is perhaps the strongest reason why so many will turn their attention inward, and try to defend the self while remaining oblivious of the potential for involvement that surrounds them. Children who feel unloved, or incompetent, or constantly guilty, or who feel manipulated and controlled by their parents, often will use up all their resources in an endless effort to prove that they are worthy of love and attention. Little energy is left over to wonder about the stars.

When such a child is fortunate to have innate talents or learned skills, the quest to validate the self might lead to great achievements. Eminent adults often had miserable childhoods, and the urge to prove themselves is often clearly visible through their adult ambition. They may not be happy, they may bring more entropy than order into their social environment, but at least they can channel their energy into a complex goal and achieve outstanding results—as did Winston Churchill, or John D. Rockefeller, Picasso, or Einstein.

On the other hand, when a child is relatively unskilled, and has no opportunities to derive enjoyment from mastering meaningful challenges, then the need to prove the importance of the self can drive a person to acts of violence and defiance. It is always simpler to make an impression by increasing entropy than by increasing complexity. A teenage girl knows that if she becomes pregnant she will get more attention from her parents than if she gets passing grades in school. And becoming pregnant would show that she has the power to resist her parents' wishes, whereas doing well in school would not. Similarly teenage boys know that violence, risky behavior, drugs, and sexual promiscuity are the quickest ways to demonstrate that they are free from the control of other people. The challenge for them is to establish independence, to show that they have the power to achieve difficult things. To invest energy in goals that increase order is not a priority for them; their first concern is to protect the self, not to enhance harmony.

Years ago I knew a young man from a prominent New England family, handsome and powerfully built, educated in an exclusive prep school, who nevertheless seemed very insecure. Behind a polite and impassive façade he occasionally revealed an inner emptiness, a lack of zest, an absence of any enthusiasm or curiosity. I still have no idea what caused the hollowness at the core of Zeke's self. It could have had many sources, and at this point it would be futile to speculate. The fact is that for two years he seemed to go through college like a sleepwalker. Then when I met him for the first time after summer vacation in the fall of his junior year, Zeke appeared transformed. He walked with assurance, he held eye contact, and smiled as he talked. He was brisk and relaxed.

Curious about what had changed Zeke's demeanor, I asked him how he had spent the summer. He didn't need prompting; he was bursting to tell. Zeke had signed up with a work crew on a steamer in Alaska, and had sailed with them from island to island in the churning Arctic seas, stopping wherever they found a colony of seals. Then they went ashore with their bludgeons and clubbed baby seals to death as fast as they could. Zeke spoke with evident pride about the hardships of the sealers' lives, about the skills required to wield the heavy club and smash it at the right place in the baby seal's neck most efficiently, and then the delicate work of ripping the fur from the carcass. Like millions upon millions of young men before him, Zeke had found in mayhem a fulfillment of sorts.

There are many ways society makes it possible for people to build their selves by hurting others and still remain within the law. Jerome Bettis, a Notre Dame fullback, speaks for many of his peers when he says, "Inflicting pain is the most important thing as a fullback." When he was a child, according to his grandmother, Bettis was a crybaby. His older siblings and their friends constantly beat him up. Now that he is 250 pounds of mostly muscle, he is going to repeat the cycle. In one of his poems, György Faludy describes how the young guards had erections as they beat the political prisoners in the cellars of the secret police. Hurting and killing other beings is a tried and true way to prove that one's self exists and is powerful, and it is something one can learn to enjoy if other sources of flow are blocked.

This kind of solution may be effective in terms of strengthening the self, but it is hardly a solution that will guide humankind into a more harmonious future. We all have the awesome potential to increase entropy around us, but if we did act on it chaos would only grow worse. So how to optimize these different goals? What does one have to do to experience flow and build a more complex self, while at the same time contributing to evolution? It is perhaps time now to gather the pieces of the answer that have been developed so far, and try putting them together.

In the first place, it is essential to *learn to enjoy life*. It really does not make sense to go through the motions of existence if one does not appreciate as much of it as possible. It is difficult to trust a righteous person who seethes in inner misery. His behavior may be exemplary, but the entropy in his consciousness is dangerous. Flow is not only its own reward, but it may be the best recipe for social order.

But enjoyment alone will not lead evolution in a desirable direction unless one finds flow in activities that stretch the self. Therefore, *seeking out complexity* is also necessary. Continuing curiosity and interest, and the desire to find ever new challenges, coupled with the commitment to develop appropriate skills, lead to lifelong learning. When this attitude is present, a ninety-year-old is fresh and exciting; when it is lacking, a healthy youth appears listless and boring.

Another trait of a transcendent self is the *mastery of wisdom and spirituality*. This means the ability to see beyond the appearance of things, to see through the deceptions of memes and parasites, to grasp the essential relationship between the forces that impinge on consciousness. It also means developing the internal discipline and the sense of responsibility that are necessary to withstand the internal pressures of our genes, and the external siren song of the memes. Without these skills it is very easy to become trapped within oneself, one's job, one's religion, and lose sight of the entire tapestry of life, of which each of us is such a tiny—but not insignificant—part.

Finally, a harmonious evolution is dependent on our ability to *invest psychic energy in the future*. A person who spends all his attention dealing with the present, or defending against possible future dangers will inevitably have a self that will be left out of the stream of evolution. There will be no kinship with, no attachment to, no participation in the future. Only those who trust what is to come, who are eager to try out their skills on unforeseen opportunities, will succeed in building the future into their selves.

When self-centered persons influence the future, they often cause an increase in entropy and exploitation. Christopher Columbus was certainly a man of great vision, but little wisdom. He could see far ahead, but the singleness of his desire for material gain and the narrowness of his drive for personal power ended up diminishing his great accomplishments. Thus evolution requires that we make an *investment in a harmonious future*. It is not just our personal advantage we must seek, or that of the causes we believe in now; it is the collective well-being of all life—whatever strange forms that may take tomorrow—that we should be willing to endorse. Individuals who transfer part of their life energy into this unconditional future are fulfilled. They have become part of the stream of evolution; the future has been grafted into them. Whatever might happen to their individual bodies and minds, the shape of their consciousness will influence the matrix of growing complexity, the forms of future energy.

FURTHER THOUGHTS
ON "THE TRANSCENDENT SELF"

What Transcenders Are Like

What would be *your* definition of a transcendent self—of a person who stands out from the common run of humanity? Do you know such a person?

What would you have to give up in your life to become a "T-person"?

What Is the Self?

Can you describe the self of some of the persons closest to you—a partner, a parent, a child, a friend—in terms of the goals they hold highest, and invest the most psychic energy in?

If goals are what defines the self, what are the priorities in your life? Which one of these goals is most likely to lead to transcendence?

Evolving Images of the Ideal Self

What do you think is currently the most accurate representation of the ideal self in our culture?

Do you have your own visual image of what an ideal person would look like? How he or she would behave?

The Development of the Self Through the Life Span

How have your priorities changed in the last five years? The last ten? The last twenty? Are the same goals still the most important ones?

What kind of a person would you like to be by the end of your life?

Flow and the Growth of the Self

Are the people you look up to and respect relatively happy and cheerful? Why?

Do you ever experience flow in an activity that leads to higher complexity? What is the activity, and could you do it more often?

Spirituality and Wisdom

Do you know any wise persons? If yes, what are their most notable characteristics?

What spiritual skills have you developed? If you have none, are there some you would like to acquire? How would you go about it?

The Challenges of the Future

What do you see as the most essential task for increasing complexity in your neighborhood or city?

How could you personally best contribute to this task?

9

THE FLOW OF
HISTORY

Building the kind of transcendent self described in the previous chapter is not an easy task. As long as individuals have to work alone to develop such selves, only a few will have the perseverance—or good fortune—to live a life filled with flow. But a few isolated transcenders cannot pull all of humanity in the direction of complexity. In order for the majority of people to take an active role in evolution, social institutions must also come to support flow and preserve order in the mind. Therefore, the topic of the last two chapters of this book is how to build complexity into the fabric of society.

If one looks more closely at what it means for complexity to evolve, it soon becomes clear that the process takes shape not so much in individual persons as in the context of information that envelops them—the culture in which they exist. A person is simply a carrier of this information. You or I can choose to invest psychic energy in the most promising values and ideas available; thus, our selves will become complex, and we do our part in advancing a more harmonious future. However, what evolves is not the self trapped in our physical body, which will dissolve after death. Rather, what will survive and grow is the pattern of information that we have shaped through our existence: the acts of love, the beliefs, the knowledge, the skills, the insights that we have had and that have affected the course of events around us. No matter how smart, wise, or altruistic a person might be, he or she is not going to contribute to evolution except by leaving traces of complexity in the culture, by serving as an example to others, by changing customs, beliefs, or knowledge in such a way that they can be passed down to future generations. It is through memes transmitted by social systems that we contribute to evolution.

Social and cultural systems are also organisms in the broad meaning of the term, and like other organisms they can be more or less complex depending on how differentiated and integrated they are. An army unit, for instance, is not very differentiated: at each level of the hierarchy individuals are more or less interchangeable. If you are a private, your identity may be interesting to you and your buddies, but as far as the army is concerned you are just a number. On the other hand, a well-run army tends to be highly integrated: each fighting unit is surrounded by smoothly functioning supply lines, medical services, communication networks. Whatever happens to one unit has immediate consequences for all the others, and produces an adaptive response from them. A typical university is in many ways at the opposite extreme: each member of the faculty operates in splendid isolation from his or her peers; the emphasis is on original accomplishment and individuality, with little sharing of information or mutual assistance. It is in fact quite rare to find social institutions that maximize complexity by being both differentiated and integrated simultaneously, and when they are, they usually are so only for a short time, after which they become again either excessively rigid, or too unstructured.

Because we spend all our lives as members of one social institution or another, and because we are so completely shaped by the roles we play in these systems, it is essential to consider how families, schools, offices, factories, and governments can be made more complex. We cannot urge our children to enjoy their lives if we don't provide them with adequate skills, and if we force them to grow up in communities that provide few opportunities for action. It is difficult to be a good person while living in a bad society. Without changing the environment, we cannot influence the course of the future. But before looking into what makes a society complex, we should consider how flow contributes to the evolution of memes, including both technological advances and changing beliefs and institutions.

FLOW AND THE EVOLUTION OF TECHNOLOGY

About half a century ago the Dutch historian Johann Huizinga proposed the provocative thesis that social institutions—even the more redoubtable ones like science, religion, or the army—start out more or less as games that only later become serious and even deadly. Science began as a series of riddling contests, religion as joyful collective celebrations, military institutions as ceremonial combat, economic systems as festive reciprocal exchanges. Originally, Huizinga believes, people came together to have a good time, and only later developed rules to make the game more lasting and interesting. Eventually the rules became binding, and people were forced to obey them. For example, the stylized behavior of today's courtroom trials originated in public confrontations between two opponents who challenged each other (*tried* each other) with various dares, each hoping to convince the audience of the justice of his case. Early trials were more or less spontaneous performances judged on their entertainment value by the entire community. As time passed, the various aspects of this impromptu game became codified; judges and lawyers became full-time roles, and written laws set down the rules by which the parts should be played. Thus, Huizinga argues, the modern trial is the codified descendant of playful spectacles. And more generally, the practices that survive and tend to become institutionalized are those that also provide enjoyment to the participants.

In fact, flow seems to be a powerful engine in history. There are three main ways in which technological progress is influenced by enjoyment. In the first place, inventors and tinkerers love what they do, and keep working on their ideas even when the odds for success seem to be very slim. Second, many inventions succeed because, like the car or the personal computer, they open up a whole new range of enjoyable experiences. Finally, technology is advanced for a third reason: because it frees time from drudgery, and promises to improve the quality of experience indirectly—like the many household appliances that are supposed to allow us to do something more enjoyable.

Most novel ideas or behaviors are generated by people who try out new things because they are bored by old routines, or because they are confounded by chaos. We have become accustomed to believing that scientists make discoveries and invent gadgets because they are driven by economic considerations. This is true only in part; the other part of the story is that inventions and discoveries would never be carried through if the inventing did not provide enjoyment to those involved with it. The Wright brothers were hoping that their flying machine would turn out to be useful and make them lots of money, but what kept them working day and night at their hare-brained scheme despite constant failures and frustrations was the challenge of a fascinating goal.

The automobile, which has changed our way of life in this century perhaps more than any other single invention, and which seems to be such a utilitarian machine, started out as a plaything, a provider of flow. Interest in automobiles started not because they were useful but because as soon as the first ones were built, stunts and races captured people's imaginations. The first drivers were gentlemen and mechanics who raced their contraptions across continents through rutted roads and dusty farmland. A recent promotional brochure from Alfa Romeo begins: "In 1910, a car company was created that was destined to distinguish itself from all others. A company built on the simple philosophy that a car shouldn't be merely a means of transportation, but *a source of exhilaration.*" The last sentence is probably true, but the claim that this was only Alfa Romeo's philosophy is not. At the very beginnings of the internal combustion engine, all car manufacturers were very aware that they were selling exhilaration.

The very quick diffusion of personal computers in the past few decades also owes a great deal to the enjoyment they provide. Many writers have commented on how utterly absorbed and fascinated the engineers and programmers who developed the first generations of PCs were with their projects. Entire mythologies have developed about the charmed Boston labs where people worked around the clock, mesmerized by the flickering screens of their experimental products, about the garage where Hewlett and Packard perfected their calculators, or about the other garage where Jobs and Wozniak assembled the first Apple computers. And what was true for the creators of the PC was also true for their consumers: at first, the great demand for the machines was fueled not by spreadsheets and word processing, but rather by games and by the intriguing options offered by these complex devices. Even now, the popularity of PCs is probably due more to the new opportunities for action they offer the user—such as desktop publishing, multimedia interfaces, tele-communications—opportunities that are more like teasing challenges rather than practical solutions to routine problems.

It would be erroneous, however, to argue that practicality has *no* impact on the evolution of technology. But it would be equally shortsighted to ignore the extent to which the desire for enjoyment has contributed to it. Two thousand years ago, when the watermill was first put to use to grind cereals in Asia Minor, a Greek poet wrote: "Spare your hands, which have been long familiar with the millstone, you maidens who used to crush the grain. Henceforth you shall sleep long, oblivious of the crowing cocks who greet the dawn." These lines summarize well the third reason why we adopt new technology: it saves physical energy, and it frees up psychic energy to do with as we wish—to sleep longer, or to do something even more pleasurable.

It has been calculated that currently each one of us in the United States uses well over four hundred electronic appliances in a lifetime. One would think that, with all these servomechanisms doing our work, we would be deliriously happy. In fact this does not seem to be the case. As we have considered at length in Chapter 5, memes that we have accepted because we expected them to be helpful can easily turn into parasites. Stefan Linder, the Swedish economist and statesman, has argued convincingly that after we have accumulated a certain number, appliances save less time than it takes to service, maintain, and store them. While it *is* certainly easier to mince onions with a sharp kitchen knife than with a seashell, a bone, or with one's teeth, is an electric kitchen knife really an improvement?

No one in his right mind would want to return to a past in which the end of daylight signaled the end of all activity, when the oceans presented an insuperable barrier, and when we had no idea that viruses and bacteria existed. On the other hand, to accept every new discovery as an unqualified benefit is dangerous. When technology adds to the complexity of experience, it makes sense to endorse it; when it adds to conflict and confusion, it makes sense to resist it. If we remember that memes multiply on their own, and if not curbed they take over our psychic energy in their blind drive to replicate, we might run less of a risk of ending up as servants of the objects we create.

Nowadays we expect public-health agencies to inoculate our children against dangerous viruses and bacteria such as polio and smallpox. Eventually, when we have come to realize more clearly that technology can spawn memes that are as debilitating to the mind as measles is to the body, perhaps we will find a vaccine to protect ourselves against them. Like the patches we have created for smokers to wear to help them stop smoking, perhaps we shall develop a patch that will make people nauseated when watching too much television, or when they are about to believe some extreme political claim. But in the long run there is no protection against information overload except the person's own control over psychic energy. Memes mutate with greater ease than genes: as soon as we learn to protect ourselves against one noxious strain, another one takes its place. So we can't rely on old solutions for protection; it is necessary to make sure, before we accept a new meme, that its promise to make life more enjoyable is not just an illusion.

For instance, in the past few decades millions of people have bought home exercise machines costing hundreds of dollars each in the hope of staying healthy and in shape while having fun like the muscular models shown in the ads. Although I could not find any hard statistics on how often such equipment is actually used, most people admit to lapsing in their exercise regimens after only a few days. And these machines are relatively benign pieces of technology: they only take up money and space, but since they are easy to forget, they make no further demands on consciousness. The really dangerous memes are the seductive ones that keep soaking up psychic energy day after day, always promising flow but rarely delivering.

FLOW AND HISTORICAL CHANGE

It is not only material things that evolve because they produce flow. Customs, belief systems, and religious and political institutions are often started because they make enjoyment possible. When they prove to reduce anxiety and increase the enjoyment of life, they are likely to be adopted by ever larger groups of people. For instance, the sinologist Robert Eno has recently described how Confucianism began and then spread in China. His controversial thesis may seem too esoteric for those who doubt that ancient history can teach us much, but it is worth considering because its main features have been repeated over and over in very different times and places.

At the time of Confucius, China was suffering one of the prolonged periods of conflict in its long history. Previously, during the Western Chou dynasty, from the twelfth to the eighth century B.C., China had seen an era of relative peace and prosperity. It was during this golden age that the Chinese came to believe that they were a chosen people ruled by a divine emperor. Unfortunately, part of this belief held that when no legitimate successor to the throne existed, Heaven revealed its wish as to who should be the emperor by making him victorious in battle. Toward the end of the Western Chou rule, the line of succession became quite muddled. This encouraged every aspirant to the throne to fight his competitors, to determine whether it was he who was destined to become Heaven's choice. By 551 B.C., when Confucius was born, internal dissensions had fragmented the nation into fiefdoms at constant war with one another. Poverty, lawlessness, and general misery became ever more widespread.

In the midst of this turmoil, bands of young men began to meet in the state of Lu, in an attempt to create for themselves a little ordered space among the spreading chaos. They did so by developing a discipline for their bodies and minds through songs and dances performed in a strict ritual fashion. Their program resembles in many respects our current obsessions with aerobics, martial arts, jogging, and other ways to focus attention on a manageable activity that produces flow. Here is, for instance, how Tseng Tien, one of the favorite disciples of Confucius, answered when asked what he would have most liked to do:

> In late spring, after the spring garments have been sewn, I would go out with five-times six capped young men, and six-times seven boys. We would bathe in the River Yi, and stand in the wind on the stage of the great rain dance. Then chanting, we would return.

It seems clear that these men had developed a successful flow activity that allowed them to ignore the troubled state of their society, while making it possible for them to enjoy complex skills based on control of the body and of the emotions. If this had been where the story ended, however, all we would have is the example of a neat formula for escape. But when Confucius joined these roving bands of dancing young men, he saw the possibility of generalizing their experience into something much more serious; indeed, he found in it cosmic implications. He conceived of *li,* the intricate rules of the ritual dances, as being one of the manifestations of the divine order that held the stars on their courses, that made the crops grow, and kept order in the state. Therefore, those who learned ritual skills helped to maintain the order of the universe, and those skills ceased to be merely occasions for enjoyable personal experience, but became duties to perform in order to keep society prosperous. Confucius's vision was so compelling that he became the acknowledged leader of the group.

Little by little the harmonious behavior and strong convictions of Confucius and his companions attracted the attention of China's rulers. Amidst the general confusion of the times, here was a band of people who seemed to be in touch with the ultimate order behind appearances, and whose very bodies communicated a sense of purposeful control. A number of warlords began to hire Confucians as court advisors. The historian Frederick Mote writes: "It became known that [Confucius's] students were a cut above the ordinary job seekers, and that made them eminently employable . . . his students advanced rapidly in government. Within a few generations the students of his widely proliferated school commanded the market—they had the talent, they got the positions."

These students were asked to draft just laws, and were given the opportunity to apply the *li* of their early joyous dances to the ruling of ever larger communities. Of Confucius's original twenty-two disciples, one was a feudal lord himself, and nine others became officials of some importance. If for no other reason, the warlords preferred to be surrounded by dependably ethical Confucian officials because their rivals were so often murdered by their own lawless retainers.

The rest, as they say, is history. Confucianism became the guiding principle of public and private life in China and neighboring cultures such as Korea, and for many centuries it exercised strong influences over much of Asia. In the process, as is so often the case, the meme Confucius helped create was infiltrated by mimetic parasites, who exploited the need for law and order for their own purposes. Respect for tradition became a convenient tool for those in power, who could justify their exalted position by referring to the heavenly purpose of which it was an expression. The oppressed poor who rebelled were accused of rejecting the divine order. Nowadays in China many people—and not just Communist ideologues—have come to despise Confucius, holding him responsible for the rigidly patriarchal, obsessively ritualistic oligarchy that made the country such a tinderbox for revolution.

Nevertheless, the history of the origins of Confucianism is instructive. It demonstrates that when people enjoy a complex activity—such as *li*—they may develop harmonious selves that make them attractive leaders to the disoriented majority. When this happens, the activity that made flow possible tends to be widely adopted and institutionalized; from a peripheral game it turns into a cornerstone of society.

A similar process seems to have taken place when Mohammed rose to prominence on the Arabian peninsula eleven centuries later. Here, too, as in China, an earlier period of prosperity had been followed by lawlessness and stagnation. "By the beginning of the seventh century," writes a historian, ". . . the national life developed in early South Arabia had become utterly disrupted; anarchy prevailed." Tribal conflicts were exacerbated by religious differences; each large family clan worshiped a different set of gods and spirits. In Mecca, where Mohammed was born, there were over three hundred shrines in the main square of the city, each dedicated to a different cult. This resulted in a veritable Tower of Babel. If, for instance, you had no heirs and wanted the gods to help you have a son, you had to go to one specific shrine to make the appropriate sacrifices; but if you wanted your camel healed, or your crops safely harvested, you had to go to entirely different sanctuaries, each with its own rituals designed for that deity and that specific purpose. One can imagine how much psychic energy the citizens wasted in conducting their spiritual affairs; little time must have been left for anything else.

The young Mohammed strongly disapproved of this spiritual chaos, and was also aware that the Jews and the Christians had prospered with their allegiance to a single God. Envying their power, and attributing it to their possession of a sacred book that recorded a covenant between the supreme deity and his people, he focused his attention on one of the gods of Mecca, an ancient god to be invoked in the times of greatest peril, by the name of Allah. Then, with the electrifying cry of *"la ilaha ill-'Allah!* There is no God but Allah!" he rallied other disenchanted youth to his cause, and began the stupendous historical movement that came to be known as Islam.

Islam acted like a huge laser: it took in the diffused psychic energy of the Arabs and concentrated it in a single beam of tremendous power. Mohammed's *Koran* became the set of rules by which life was ordered and simplified; the recitation of its harmonious verses, and its daily prayers, gave people a spiritual activity that bound them to a common goal. With clear goals, clear rules, new challenges, and a new self-confidence, the followers of Islam could approach life as a unified flow activity. The energy thus liberated was directed first to the military conquest of much of North Africa and Asia, and later to the development of one of the most sophisticated civilizations the world has known.

Another historical example from a thousand years after Mohammed's birth can likewise be used to illustrate the way flow helps to establish powerful and long-lasting institutions. By the mid-sixteenth century, the temporal and spiritual order that the Catholic Church had slowly built up was in tatters. Under the impact of the Reformation, Europe had broken into warring states divided by conflicting religions as well as economic interests. The psychological effect of this fragmentation on those who remained faithful to Rome was severe. Especially for the more educated and idealistic young men, it was no longer clear what a Christian lifestyle entailed;

doubts about the proper way to conduct oneself led to widespread anxiety and confusion.

It was to this spiritual chaos that Ignatius of Loyola, a pious Spanish officer, addressed himself in 1540 when he founded the Society of Jesus. He collected around himself a group of enthusiastic young men, whom he organized into a religious order modeled along military lines, with the goal of renewing the faith and helping the Pope triumph against its opponents. A notable aspect of the Jesuit order is that it provided its adherents with a finely calibrated set of challenges and skills that made it possible for them to concentrate their entire psychic energy on a coherent flow activity.

The daily schedule of the Jesuits was laid out in minute particulars from early morning till late evening, punctuated by specific devotions. For example, twice a day they had to stop and reflect on what their goals for that day had been, and evaluate how well they had accomplished them. Every gesture, every movement of the body was shaped by the *Rules of Modesty,* an official manual that prescribed the right way to hold one's head, how tightly the lips should be compressed, and what to do with one's hands on every occasion.

Yet paradoxically this obsessive concern with small, detailed rules was matched by a tremendous flexibility and unusual freedom in facing political and social challenges. Jesuits were given an excellent education and a very severe character training, and were then encouraged to embark on adventures in which their resourcefulness would be tested to the utmost. Solitary Jesuits were the first Europeans to explore much of the Canadian wilderness and the region of the Great Lakes, trying to convert the natives; others went to South America, where they set up native states free of colonial oppression. Jesuits in China, India, and Japan often spent dozens of years as the only Europeans in a foreign and often hostile culture, yet kept their beliefs and continued their work of scholarship and conversion.

It was this combination of a strict order with an emphasis on individual initiative that was so attractive about the Society of Jesus. The order was successful beyond anyone's expectations; by the time Ignatius died, 1,000 Jesuits were already at work, and despite their very demanding training their numbers climbed to 15,544 by the year 1626. One of the main challenges the order took on was the reform of Catholic education; they opened their first college at Messina in 1548; two hundred years later, the number of Jesuit colleges had risen to 728. One may have grave reservations about the political effects that the Jesuits eventually had in the countries in which they became powerful, but one cannot deny that this institution was an ingenious solution to the spiritual entropy that threatened Catholicism in the sixteenth century.

The same crisis that prompted the Jesuit response also stimulated another kind of flow activity, which had an even more momentous impact on history. This was the so-called Puritan work ethic, which became the foundation for the capitalist entrepreneurship and industrial productivity of northwestern Europe, as well as North America. Having rejected the Pope and the sacraments through which the Catholic Church claimed to guarantee salvation, the early Protestants were left unsure about how they were to know whether their souls were to be admitted to eternal life or not. In a culture in which the fate of the soul was, at least in theory, more important than that of the body, this was a critical matter. One solution, proposed by John Calvin, gained credibility. It stated that one knew whether one was saved by how successful one was in one's work. God would not let you become wealthy and respected if you were not destined for heaven.

As a result of this meme that established a connection between industriousness and eternal happiness, the Puritan merchants and craftsmen felt justified in working much harder than they had before, because now they could, so to speak, kill two birds with one stone: They could get rich and holy at the same time. Those who embraced this ethic generally did not reap the fruits of their labor; in fact they enjoyed fewer pleasures and had less free time than they had earlier. "He [got] nothing out of his wealth for himself," writes the sociologist Max Weber, "except the irrational sense of having done his job well." Like a chess player or a rock climber, the worker at the dawn of modern capitalism shunned comforts and enjoyment, yet was motivated by the intrinsic rewards of the activity itself.

The Protestant ethic offered a consistent set of rules, with clear goals and clear feedback, by which the faithful could order their lives and avoid the anxiety induced by the fading certainties of their faith. In Weber's words:

To attain . . . self confidence, intense worldly activity is recommended as the most suitable means. It and it alone disperses religious doubts and gives the certainty of grace. . . . The moral conduct of the average man was thus deprived of its planless and unsystematic character and subjected to a consistent method for conduct as a whole.

In other words, the Protestant ethic provided a great new "game" that made it possible to concentrate psychic energy; a worker (or, more exactly, "player") in such a system "will carry out his work in order, while another remains in constant confusion, and his business knows neither time nor place." It is ironic that the Puritans placed so great an emphasis on condemning all forms of enjoyment. According to this interpretation, however, they must have enjoyed the very rigors of their ascetic way of life, and frowned only on those less complex forms of pleasure and entertainment that conflicted with it. Even now, many hard-working people, who are sometimes called workaholics, would disdainfully deny that they enjoy their jobs, an admission that would rob those jobs of their importance. The workaholic is unlikely to admit that he is getting more pleasure from work than from going on a vacation, watching a show, or relaxing.

For quite some time now, no new games with the same wide scope as these earlier examples have appeared. Perhaps at their beginnings socialism and then communism offered the same opportunity to those few individuals who met in secret party cells and devoted their entire lives to the inevitable, scientifically guaranteed success of the proletarian revolution. While it is difficult to associate flow with the dour, humorless, and often vicious intensity of the Bolshevik cadres, they by all accounts also found ordered goals and a clear set of challenges in their calling, and pursued it with relish regardless of hardships and dangers. Some of their dedication can be explained by the attraction of ideals, and much of it by a drive for power, fame, and material rewards. Yet, if playing the revolutionary game had not been so enjoyable, it is doubtful that so many would have played it to the end, after ideals had lost their credibility, or when material rewards had proven illusory.

By the middle of the last century, according to Weber, capitalism had changed from a freely chosen, exciting personal adventure into an "iron cage." The rules of the game had become rigid, inherited capital made the playing field unequal, and huge monopolies and oligarchies had coopted the government apparatus to protect themselves from competition. It was no longer fun. As it turns out, Weber may have sold capitalism short; seventy years after he wrote his analysis, capitalism seems still to be the best game in town, while the rules of socialism turned out to be even harder to police, and thus its hierarchy was immediately infiltrated by parasites who exploited the idealistic memes for their own selfish advantage.

Two conclusions are suggested by this quick journey to some of the milestones of history. The first is that the ability to reorder everyday experiences into a meaningfully related, goal-directed activity is a powerful force. Whenever entropy engulfs society, the resulting anxiety makes people yearn for clarity and order. A new set of memes that allow people to be in flow again will be very attractive, and will often triumph. And just as there are many very different activities that produce flow—from music to wrestling, from reading to parachute jumping—so, too, can many very different cultural solutions emerge to deal with chaos. For instance both the Jesuit order and the Protestant work ethic arose roughly at the same time, in response to the same chaotic socio-cultural situation. The Jesuit and the Puritan believed in different memes, and acted in very different ways from each other, yet their selves were shaped by rules that provided a similar focus to psychic energy, and resulted in similar experiences of order and enjoyment.

The second conclusion is that no new cultural game is immune to exploitation. The Confucian system was from its very beginning manipulated by selfish rulers. It is true that for many centuries it was probably a more complex solution than any alternative would have been, but eventually it sapped the energies of the Chinese people. Islam succumbed to a sense of complacency, the Jesuits were often corrupted by power, and the work ethic without its transcendent justification runs the risk of turning into an obsessive need to control. These and innumerable other liberating solutions turn into obstacles to evolution as soon as they become rigid. Eternal vigilance may be the price of freedom, but nobody wants to be eternally vigilant. And as soon as vigilance is relaxed, the parasites move in.

What is the new game that will make it possible for us and our children to experience flow in these troubled times? It is important to realize that among the innovative memes that are bound to arise in the coming years, some will be shortcuts that will increase entropy in the long run, like the National Socialist solution, which had such a strong appeal to Europeans confused by the anarchy that followed after the First World War. Others will be more complex, more in tune with a harmonious future. Which direction evolution will take depends on our choices, so to improve the likelihood that the more complex choice is made, it will be useful to consider what makes a society "good," or in line with the course of evolution.

THE GOOD SOCIETY

When the French Revolution for the first time successfully challenged the order of the Old World, its leaders adopted a motto that described their expectations for a good society: *Liberté, égalité, fraternité*. Freedom, equality, and brotherhood are in fact a good, short summary of the essential elements of a complex society (if we are willing to forgive the sexism of that "brotherhood"). Freedom is certainly one of the ways differentiation is manifested: a free society allows its members to formulate their own goals, develop their own skills, take the actions that will make them unique individuals. But differentiation without integration breaks up the social order into centrifugal fragments; therefore we need brotherly love as a counterweight. And equality must stand between the two opposing principles because it is the link that connects them: equality of opportunity and equality before the law are what make it possible for a group of individuals bent on pursuing their own interests to coexist in peace with one another.

Of course, ideals are rarely implemented in the real world. Memes that instruct us to be "brothers" have to compete with the instruction of genes that tell us to take care of ourselves first, and our relatives next, as well as with the instructions of older memes that tell us that a Muslim, or a black, or a rich man can never be our brother. In this competition, the older instructions usually win out. Nevertheless, in the past two hundred years the memes for freedom and equality have spread to an unbelievable extent all over the world. Slavery is no longer an option, and nobility and wealth are no longer believed to be God's gifts, gifts that entitle a few fortunate persons to make life miserable for everyone else.

But what about *fraternité?* Here the record is more mixed, for it is difficult to claim that the principle of integration has progressed in the last few centuries. Unfortunately, while freedom and equality can be legislated, brotherhood cannot. Neighborly love is a spontaneous feeling that can be affected by external information, but cannot be controlled from the outside. Since the religious beliefs that once bound Europe and the Americas to a common set of principles have lost much of their connective power, other memes have arisen to give people a feeling of solidarity and belonging. But none of them have been universal enough to unite everyone into a single community of values. In the last century (and again now, at the end of the present one) nationalism became a powerful force, and then the political ideologies of communism and fascism gave the comfort of solidarity to some people, but only at the expense of a feeling of separation from those excluded.

The same trend favoring differentiation over integration took place in the United States. When John Locke developed those doctrines of individual freedom that shaped the thinking of the founding fathers of the American Constitution, he simply assumed that a strong Christian morality would continue to moderate the self-seeking unleashed by the removal of political restraints on individual initiative. As John Adams, our first vice-president, succinctly stated: "Our constitution was made only for a moral and religious people. It is wholly inadequate to the government of any other."

Locke's vision was so attractive because it advocated an unlimited opportunity to compete for the good things in life, free of government interference. Yet living in a tradition-bound community, he probably could not have anticipated a condition in which people were also going to be free from the restraints of mutual respect, criticism, and evaluation provided by stable, face-to-face interactions. He must have expected that political freedom and equality would be tempered by the common sense of citizens who had to live close to one another, dependent on one another. While all people may have been created equal—however vague a concept that remains—most people living in the same village or small town know very well that some of their neighbors are more responsible than others. They contribute more to collective well-being, while others only cause waste and dissension.

Locke and the shapers of the Constitution took for granted that a common religion would keep providing integration, and that the moral pressures of face-to-face communities would continue to moderate freedom and equality. Thus they did not worry too much about limiting the forces of differentiation, because it was difficult to conceive, at that time, that they would ever grow to be too strong. How could they have foreseen universal suffrage; universal education; the easy mobility brought about by railroads, cars, and planes; the revolution in productivity that made the landed gentry obsolete; the erosion of the power of community control—all developments that supported freedom and equality, but reduced integration?

In the course of our history, both the political memes that rule public behavior and economic and technological changes have conspired to diminish drastically the feeling of belonging and mutual responsibility in the United States. Not that John Locke and the free market are alone to blame for this loss of integration. In fact, our predicament on this score is still less severe than that in many other societies. One sees worse forms of social entropy in the former Communist nations, and Swedes complain more than is acknowledged of the loneliness and alienation they feel in their affluent socialist state. The problem is not limited to technologically advanced societies, either. What could be a more heartrending example of it than the Somali proverb "I and Somalia against the world; I and my clan against Somalia; I and my family against my clan; I and my brother against my family; I against my brother"?

One difficulty about achieving social improvement is that we tend to uncritically regard any advance in either differentiation or in integration as a good thing. If a new law increases freedom, it must be progress, as is a new movement that fosters the feeling of solidarity among people. Yet neither of these programs is likely to improve matters without the complementary contribution of the other. Complexity requires the synergy of these dialectically opposed forces; a gain in only one is likely to promote confusion and chaos. We think of social entropy as being caused by a loss of liberty or a loss of common values; but gains in either at the expense of its complement are just as dangerous. Freedom without responsibility is destructive, unity without individual initiative stifling, and equality that does not recognize differences is demoralizing.

A good society is one that helps each individual develop his or her genetic potential to its fullest. It provides opportunities for action to everyone: to the athlete and the poet, the merchant and the scholar. It does not bar anyone from doing what he or she does best, and guides everyone to discover what that is. A good society makes it possible for each person to develop the skills necessary to experience flow in socially productive activities. At the same time, it guards against anyone's exploiting the psychic energy of another person for his or her own advantage. There is a constant watch for oppressors and parasites. According to this perspective, freedom does not apply to *doing*, but to *being*. Each person is free to develop a self to the utmost level of its potential complexity, but not to curtail another person's freedom to do so.

But a social system that will assist evolution cannot stop even at this point. It must also take into account differentiation and integration beyond the needs of individual human beings, and of humanity as a whole. It has to be a system that recognizes the laws of nature as well as the laws of men. A society that ignores how denuding forests affects the quality of air, how manufacturing poisons affects the quality of water, how destroying plants and animal species affects the complexity of our planetary home is not likely to lead us forward. Just as we need selves that invest energy in goals that transcend its narrow interests, so too do we need transcendent cultural values, transcendent institutions to help shape our behavior in the interest of evolution.

CREATING A GOOD SOCIETY

We can all readily agree that we need to build social systems that are just and complex—even transcendent. But how do we go about accomplishing this? One thing is clear: No one has a simple solution that can be followed step by step to a satisfying conclusion. Does this mean, then, that any speculation about what makes a good society is just pious but pointless woolgathering? I don't believe so. For while it would be useless, and even dangerous, to suppose that we already know *what* needs to be done to bring our institutions in line with evolutionary requirements, we are on safer grounds in suggesting *how* we may find out what needs to be done.

The model for how to go about improving the memes that control our psychic energy—the laws of the land, the rules of conduct, the beliefs, the institutions in which we live—comes straight from evolution itself. As the psychologist Donald Campbell has argued, species increase their competitive edge by developing organs that allow them to gather increasingly more systematic information about their environment. At first this involves refining sensory receptors so that the organism can find out what is happening around it with greater precision. The ear of the bat, the nose of the bloodhound, the eye of the hawk are exquisitely sensitive devices for bringing information to these animals' attention.

Where we humans have an advantage is in the cultural tools created to bring us news about aspects of reality that presumably no other species living on this planet has access to. Egyptian pharaohs could learn what their enemies were about to do hundreds of miles away through messages written on papyrus sheets. With the aid of the telescope, Galileo could count the moons of Jupiter. Peering through his microscope, Van Leeuwenhoek could wonder at the intricate life contained in a few drops of water. And the likes of Newton and Pasteur made sense out of the data these instruments revealed. The most exhilarating aspects of our evolution, where the record of progress is clearest, are those in which we have increased our ability to discover what is happening around us, and to understand at least some of the laws of nature that underlie the news we have gathered. Through religions as well as science, our ancestors have been able to create increasingly sophisticated representations of the way things work in the world.

In one respect, however, our strides have been small. That is the matter of knowledge about individual and social needs, and understanding the laws governing human affairs. One could object that, for instance, universal suffrage is an enormously important invention that provides information about the needs of every single adult in the nation, thus making it possible for our representatives to steer a course of action responsive to these needs. But the vote, certainly at the national and usually also at the local level, is such a crude way of learning what the voters want that it rarely provides any useful information.

First of all, voters express their needs mainly by discriminating between two or more candidates who claim to represent different goals. By voting for a Republican candidate, I may express a preference for free enterprise; by voting for a Democrat, one might suppose that I endorse more extensive social services. But how reliably does my vote represent my goals and needs, especially in an election year like that of 1992, when neither of the presidential candidates spent much time explaining what they actually intended to do for us, the nation, or the world? Since they lacked cogent data about the candidates' agenda, it was impossible for voters to endorse the goals that best matched their own. Even if we forget for the moment the unlikelihood of compressing the dreams of a quarter-billion people into the planks of two parties, the amount of information we receive and transmit through an election is woefully meager.

If we want our political institutions to represent more clearly our goals, we must find better ways, first, to understand what those goals are, and second, to communicate them to others in a convincing manner. It is incredible that in our society we are spending trillions of dollars on armaments, space exploration, supercolliders, and inefficient social-service bureaucracies, yet we have no budget and no program to enhance the match between our dreams and the institutions that are supposed to help make them real. At the very least, one would expect every community or neighborhood to have a beautiful space—an amphitheater in a park, a lofty hall—where people could meet to discuss their public concerns, and where decisions affecting their representatives could be made. Such town meetings would be cheap even if free caviar and vintage champagne were served, compared to the sums now wasted in programs nobody really benefits from.

Hannah Arendt, the political philosopher, argued that real democracy existed only once in this world, among the free Athenians twenty-five centuries ago. The reason this was so, in her opinion, was that the Athenians had instituted a "public sphere" in which each citizen could debate any issue affecting the city, and be evaluated by his peers on the merits of his argument. And the debate was not academic: when the men in the agora had heard every opinion, they voted and their decision became law.

Arendt's thesis can be easily challenged. First of all, Greek democracy included only affluent males; second, one could certainly find many other examples of "public spheres" that had the essential characteristics of the Athenian agora, from the councils of American Indian tribes to the Swiss cantonal meetings, from the town meetings of New England to the gatherings of the Don Cossacks. But she is correct in her perception that such an institution is indispensable in any democracy worth its name, and that there are still few places in the world where such spaces exist.

Politics has lost much of its luster since the heyday of Athens. Many of us have effectively left the reins of the community in the hands of real-estate speculators, the owners of large construction firms, and others whose interest in the common good is usually limited and self-serving. It has been said that of the three million inhabitants of Los Angeles only a hundred lawyers and newspersons are more than vaguely aware of the policies being implemented in their city hall. As long as most citizens ignore politics, regarding it as a necessary evil, it will always remain an unsavory practice controlled by selfish interests. But if we take the shaping of the future as the great challenge it is, we shall discover that the Greeks knew what they were saying when they spoke of politics as the highest form of leisure. The most satisfying way to actualize the self is by building that most complex system—a good society.

EDUCATING FOR THE GOOD SOCIETY

Of course, even the most decentralized decision-making institution will not work unless its components—the individuals who make it up—know what they want, and want what is good for the community. To a certain extent, it is a vicious circle: a complex social system requires complex selves, yet complex selves usually thrive in complex systems. But this very circularity makes it possible to achieve progress, one small step at a time: any increase in complexity at the personal level can be translated into a societal improvement, and vice versa. Gandhi's idea of passive resistance spread all over the world, and was adopted by political movements from Amsterdam to Alabama. Conversely, millions of immigrants from feudal societies, without any experience of democracy, have been lifted to a higher level of political awareness after being exposed to the laws of the United States.

Ever since the beginnings of this nation, Americans have expected education to provide the instruction necessary for children to grow into informed citizens who will be able to support the growth of a complex democracy. Unfortunately, education has always been narrowly conceived of as merely book learning, or the transmission of abstract information. The old wisdom contained in the African proverb "It takes a whole village to educate a child" has been forgotten. Instead, education has been delegated to schools modeled on the mass-production methods that had proved so efficient in factories. Yet, as many critics of education have pointed out, direct experience teaches at least as many lessons as do books. If the school is repressive, children will distrust academic learning and avoid it in the future. No matter how important an idea, if it is presented in a boring way, children will tune away their attention from it. No matter what lofty ideas about democracy one reads in books or hears from teachers, if the local government is corrupt, cynicism is what will be learned.

A good society needs more than schools with a broad curriculum and up-to-date science labs. Education takes place in the whole community. It is the malls, the highways, the media, and their parents' lifestyles that give young people their clearest ideas of what reality is about. It is true that much of what they perceive is the kind of illusion of which the veils of Maya are woven; nevertheless, for a self that is not yet trained to distinguish between useful and entropic memes, it is such appearances that will shape the mind. If we wish to have a society in which freedom coexists with responsibility, we must ensure that the environment in which young people grow up provides complex experiences.

Utopian thinkers from Plato to Aldous Huxley have proposed educational ideals that, even though they are still challenging and perhaps impractical to implement, contain such important insights that we cannot ignore them without peril. What is common to these ideals is that they emphasize the training of the whole person, building on spontaneous interests and potentialities, and they stress risks and responsibilities, while making possible a joyous experience of growth. For instance, Plato understood that it didn't make sense to expect children to grasp abstract ideas until they had learned how to control their bodies in athletic exercise, and until they had learned about order through the rhythm of music and other forms of sensory harmony.

Huxley suggested rock climbing as an ideal basic training for citizenship. This sport teaches young people that survival depends on developing skills and on preparing oneself to face risks and unexpected contingencies. They discover that every move they make has real consequences involving life and death. In addition, a rock climber learns to take responsibility for another person's life, and learns to trust his life in the hands of the companion who holds the other end of the rope to which he is attached. What could be a more concrete way of shaping a complex self?

The anthropologist Gregory Bateson believed that the first thing children should learn was how the various life systems are interconnected: What is the relationship between the food we eat, the garbage we produce, and the survival of fish in the sea? How does the choice of the clothes we buy affect the life of families in Arkansas and in Sri Lanka? How does smoking affect longevity? Rather than analyzing reality via different disciplines that have no connection to one another, such as chemistry and history, we have first of all to learn how every process in this world depends on every other.

These radical visions hinge on the insight that true education involves growing to appreciate the direct links that exist between actions and consequences—in one's body, in one's social network, in the planetary environment as a whole. Nowadays learning is generally mediated by abstract information: no appreciable risk is involved, no direct experience of effects is possible, except through a failing grade. But a bad grade only tells you that you haven't convinced the teacher that you have studied, and it does not give any clues about the truth of what you have learned.

Only a few generations ago, a person who grew up on a farm knew what he or she had to know, and why. Information was concrete, familiar, and relevant. Knowledge was integrated around survival tasks—planting crops, caring for domestic animals—or around crafts like building barns and weaving cloth, or around symbolic necessities like playing music, dancing, or religious rituals. The usefulness of information was obvious. Now, however, a young person is rarely involved in serious, responsible activities outside of school. What he or she has to do is learn a great amount of abstract material, such as chemistry, biology, genetics, physics, mathematics, world geography, and history—most of the time without understanding what purpose these subjects will actually serve.

But even if someone learns enough about these separate disciplines, almost no one knows how to put them together. Yet any meaningful understanding requires bringing together the insights we have gathered from the various representations of reality, including the insights of art and religion. The great advances of Western science and technology have come about because we have learned how to funnel knowledge into increasingly narrow channels. This has resulted in great physicists as naïve about social and political issues as a little child, in famous molecular biologists who study brain chemistry and understand less about how the mind works than Australian aborigines, and in social scientists—like the present one—who couldn't solve a differential equation if their lives depended on it.

Perhaps the most urgent task facing us is to create a new educational curriculum that will make each child aware, from the first grade on, that life in the universe is interdependent. It should be an education that trains the mind to perceive the network of causes and effects in which our actions are embedded, and trains the emotions and the imagination to respond appropriately to the consequences of those actions. What is the real price of driving cars, when all the costs to the environment are included? Of waging wars, when we consider the long-term impact of lives lost without reason, of cultures and social systems destroyed? What are the likely effects of letting all the hundreds of varieties of rice die out except the few most commercially profitable ones? What do "good" and "bad" mean, in terms of the total effects of a person's actions?

We teach children conservation in physics—that each action produces an equal and opposite reaction—as if it were a law that applied only to billiard balls or pistons in an engine, without making them aware that the same principle applies to human psychology, to social action, to economics, to the entire planetary system. We bring up children to take their places in a culture that, in reality, no longer exists. The basic skills they learn have little to do with survival in the future. Each academic subject is presented as if it had an existence independent of all others. History is taught with little regard to the ecology, the economics, the sociology, or psychology—let alone the biology—that are necessary to understand human action. The same is true of all other academic subjects. Yet if we continue to teach physics separately from ethics, or molecular biology without concern for empathy, the chances of a monstrous evolutionary miscarriage are going to increase. To avoid these possibilities, it is imperative to begin thinking about a truly integrative, global education that takes seriously the actual interconnectedness of causes and effects.

A good society, one that encourages individuals to realize their potential and permits complexity to evolve, is one that provides room for growth. Its task is not to build the best institutions, create the most compelling beliefs, for to do so would be to succumb to an illusion. Institutions and beliefs age rapidly; they serve our needs for a while, but soon begin to act as brakes on progress. Even the Bible, even the Constitution are only steps in the process of continuing enlightenment. They are glorious achievements, to be admired and revered with the awe with which we approach the Parthenon, the Sistine Chapel, or Bach's *Brandenburg* Concerto. And we should certainly not abandon their wisdom until we discover more compelling formulations. But the task of a good society is not to enshrine the creative solutions of the past into permanent institutions; it is, rather, to make it possible for creativity to keep asserting itself. Its task is to give people a chance to bring forth new memes to be evaluated, selected, and joyously implemented by informed, free, and responsible peers.

FURTHER THOUGHTS
ON "THE FLOW OF HISTORY"

Flow and the Evolution of Technology

My first books were written by hand on yellow legal-size pads. I used to love the process of writing, the shaping of letters, words, and sentences. Now I am writing these lines on a PC, to which I have become addicted because I love the enormous flexibility in changing and editing that a PC provides. But the computer uses silicon chips that require powerful acids to manufacture, acids that after being used seep into the ground and make the water undrinkable. Is the change worth it? Who should pay for the poisoning of the water table?

What kind of technological advances would make your life more meaningful and enjoyable? Could you achieve similar results by devoting more attention to relationships with other people, or to developing "spiritual" skills?

Flow and History

Of the many historic changes taking place at this time, which ones do you think are leading toward higher complexity?

Is there a social movement—a religious sect or political party—that would make your life more enjoyable if you joined it? Is this a movement that is likely to lead to higher complexity?

The Good Society

Which of these three dimensions is most lacking in your present social environment: freedom, equality, or close personal relations? Why do you think this is so?

What unused personal qualities do you have that might help to improve your societal environment?

Educating for the Good Society

What is the most important bit of knowledge that you have learned in your life? Where did you learn it and in what way? Could it be taught to others?

If the task of education were again to become a community responsibility, what could you teach young people that would increase the complexity of their selves?

10

A Fellowship
of the Future

Our visions of the future usually contain an interesting contradiction. In the novels, movies, or essays predicting how we will live a few hundred years hence, the technology tends to be very sophisticated and advanced. Spaceships hop from galaxy to galaxy at the speed of light, self-contained cities rise through the clouds or swim submerged in the oceans. Until recently, the technological aspect of these visions tended to be utopian—it assumed that the material conditions of life would be getting easier and more efficient. At the same time, the vision of the human dimension in these glimpses into the future has generally been dystopian. In other words, it either projects the quality of personal life and the quality of relationships between individuals as just an extension of those of the present, or it actually portrays them as deteriorating. (Recent popular science-fiction books and movies, such as *A Clockwork Orange, Escape from New York,* the *Terminator* series, and *Blade Runner,* present worlds that are worse in both the material and the spiritual sense.) It is clearly easier for us to imagine ourselves living among better appliances than among better human beings.

We should not surrender to the cliché that the quality of life has been much better in the past, and is just recently growing worse. One need only read accounts of how people lived in Chicago and other large American cities earlier in this century to be grateful that the "good old days" are past. The urban sociologists of the 1920s described mile after mile of rickety boardinghouses, where the workers of the huge factories, stockyards, and railroads led a zombielike existence, spiritually isolated from one another, like anonymous termites. Nor did most of the millionaire bosses enjoy complex, fully human lives. Their major concern seems to have been how to impress their peers with a display of their wealth and barely developed taste. Mindless competition in consumption and an uncomprehending attempt to mimic "cultured" behavior appear to have consumed most of their time away from the office. Reading these clinical accounts, one feels a deep sorrow for the stunted lives, the opportunities missed, the joyless existence forced on millions by the wildly reproducing memes of a rapidly industrializing civilization.

The situation has hardly improved. Even if one sets aside the slums for the moment, many areas of our cities are no better than recharging stations for a race of robots. Block after block of tidy bungalows stretch out as far as one can see, all equipped to make it possible for workers to eat, rest, and reproduce. On the corner of every fourth block there is a church, alternating with a saloon, to provide spiritual solace and a feeling of community. Occasionally a park interrupts this monotony, with baseball diamonds and other athletic facilities. In the topography of these living arrangements it is easy to read the poverty of our lives.

In fact, it is pointless to expect that, left to itself, society will become more complex, and people more willing to transcend their limitations. It takes effort to defeat entropy, the force of inertia that constantly gnaws at the heels of order. During much of evolution, organisms evolved not because they intended to do so but because external forces, competition, and accident steered them in that direction. But in those few moments of history when the quality of life has flared up in sparks of spiritual incandescence, when flow and complexity were part of everyday experience, it has not been by chance. A creative response had to be involved.

So how, finally, can we help steer the course of events in the direction of higher complexity? One solution is simply to improve one's own self, and work toward a better society within existing institutions. As Robertson Davies wrote: "If a man wants to be of the greatest possible value to his fellow creatures, let him begin the long, solitary task of perfecting himself." The same sentiment was expressed many years earlier by Thomas Carlyle to a young man who had asked him how to go about reforming society: "Reform yourself. That way there will be one less rascal in the world." It is no small accomplishment to be a decent person, an honest citizen with a contented family. If everyone achieved these goals, we would not have to worry too much about the future. But it is almost impossible to live a decent life when the social system is devoted to greed and blind exploitation. And to change the system, one needs to step out of the cocoon of personal goals and confront larger issues in the public arena.

FORGING A FELLOWSHIP

The desire to achieve complexity will have limited value as long as it is held by separate individuals, each nursing it in the privacy of his or her own consciousness. It must be shared to become effective. Only a community of individuals sharing similar convictions can generate the feedback that confirms each individual's private belief. *Sine ecclesia,* went the old saying, *nulla religio.* Or, "There can be no religion without a church." But this is not just true of religion. Science could not survive without a community sharing scientific values. Moral systems do not continue unless individuals subscribe to a common set of ethics. Values are so ephemeral that they require the joint psychic input of a group to retain their hold on each person's attention. They may be created by individuals, but they must be maintained by a collectivity.

For this reason, we will need to develop a community that shares a belief in the evolution of complexity—something on the order of a Fellowship of the Future, a group of kindred spirits dedicated to supporting trends that move in the direction of greater harmony and greater individuation, and to opposing the encroachments of chaos as well as conformity. Political parties are based on values developed hundreds of years ago, when the systemic interdependence of the planet and its resources was not yet understood. Religions express the wisdom of previous centuries. Special-interest groups often focus on important but isolated issues. To face the third millennium with confidence we must join together in a community of shared belief about the future.

Arnold Toynbee, the British historian who wrote extensively about the rise and fall of the great civilizations, believed that a vital culture is always the product of a small "creative minority." For instance, if people around the world respect the United States it is not because of its wealth, not even its advanced technology, but because of the conception of a free and humane representative government hammered out by a few white European males (now dead) in earnest dialogue with one another over the course of many years, more than two centuries ago.

Similarly, the glory of Renaissance Florence was not a product of the masses, but the conscious achievement of a few dozen merchant banking families bent on developing an international financial network and on making their city the most beautiful in the land. When we speak of Pharaonic Egypt, Han China, Athens, Rome, or nineteenth-century Paris, what we are referring to are unique human systems shaped by relatively small minorities with unusual skills and individual visions.

To point this out nowadays would seem elitist. But creative minorities do sometimes arise from the least advantaged strata of the population; their achievement is due, at least initially, to personal commitment and merit rather than to inherited status or economic advantage. For instance, the disciples and apostles responsible for the spread of Christianity were fishermen, tax collectors, and other insignificant members of a backward province of the Roman Empire. Science is definitely an elitist domain; a small creative minority sets the agenda and determines priorities. So are the arts. Yet both science and the arts tend to be meritocracies, where the most able individuals emerge and prosper. To oppose "elitist" interpretations of history is tantamount to trying to deny individual differences among people; it may be a politically correct attitude at certain times, but it does not support the facts very well.

Also, to recognize that it is small groups who give history its peculiar texture does not mean endorsing this fact in every case. Individual leaders like Napoleon, small elite groups like the Bolshevik cadres in Russia arise out of and contribute to the differentiation of social systems. Unless they also achieve social integration in the process, however, their efforts do not lead to greater complexity; in fact, they can be very destructive. Societal integration—the great religious unification of early Christianity, the tide of Islamic conversions, the nationalist movements of the last century—are by definition mass phenomena, bringing together people from all walks of life. Yet here, too, such movements begin with visionary individuals and small groups: the Buddha and his disciples, Christ and the twelve apostles, Cavour, Kossuth, and Bismarck.

I do not intend to debate here whether creative minorities are autonomous agents of social transformation or simply the tools of much larger historical forces. The fact is that, one way or another, they are necessary to spark new ideas, and to nurture new institutions into being. The question is, how can they do so today?

There is no recipe for establishing a nucleus of social change, but there are many models to draw from, ranging from the alternative lifestyle communes popular a few decades ago, to special-interest groups like the Sierra Club. They all involve individuals who grow tired of the same routines, who are dissatisfied with the status quo, and who then get together with a few like-minded people and try a number of solutions until one works out. More often than not the attempt fails, but generally those who have committed themselves to an ideal of change do not regret their efforts even when they do not succeed.

A simple example concerning education, and one with which I am personally acquainted, is the creation of the Key School in Indianapolis, Indiana. This K–7 public school was founded by eight teachers who had been working in Indianapolis schools for many years, and who saw many more dull and drab years stretching ahead of them if they remained at their jobs. They were all dedicated to teaching children, but they felt that the constraints of the system made it increasingly difficult for them to do their work with enthusiasm and conviction.

Instead of resigning themselves to "reality," transferring out to private schools or to the more affluent suburbs, these eight teachers decided to start a radical reform project. As a first step, they agreed to bring themselves up to date on the most recent thinking on educational innovation. For over a year, each teacher spent much of her free time reading, and then presented what she had learned to her colleagues in informal evening workshops they organized at one another's homes. As a result of this preparation, the group decided to use Howard Gardner's theory of multiple intelligences—that education should deal not only with words and numbers, but also with sounds, colors, movement, and feelings—as a basis for their intended school reform.

Once the overall conceptual direction was agreed upon, the group visited as many already existing innovative schools as time and funds allowed. They applied and got grants for traveling, and different teachers went to different schools around the country, learning about their goals and methodologies. The information thus gathered by individual members was again shared with the group as a whole. The next phase consisted in drawing up a plan for a school that would function within the public school system, but that would be much freer—yet at the same time more unified—than schools usually are. In addition, the school was willing to accept every child who applied, provided the parents were ready to make some small sacrifices of time and comfort in order to facilitate the child's attendance.

Finally the group had to convince the schools' superintendent and the educational bureaucracy of the soundness of their plans. After many discussions and some painful compromises the teachers were given the go-ahead by the authorities. The superintendent, who, despite many practical difficulties, had been supportive of this initiative all along, found an old building, had it renovated, and the teachers of the new Key School were in business.

Each teacher invested many years of volunteer work in the planning and execution of the Key School. They felt somewhat guilty about diverting so much time away from their families to make this educational dream come true. They explained to their families that the sacrifice was worth the future gain that would come when the children themselves would be able to attend the ideal school their mothers were designing.

The entire enterprise almost collapsed when, before opening day, so many prospective students had applied that the district authorities insisted a lottery should be used for admission, and no exceptions made—and then it turned out that none of the eight teachers' own children were selected by the draft. Imagine working for nearly four years on a plan that would benefit education and your own family, and then finding out that your children were to be excluded from the advantages you spent so much effort fighting for. Despite this disappointment the teachers persevered, and the new school has been a great success. Visitors are constantly impressed by the air of joyful, purposeful activity in hallways and classrooms. One rarely sees a bored child or a listless adult anywhere; teachers and pupils are involved together in an exciting learning adventure.

The Key School, a small project, is not perfect, and it is possible that it may fold at any time. Nevertheless, even this modest success story shows that it is possible to change the system if a few individuals get together resolved to make a difference. And fortunately there are many other schools, businesses, and enterprises that, like the Key School, are determined to make things better than they are now. The best hope for the future is not in huge government programs, in presidential promises, and complicated bureaucracies. Of course, we need federal resources to implement large-scale programs such as Head Start or initiative zones in the inner cities. But it is from the grass roots, where enthusiasm and commitment are strongest, that new solutions are likely to emerge.

The problem with individual initiatives like the Key School is that they tend to be fragmented and specialized, and they rarely attain enough momentum to have an effect beyond the immediate range of the individuals who participate in them. So how can the energy and imagination of people like you and me be harnessed more effectively to direct the course of evolution? It seems that two goals must be accomplished above all else. First, we need to find ways of organizing interested individuals into functional groups. This will allow creative minorities to gather the necessary information and skills to make change possible, and then to organize themselves into effective political forces. And second, we need common goals and values to focus the energy thus generated into the direction of increasing complexity.

CELLS OF THE FUTURE

The ideal social unit for accomplishing a task is a group small enough to allow intense face-to-face interaction, one in which members participate voluntarily, and in which each person can contribute to a common goal by doing what he or she knows best. A "cell" of this type is likely to be a complex social unit, and one that allows the greatest amount of flow for its members. These days there aren't many opportunities to belong to such groups. The institutions in which we participate tend to be large, involuntary, and anonymous. Few people feel that their contributions make a unique difference to the company for which they work, the political party for which they vote, or the community in which they live.

Now let's imagine that one is determined to create a cell suitable for making a difference to the course of evolution. How to get started? According to those who study social systems, every social organism must attend to four major tasks in order to keep existing. It must acquire resources from the environment to keep the members of the group alive: a hunting group must find game, a university must find students, a bank has to find deposits. Second, it must coordinate its activities with those of other groups in the pursuit of its goals. Third, it must divide the resources and the tasks within the group while maintaining harmony and cooperation among members of the group. And finally, it must develop and maintain values and beliefs that give the group hope, identity, and purpose. These four functions are usually performed by different individuals, or subgroups within the system.

If these premises are correct, one would conclude that the smallest viable evolutionary cell would consist of a minimum of four persons. Suppose you make a commitment, with three other people in your neighborhood, to form such an "evolutionary cell." The initial purpose of this union is to become as well informed about the environment in which you live as possible, so that you can make an intelligent estimate of the forces that lead toward complexity, and those that are likely to increase entropy.

One person in the cell—or more than one, if the group is larger—would become specialized in assembling information about the economic conditions of the neighborhood or community in which the cell is located. What are the manufacturing, service, and financial resources? What are the investment policies of the banks? What are the interests of developers, of the owners of real estate? What are the prospects for small businesses, for the work force?

Systematic summaries of what the economic specialist has learned can then be shared with the rest of the cell whenever its members meet.

The second person would collect information about the network of political forces in the community. Who are the major players, and from where do they derive their strength? Whose interests are represented, and whose are not? What are the major lines of conflict among the elected representatives, and among interests that find no expression in the political arena? What latent political forces are ready to be organized in the community? Again, the information thus collected would be shared within the group on a regular basis.

The person who fills the third role in the cell is the one responsible for the internal organization of the group. This involves, first of all, having good information about the skills of the individual members, and about the internal functioning of the cell. A further task is to make sure that meetings are held, information flows smoothly, the members of the cell know what they are supposed to do and are doing it, and when action is called for, it is implemented. The role involves instrumental leadership, the practical, operational running of the cell.

And finally, the fourth member is the one who integrates the information flow and makes sense of it. The task of this person would be to keep the standards of complexity clear, and to apply them to the particular situation in which the cell finds itself. With the help of his input the group as a whole can evaluate the entropy in the community that surrounds it, and perhaps find ways to make more room for harmony instead.

At first glance it might seem that such groups would not be very different from existing political units. But the differences are indeed quite marked. Political parties form with the goal of advancing the self-interest of their members, regardless of broader consequences. The purpose of evolutionary cells, in contrast, is to collect information, understand as much of the reality of a given situation as possible, and then take such action as promises to advance the cause of evolution. This also is a selfish agenda, but one in which individual interests are merged with the best interests of not only humanity but of life as a whole.

But what would an evolutionary cell actually *do?* The first, and

in many ways most important, task is simply to provide its members—and eventually the public at large—with accurate and relevant information. Most of us have very little idea of what actually occurs in the communities in which we live. Our knowledge is too specialized for us to grasp how the intricate links within the system work, how decisions about zoning, public contracts, or taxes are made. The media, whose job it is to inform us about such issues, are generally too concerned about selling advertising space to make it a priority to keep tabs on the complex workings of the communities they serve. If the majority of readers prefer to be kept up to date on the sexual routines of stars rather than the fiscal moves of speculators, the media will dutifully oblige. Lost in the cacophony of pointless news the mind boggles trying to sift out the meaningful data. It is for this reason that a cell's most effective strategy would be to first gather information about the situation in its immediate vicinity, where the facts are likely to be most accessible and least distorted.

The second activity consists in understanding the facts thus collected in their systemic relationship with one another. A major problem with the news that we get from the media is that it is usually presented in a disconnected way: each item stands on its own, its causes and correlates barely sketched in. A newspaper editorial may lament the increase in gang violence in a neighborhood without mentioning the political and economic decisions responsible for it. By necessity the media have a short memory and a short attention span; to get a sense of the systemic forces underlying the superficial facts one must make an extra effort.

The major advantage of an evolutionary cell is that it would have a principle for evaluating facts, and for making principled decisions about them. The issues confronting a community, such as redistricting, redlining, closing schools, or building golf courses would not be evaluated in terms of short-term self-interest or in terms of staid dogmas derived from free-market or socialist ideologies. Instead, the question would be, How do these issues affect the complexity of the community in the long run? The principle of complexity is stable and constant; but its application to real issues is going to change and become more complex itself from year to year, as new knowledge and experiences accumulate. It is in this sense that the cells will

embody the principle of evolution in the very way they operate.

What will a cell do after collecting all this information and reaching all this understanding? At first, its conclusions may simply be an end unto themselves. It is no small accomplishment to have lifted even a small corner of the veils of Maya. Each member's life—her sense of belonging and participation in a community, his sense of appreciating his place in the complex tapestry of history—will be enriched and made stronger. In this sense, the pursuit of knowledge provides flow experiences that are much more satisfying than the forms of entertainment we now rely on to fill our free time. To share with a few like-minded people a realization of how things really are around oneself is much more gratifying than watching yet another installment of *The Tonight Show,* or sniffing cocaine while listening to tapes.

After the individuals in the cell have achieved a certain sense of clarity about the conditions in which they live, the next step involves translating knowledge into action. At first this might involve endorsing one local candidate against another, working within the already existing political institutions. With time, however, single evolutionary cells may start sharing information with others in the same community or in neighboring ones; at that point, new forms of political action will become possible. They may start spreading more widely the information they have accumulated; they may form new institutions to implement their decisions. Eventually, the isolated cells may coalesce in a loose confederation, an evolutionary fellowship that could provide a vision and a conscience for society as a whole.

A FAITH OF THE FUTURE

The basic tenets on which to base the work of such a fellowship could be very simple. If we believe that making the future more complex is something worth striving for, we should be guided by the following axioms suggested by the logic of evolution:

1. *You are a part of everything around you: the air, the earth, and the sea; the past and the future.* If you bring disorder to any of these, you bring harm upon your own self as well.

2. *You shall not deny your uniqueness*. You are the only center of consciousness in your space-time location. Therefore, your thoughts, feelings, and actions shall be rooted in your personal knowledge and experience.

3. *You are responsible for your actions*. If you achieve control over your mind, your desires, and your actions, you are likely to increase order around you. If you let them be controlled by genes and memes, you are missing the opportunity to be yourself.

4. *You shall be more than what you are*. The self is a creative construction. No one is ever complete and finished. It is what you will do in the future that determines who you are. Transcending the limits of a self-centered selfhood is the path of evolution.

This list could be extended, but by its very nature it could never be complete, or written in stone, as the Biblical commandments were. The suggestions we might glean from reflecting on evolutionary processes must by definition change as our understanding expands. There is no end to be found, no ultimate wisdom—just a slowly growing awareness that with time becomes ever more rich and complex.

Following these suggestions does not guarantee the kind of eternal life that the cartoonist's rendering of the medieval imagination has made familiar. They do not promise that we shall be reborn with airbrushed features, dressed in white, billowing nightshirts, and allowed to sit forever in the blue air in concentric circles around the Creator on a white, fluffy cloud. As far as we know now, death is final. When the physical structure of the body dissolves, so does the consciousness that for a few decades sparkled in the network of brain cells.

But to the extent that during life we invest psychic energy in directing the evolutionary process toward greater complexity, our contribution will continue to grow after the body dies. The information contained in the genes and in the memes that were once part of us will go on shaping the future. The echo of our actions will reverberate down the corridors of time. So of what benefit is this strategy to us now, afraid of personal death, of the dissolution of consciousness? There is, of course, no definitive answer to this question. Perhaps, in some future dimension of being, human individuality will indeed be preserved. Perhaps a copy of one's being will live on after death, perched on a metaphysical cloud in some region of eternity. It could be true, as some claim, that consciousness will be reborn in a more advanced physical entity.

To believe these consoling notions requires faith that goes far beyond present knowledge. Some might feel comfortable making the leap, but many will balk, unwilling to suspend disbelief. There is one source of faith, however, that needs no great leap and thus requires no compromise with reality as we know it now. It simply involves accepting our role in the unfolding complexity of life. The fear of death is the result of being too closely identified with an individual self. The more psychic energy we invest in personal goals, regardless of broader purposes—that is, the more exclusively we are involved in differentiation without concern for integration—the more frightening the dissolution of individuality is likely to be. Whereas to the extent that we identify with evolution, with the process of increasing complexity, the threat of death retreats.

Identifying with evolution does not mean we can rest safely in the belief that complexity is bound to increase forever, and that our genes and memes will stay at the cutting edge of this development. The possibility of reversal is always present. An enterprising new virus that feeds on human brain tissue may be born at any moment, or a century from now we may drown ourselves in the useless waste we have produced. There is no assurance that the complexity of the brain is destined to generate ever higher levels of differentiation and integration. Perhaps the adventure of life will prove to have been merely an aberrant blip on the immense time line of the cosmic ages, and we are destined to devolve, through apes and cockroaches, back to inorganic dust.

Because these possibilities are very real ones, faith in evolution is a vital necessity. If we knew for certain what the future held, faith would be superfluous. It is precisely because the unknowns are so great and dangerous that we require some manner of faith to choose our path and to give us courage. If we cannot believe that our existence is part of a meaningful, unfolding design, it will be difficult to maintain the resolve needed to make it come true. So even though faith in evolution does not require belief in a foreordained outcome, it does require trust in the unknown.

It is with the help of such a faith that giving direction to evolution will become a possibility. This process involves, first of all, a recognition of the many layers of illusion that prevent a clear view of reality. A sustained effort of will is necessary to liberate consciousness from the determining force of genetic instructions, of habits, of cultural conditioning. Like the alcoholic who must admit his helplessness before trying to grow out of his addiction, we must first realize our limitations before building a self in harmony with the universal order. And when we start to identify with the evolution of complexity, when we begin to recognize our kinship with the rest of creation, then it will be easier for us to free ourselves from the constricting needs of the self, from the terror of meaningless mortality.

Strange as it may seem, life becomes serene and enjoyable precisely when selfish pleasure and personal success are no longer the guiding goals. When the self loses itself in a transcendent purpose— be it to write great poetry, craft a beautiful piece of furniture, understand the movement of galaxies, or help children be happier— it becomes largely invulnerable to the fears and setbacks of ordinary existence. Psychic energy becomes focused on goals that are meaningful, that advance order and complexity, that will continue to have an effect in the consciousness of new generations long after our departure from this world, even after we are long forgotten.

The knowledge that we are not alone, that we don't have to defend our isolated selves against the rest of the universe, results in an intoxicating feeling of relief. We can act with joyful abandon, trying with the strength of all our fibers to reach the goals we have set for ourselves, yet ready to face failure with serenity. After all, why should our own goals take precedence in the enormous complexity of the universal mosaic? If they work out, so much the better. But we cannot really lose as long as our ultimate goals are at one with those of the cosmos. It is not only while playing an exhilarating game of touch football, or singing a beautiful tune, or becoming lost in painting a canvas that we will experience flow;

flow will become the normal experience of everyday life, permeating everything that we do.

If we could keep constantly fresh the belief that every one of our actions, when carried out with full consciousness, leads to a better future, we could stop right there. The evolution of complexity would be assured. But it is very difficult for a person acting alone to keep intact the vision of a goal that is by necessity always changing and impossible to pin down. It is for this reason that to have a sustained impact on the direction of evolution one needs to create larger social systems that share the goal and help implement it in concrete, manageable steps.

A Fellowship of the Future is one possible solution. Its evolutionary cells would increase exponentially the relevant information individuals need to understand the reality in which they live, to remove the veils of illusion woven by those whose interest lies in exploiting the psychic energy of others. And by combining information with like-minded individuals, we shall have a better chance to distinguish memes that are useful for the future from those that drain energy for their own purposes.

Evolutionary cells will make it possible to experience flow while working for the most ambitious goal available to the human imagination: to blend our individual voice in the cosmic harmony, to join our unique consciousness with the emerging consciousness of the universe, to fold our momentary center of psychic energy into the current that tends toward increasing complexity and order.

Even if nothing were to change in our own lifetime, even if signs of a new dark age proliferated, if chaos and apathy were on the ascendant, those who cast their lot with the future would not be disappointed. Evolution is not a millenarian creed, expecting a Second Coming next year, the next century, or the next millennium. Those who have faith in it have literally all the time in the world. The individual life span with all its woes and disillusions is only an instant in the awesome cosmic adventure.

At the same time, our actions have a decisive impact on the kind of future that will evolve on this planet, and perhaps on other planets as well. Barring some unfortunate collision with a disoriented comet, or the exuberant multiplication of a deadly virus, the future is in our hands. Abrogating this responsibility will leave us at the mercy of indifferent chance, or even worse, of parasitic exploiters in various guises. Taking sides with the patterns of evolving order will not guarantee that we will achieve success, or even that we will be happy as defined by the illusory values of the culture. But it will offer the opportunity to lead as full and as enjoyable a life as is possible in this world, secure in the knowledge that it was well spent.

FURTHER THOUGHTS
ON "A FELLOWSHIP OF THE FUTURE"

Forging a Fellowship

What kind of information about your social environment would be most useful for you to have first? How could you get it?

At present, what are the major obstacles that prevent complexity from developing in your community? Are the problems mainly economic, political, or moral? Do they involve lack of vision or creativity?

Cells of the Future

Have you ever been involved in grass-roots action? What did it accomplish?

Do you know three other persons with whom you might form an evolutionary cell?

A Faith in the Future

Are you comfortable with the idea that the shape of the future depends on how you invest your psychic energy now? What consequences do you draw from this fact?

If you have written down a few ideas in response to the questions listed at the ends of the chapters of this book, or even if you have just taken a few moments to think about them, your consciousness may have changed somewhat. Do you think that there has been a change? How would you describe it?

ACKNOWLEDGMENTS

The ideas contained in this book derive from innumerable sources, some of which are indicated in the notes at the end of the volume. But there are some persons who have helped this work through their direct support and assistance, and it is a pleasure to recognize their contribution here—hoping that what follows will not embarrass them too much. First of all, I must thank my wife, Isabella, whose encouragement, inspiration, and assistance has enabled my research and writing for almost thirty years. Our son Mark has provided insightful comments on various drafts, and Christopher added his refreshing perspectives.

Howard Gardner of Harvard University has been the kind of stimulating colleague one always dreams of having at one's side. The group of psychologists at the University of Milan, led by Professor Fausto Massimini, have contributed more than anyone else to the development of the ideas about cultural evolution. George Klein of the Karolinska Institute in Stockholm, Elisabeth Noelle-Neumann of the University of Mainz, and Hiroaki Imamura of Chiba University have continued to inspire my work through their friendship. Martin Greenberger of UCLA suggested the interactive format of the book. Philip Heffner, editor of *Zygon,* and Steven Graubard, editor of *Daedalus,* have been very receptive to some of the ideas contained in this volume. At my own university I would like to thank especially Edward Laumann, Wayne Booth, Martha McClintock, and my colleagues on the Committee on Human Development, whose scholarship and friendship has meant much to me over the years.

Of the many former and present students who have enriched this volume I shall single out Kevin Rathunde, now at the University of Utah; Maria Wong, at Connecticut Wesleyan; and Samuel Whalen. Particular thanks are due to the Spencer Foundation, which has generously supported my research over the past several years. I should also like to recognize John Brockman, who helped make this project come true; and Rick Kot, whose careful editorial skill greatly improved the manuscript. Finally, I would like to thank the hundreds of readers of *Flow* who took the trouble to tell me what they liked and disliked about my writing. Their reactions convinced me that it was worthwhile to take this next step.

Chicago, June 1993

NOTES

PAGE   The description of the flow experience for a general audience is to
ix   be found in a book entitled *Flow: The Psychology of Optimal Experi-
        ence* (Csikszentmihalyi 1990a). It was based on two earlier technical
        volumes (Csikszentmihalyi 1975; Csikszentmihalyi and Csikszent-
        mihalyi 1988), and on a great number of scholarly articles refer-
        enced in the above sources.

   The concept of flow is similar to the ideas of many previous
writers, although its basic elements emerged from psychological
research, not from reading other authors. For example, after my
first publications appeared, it was brought to my attention that the
Hindu Vedas, and especially the *Bhagavda Gita,* contain similar
notions; so do Taoist writings. The Taoists had a word, *yu,* which
has been translated as "walking without touching the ground,"
"floating," or "flowing," and refers to the way a wise person lives.
In the West, Aristotle's notion of virtue was based on acting for the
sake of excellence in the action itself (MacIntyre 1984). Marcus
Aurelius and the stoics had said many of the same things, and Dante
Alighieri in the *De Monarchia* describes the fullness of being as
acting with total involvement and joy.

   In terms of more recent parallels, I was influenced as a student
by the writings of the psychologist Abraham Maslow (1968, 1971),
whose descriptions of "peak experiences" are very similar to flow.
In fact, it is surprising how many people have come independently
to the same conclusions regarding the real sources of human happiness. For instance, in the spring of 1992, two years after *Flow* was
published, as I was browsing at a newsstand while waiting for a
flight at the Zurich airport, my eyes were caught by a paperback
with the title: *La Conquista della Felicità,* which turned out to be a
new Italian translation of an old work by Bertrand Russell originally entitled *The Conquest of Happiness* (1930). I bought the book,

started reading it, and almost missed the plane, so immersed had I become with Russell's ideas, which were remarkably similar to my own conclusions. More recently, Dr. C. Wayne Callaway sent me a book originally written in 1928 by a French philosopher entitled *Alain on Happiness,* which is also full of insights that match the results of my investigations. I think these parallels are not just curious coincidences; they demonstrate that in this case minds reflecting on experience independently of each other have come to almost identical conclusions.

In the past few years, research on flow has taken many directions. In addition to our laboratory at the University of Chicago, the most vital investigations have been carried out by Professor Fausto Massimini, Dr. Antonella Delle Fave, and their group at the Medical School of the University of Milan. Among many other important researches, they have organized a Himalayan mountain-climbing expedition to study flow in extreme situations. Other recent applications of flow have been to clinical psychotherapy (DeVries 1992), to the study of stress among business executives (Donner and Csikszentmihalyi 1992), the study of television viewing (Kubey and Csikszentmihalyi 1990), and the study of talent development in adolescence (Csikszentmihalyi, Rathunde, and Whalen 1993).

Interest outside academia in flow has also become strong. It has inspired automobile manufacturers to understand better the enjoyment of driving, computer software designers to create "seductive software," educators to design new curricula, managers to change work environments, and a garden magazine to understand the attraction of gardening. During the 1993 Superbowl, Jimmy Johnson, coach of the Dallas Cowboys, told the Press that *Flow* helped him and his team prepare for the victorious game. These developments appear to support the saying that there is nothing more practical than a good theory.

ix   **artists at work:** The research with artists was summarized in a book published almost twenty years ago (Getzels and Csikszentmihalyi 1976). A recent update is in Csikszentmihalyi (1990c).

x   **play:** Initially, *play* and *flow* were seen as being practically synonymous. This was, in part, because recognition of phenomena similar to flow could only be found in the literature on play (e.g., Piaget 1951; Bruner, Jolly, and Sylva 1976; Huizinga [1939] 1970). Soon, however, it became apparent that not all play produced flow, and flow could occur in work as well. In fact, one of the most important contributions of the theory of flow has been to point out that from a psychological point of view, work and play are not necessarily opposites (Csikszentmihalyi 1981).

x   **external goals:** After many years in which only external rewards were thought to motivate people to act, psychologists have recently discovered the importance of intrinsic rewards (Amabile 1983; Deci and Ryan 1985; Lepper and Green 1978). Some believe that *intrinsic rewards,* which are derived from the activity itself, are undermined when the person is also given *extrinsic rewards* such as praise or money. However, it now seems that the two kinds of rewards are often synergistic and can reinforce each other.

xiii **religion:** My views on the role of religion in evolution have been discussed in more detail in Csikszentmihalyi (1991) and Csikszentmihalyi and Rathunde (1990).

CHAPTER 1

PAGE **Pascal:** "Man is but a reed, the weakest in nature, but he is a
3   thinking reed." *Pensées,* no. 347.

Consciousness: My views on what consciousness is and how it works were developed in Csikszentmihalyi (1978, 1990a) and Csikszentmihalyi and Massimini (1985). Basically, what we can be aware of at any time is limited by our ability to pay attention, which is a limited resource. Attention is the psychic energy that we need to think with, to act with, to remember with. What we attend to, how intensely, and for how long, are determined by goals—which in turn are largely shaped by instincts and learning. The sum of what we attend to over time is *our life.* This view of attention as the organizer of consciousness is very similar to the one presented by William James in his masterpiece of 1890, *The Principles of Psychology;* see especially Volume 1, Chapter 11.

The "self" is one of the contents of consciousness, and to protect and enhance it becomes one of each person's primary goals. The description of the origins of consciousness in this chapter is indebted to the work of Dennett (1991) and seems congruent with the research conducted on the same topic for many years by Edelman (1993).

9   **the first millennium:** Throughout the history of Christianity, some people have taken seriously the book of Revelations to John, especially 20:4, where it is written that Satan would be chained for a thousand years in the abyss before the end of the world would come. Belief in the Apocalypse was especially widespread at the turn of the first millennium, and it seems to be growing again, a thousand years later—witness the events in Waco, Texas, earlier this year. But the expectation of a fiery end to the world followed by a just divine retribution is held by other cultures and religions as well. A good introduction to the subject is the classic work of Cohn (1957). For a review of messianic and millenarian cults around the world, see Lanternari (1965).

10   **Jacques Monod:** The speculations of this French biochemist (Monod 1971) have had a wide influence on the way evolution and natural selection are currently perceived.

         Were past ages happier: There is really no way to compare with any degree of precision our happiness with that of people who have lived in the past. It is even questionable whether we can compare the happiness of individuals living now in one country with that of people living in a different one, or even compare the happiness of two people living in the same country. However, in the past few years psychologists and other social scientists have begun systematic studies of happiness (e.g., Argyle 1987; Strack, Argyle, and Schwartz 1990; Bradburn 1969; Myers 1992). Descriptions of the conditions of life in the past that have bearing on happiness can be found in the accounts of everyday life edited by the team of French historians led by Aries and Duby (1987).

11   **Johann Huizinga:** His account of how men and women lived in medieval Europe can be found in Huizinga (1954). Incidentally, this same Dutch historian wrote *Homo Ludens* (Huizinga [1939] 1970), certainly one of the most insightful analyses of the play experience—and another influence on the development of the flow concept.

15   **Plato was not alone in the Golden Age:** A controversial but stimulating treatment of "historicist" thinkers (especially Plato) is Karl Popper's *The Open Society and Its Enemies* (Popper [1945] 1963).

16 **New Age movements:** Material for this brief discussion of human potential and New Age movements was drawn from Hulme (1977), Keen (1982), and Peters (1991).

17 **94 percent of our genetic material:** The actual overlap between the genetic instructions in human and chimpanzee chromosomes ranges from a low of 94 percent to a high of 99 percent. For example: "Nucleotide-by-nucleotide comparisons of DNA sequences in chimpanzees and man have shown so few differences—less than one percent—that biologists wonder why the two species appear as different as they do. The latest studies indicate that chimpanzees are genetically closer to humans than they are to gorillas." (Dozier 1992, 105). Diamond (1992) places the genetic overlap between humans and chimps at 98 percent.

18 **entropy:** I have been using this term borrowed from physics primarily to describe the state of confusion and inability to act that occurs in consciousness when one's goals are frustrated, and the consequent negative emotions one feels. It can also be applied at the level of social systems to the disorder that arises when community goals are threatened. The opposite of this state is *negentropy,* which describes the ordered state of systems—consciousness or community—working effectively. At the individual level, psychic negentropy manifests itself as optimal experience, or flow. Although I have been often warned that it was inadvisable to borrow these terms with a precise meaning and a long pedigree in other fields like physics and information processing, I still keep using them in a quasi-metaphorical sense in the context of human experience, because it seems to me that their heuristic value outweighs any confusion they might cause.

19 **William Hubbard:** The description of the American natives as evil comes from Hubbard (1677).

CHAPTER 2

PAGE 29 **Hsün Tzu:** For a translation of this Chinese classic, see Latourette (1959); and for a commentary on its ethical implications, see Ivanhoe (1991).

30   The lines from Faust were translated by this author, with apologies for the presumption.

31   **. . . a wired-in function of the nervous system:** Neurological bases of dissatisfaction are discussed in Konner (1990).

Escalating expectations have been reported by many investigators including Campbell, Converse, and Rodgers (1976), Martin (1981), and Michalos (1985).

32   **Overriding the genetic instructions . . . :** Ernst Mayr (1982), among other evolutionary biologists, has written eloquently about "open" genetic programs, and has claimed that humans have an instinct for learning. Nevertheless, each individual is born with a quantity of hard-wired propensities that are difficult to modify during one's life.

. . . the natural state of the mind: Distraction is a natural result of the mind's inability to focus attention on the same stimulus for long. Already a hundred years ago, James remarked, "There is no such thing as voluntary attention sustained for more than a few seconds at a time" (James 1890, 490). But the fact that people have a difficult time ordering their minds and enjoying themselves when there is nothing to do was something that emerged slowly during our investigations (Csikszentmihalyi and Larson 1984; Kubey and Csikszentmihalyi 1990). Being alone in unstructured situations produces a mental state similar to that reported in conditions of stimulus deprivation (Bexton, Heron, and Scott 1973; Zuckerman 1964; Csikszentmihalyi 1975).

33   **Mind needs ordered information:** This relationship was colorfully expressed by the neuropsychologist George Miller: "The mind survives by ingesting information" (Miller 1983, 111).

Even the experience of working at a job . . . : Our studies suggest that most dimensions of inner experience are more positive when people work on the job than at home—people report being more active, creative, and satisfied when they work—yet they generally say that they would prefer to work less and spend more time at home (Csikszentmihalyi and LeFevre 1989; Delle Fave and Massimini 1988).

Sunday morning: That Sundays are dangerous to mental health was already observed at the turn of the century by the early psychoanalysts, who coined the term "Sunday neurosis" (Ferenczi 1950). Since then it has been found that all sorts of vacations and holidays present the same problems, and for the same reason: people deprived of routines tend to become anxious (Boyer 1955; Cattell 1955; Grinstein 1955). In 1958 the Group for the Advancement of Psychiatry reported that "Leisure is a significant danger for many Americans." Workers who had not developed alternative interests suffer after retirement for similar reasons.

34 **internal discipline:** A good summary of the various ways people in different cultures have learned to control their minds, drives, emotions, and behavior (such as Yoga, meditation, religious disciplines, and self-help methods) is given in Klausner (1965).

36 **seventy thousand murders on television:** The estimates of how many murders the average American child will see being committed on his television screen before adulthood varies from a low of seventy thousand to a high of more than double that figure. Of course, such numbers are notoriously imprecise and useful mostly for bolstering ideological arguments. Nevertheless, it is clear that the amount of violence presented in the media is both excessive and dangerous for the development of a complex self.

Negative emotions are not necessarily bad: It has been documented again and again that the early lives of succesful men and women are often filled with an unusual amount of trauma and hardship (e.g., Csikszentmihalyi and Csikszentmihalyi 1993; Goertzel and Goertzel 1962). Consequently creative and successful adults often show symptoms of depression and other mental illnesses (Andreasen 1987). However, the question remains as to whether success at the expense of serenity is worth the price.

37 **The mind as separate from the body:** For psychological studies of the mind-body relation see Fisher (1970), Piaget (1971), Wapner and Werner (1965), and Mandler (1975). Ideas about the origins of the mind and its relation to the rest of the body are discussed in Jaynes (1977) and Donaldson (1993). Eastern ideas on the same subject are discussed by Granet (1934), Radakrishnan (1956), Fingarette (1979), Lau (1953), and Munro (1988).

39– **By studying how computers work they will discover how**
40 **we think:** There is a long controversy about the extent to which it is possible to learn from computers about the way the mind

works (see, for example, Dreyfus 1979; Anderson 1964; Hofstadter and Dennett 1981). For a small contribution to this debate, see the exchange between Csikszentmihalyi (1988c) and Simon (1988).

41   **Economic behavior:** Historical changes in economic motivation at the cultural level are described in the volume by Karl Polanyi, *The Great Transformation* ([1944] 1957). See also Scitovsky's (1976) description of economic irrationality at the individual level.

42   **The Addiction to Pleasure:** The entire section on addictive pleasures relies heavily on the interesting book by Lionel Tiger (1992). See also Cabanac (1971) and Burhoe (1982) on the same subject. The distinction between pleasure and enjoyment—or flow—is that pleasure involves the satisfaction of a homeostatic imbalance in a genetically programmed need (such as eating, drinking, resting, sex, sociability, and so on), whereas enjoyment is usually the result of using one's skills to match an opportunity for action that is not genetically programmed. Pleasure is easily sated, but also easily replenished—one can derive pleasure from eating more or less the same food several times a day.

      Enjoyment can last much longer, but one can get easily bored by what provides it unless the challenges become progressively harder, or different. It is for this reason that enjoyment leads to evolutionary change while pleasure does not. An old proverb encapsulates these relations well: "If you want to be happy for a few hours, get drunk; if you want to be happy for a few years, get married; if you want to be happy forever, get a garden." Of course this old saying misses the point that marriage can also remain enjoyable if, like a garden, one learns to cultivate the relationship.

      Apollo and Dyonisius: The dialectic between these two tendencies has been one of the oldest themes in cultural history; see, for instance, Nietzsche (1883–1892, Vols. 1–4, *Also sprach Zarathustra*) and the anthropologist Ruth Benedict (1934).

      Pitirim Sorokin: Sorokin (1962) has summarized many of the theories of cultural change, as well as doing painstaking research of his own on the subject. See also Csikszentmihalyi (1991).

45   **Buddhism:** The importance of the Four Noble Truths and the Noble Eightfold Path is described in Ikeda (1988). However, there are many sects and subdivisions of Buddhism, and like their Chris-

tian counterparts, they do not speak with the same voice, or value equally the same ideas.

46   **Roger Sperry:** Some of Sperry's ideas concerning the interaction of thoughts and emotions on the one hand, and the structure of the nervous system on the other, can be found in Sperry (1984, 1988).

46–   **Stress, strain, and hormones:** This entire section has been in-
47   fluenced by my colleague Martha McClintock, whose lectures I have heard during several summers when we both taught in the Vail Management Seminars. Some of her pioneering work on the interaction between mental states and physiological processes are in McClintock (1979, 1987). See also Sperry (1984, 1988) and Selig-man (1975, 1990).

50   **Louis XVI:** A good biography of the unlucky monarch is by Bernard Faÿ (1966).

51   **Men's movement:** One of the inspirations for this movement was the work of the analytic psychologist Carl G. Jung, as ex-panded by some of his followers (e.g., Moore and Gilette 1990). An interesting commentary on repressed masculinity has been Robert Bly's (1990) book *Iron John*. Some of the dangers poten-tially inherent when this movement is embraced uncritically were pointed out by Aeschbacher (1992), who fears that a mythical masculine ethos can easily degenerate into proto-fascist ideology. The literature on the women's movement is so large that it defies summary. However, among the best psychological works about this issue are by Gilligan (1982; see also Gilligan, Ward, and Taylor 1988) and Miller (1976).

CHAPTER 3

PAGE   **Democritus:** The quote is from Diogenes Laertius, *Lives of the*
56   *Philosophers,* vol. 9, 72.

        Evolutionary epistemology: The term was given currency by the psychologist Donald Campbell (1976). For some applications of the concept, see also Csikszentmihalyi (1992) and Csikszent-mihalyi and Rathunde (1990).

57   **Extrasomatic storage of information:** The effects—on the sense of self and on the culture—of being able to store information

outside the nervous system is discussed in Csikszentmihalyi (1992) and Csikszentmihalyi and Massimini (1985).

59 **Cultures can inculcate their values:** A comprehensive study of ethnocentrism around the world is in LeVine and Campbell (1972).

Social construction of reality: A classic and easily accesible treatment of this theme is the book by Berger and Luckmann (1967).

60 **Cognitive map:** The term was coined by the psychologist Edward C. Tolman almost 50 years ago (Tolman 1948). Contemporary applications of the idea can be found in Neisser (1976), who uses the term "schemata" to describe the same idea.

Individual differences develop with time: The psychologist Howard Gardner (1983) has developed the concept of "multiple intelligences" to account for the gifts—such as kinesthetic, or interpersonal abilities—that are distributed differentially among children.

61 **Ilya Prigogine:** His ideas can be found in Prigogine and Stengers (1984).

Physicist John Wheeler: See Wheeler and Zurek (1983).

When the Australian aborigines tried to explain the monsoon: The aborigines' worship of Yurlingur, the name given to the yearly monsoon that fertilized Australia, is described by the anthropologist W. Lloyd Warner (1958).

64 **Babies are programmed to imitate adults:** The importance of imitation in the development of infants has been studied by Kaye (1977) and Rosenblith and Sims-Knight (1985).

65 **Genes are not our little helpers:** The biologist Richard Dawkins (1976, 1982) has helped make this notion popular. The idea is well expressed in the saying: "A chicken is just an egg's way of making another egg."

Unwed teenagers and pregnancy: Genetic programming for early pregnancy is discussed in Csikszentmihalyi (1993a). The problems this trend causes in contemporary society has become the central issue studied by the foundation *An Ounce of Prevention,* established by the Chicago philanthropist Irwing Harris.

66 **The example of Jerry, an imaginary lawyer:** Any understanding of human psychology benefits from being placed in the context of daily time budgets. Only in comparison with other everyday activities and experiences can the significance of a given behavior or emotion be evaluated. We can find out what people do during the day either from diaries (e.g., Szalai 1965, Robinson 1977, deVries 1992), or from the use of the Experience Sampling Method, or ESM, which consists in having people fill out short questionnaires whenever a pager activated at random moments during the week signals (Csikszentmihalyi, Larson, and Prescott 1977; Csikszentmihalyi and Csikszentmihalyi 1988).

67 **Teenagers think of sex . . . :** I must say, however, that our ESM studies suggest a much lower preoccupation with sex, presumably because the method used for gathering the data is different.

Food has a similar grip: The amount of time spent thinking about food is reported by Johnson & Larson (1982).

68 Facticity is the term existential philosophers like Sartre (1956) and Merleau-Ponty (1962) use to refer to the biological or social conditions that determine a person's consciousness. In contrast *possibility* refers to the margin of freedom that a self-reflective person has when choosing a course of action that is not entirely determined by genes or memes.

69 **Peasants . . . of the Hungarian plains:** The ethnocentric villagers are described by Fèl and Hoffer (1969). In Italian, ethnocentrism is called *campanilismo,* literally "church-spire-itis," for the same reason—namely, the tendency to believe that one's church steeple is the hub of the world. However, the church was never the only center in the life of peasants; for instance, painted over the entrance to the *kocsmas,* the Hungarian equivalent of English pubs, one could usually find the following rhyme (Lang 1971, 40):

> *Here is the world's center*
> *If you don't believe it,*
> *Just enter.*

70   **The Chinese believed . . . :** That the Chinese sincerely believed themselves to be the only civilized culture, and the only one fit to rule the rest of the world, is mentioned, for instance, by Latourette (1970, 152). Of course, most Americans now hold the same view of the United States.

72   **The Gusii of West Africa:** The world of this West African people is described in detail by Robert LeVine (1979).

74   **Creative geniuses are often marginal people:** The analysis of the lives and thoughts of seven exemplary creative geniuses of this century is the latest work of the psychologist Howard Gardner (1993).

76   **Self-reflective consciousness is a recent development:** One of the latest books on the evolution of consciousness is by the neuroscientist Gerald Edelman (1993); for a review of this field, which is undergoing a renaissance after many years of neglect, see Sachs (1993). Other perspectives on how consciousness may have evolved are those of Jaynes (1977) and Donaldson (1993).

77   **Let us consider Zorg:** The imaginary Zorg's motivation is not that different from what the anthropologist Marshall Sahlins (1972) found among pre-literate people living in our days. For instance, contemporary hunters and gatherers hate to be given presents because they feel obliged to carry them in their bundles as they move from one camp to the next, and each item they own just adds to the weight they have to carry.

79   **"A man's Self . . . :** The quote is from James (1890, 291).

        The sudden loss of one's possessions: For the role of possessions in human psychology see Csikszentmihalyi and Rochberg-Halton (1981) and Rudmin (1991).

CHAPTER 4

PAGE   The term *memes* was given popularity by Richard Dawkins
87   (1976). The root of the word comes from the Greek for "imitation" (c.f., mime, mimetic). It refers to units of cultural instruction that affect phenotypic human behavior. For instance, a recipe for stuffed artichokes I learned as a child and then teach to my children is an example of a meme. So are the injunctions of

the Ten Commandments, the rules for long division, or the bars of a favorite song. Memes are passed on from one generation to the next; they make us do things in certain specific ways, but unlike genetic instructions, they are not coded chemically on our chromosomes.

Yet a meme is functionally equivalent to a gene, in that it contains instructions to be implemented by a (human) organism; a major difference is that the information in memes is encoded and decoded by the mind, and thus must pass through consciousness, instead of being implemented more or less automatically as genetic instructions are. Memes must be learned to be effective; hence they follow a Lamarckian rather than Darwinian model of evolution.

89   **Power can be dangerous:** The line "Power tends to corrupt and absolute power corrupts absolutely" was contained in a letter by Lord Acton to Bishop Creighton dated April 5, 1887. The philosopher Karl Popper thought that this claim about power was one of the most basic universal statements in the social sciences, and that an entire theory of human behavior could be derived from it.

90   **Class differences in the U.S.:** In 1991, at the end of a decade of legislation that facilitated the rich getting richer and the poor poorer, the wealthiest 20 percent of Americans earned 44.2 percent of the total household income in the United States, while the poorest 20 percent earned only 4.4 percent of the total income. Only Brazil had a more skewed distribution of income (66.4 percent to the top quintile, 2.4 percent to the bottom quintile), while other developed nations that make such statistics available (i.e., Canada, France, Germany, India, Italy, Japan, the United Kingdom) are more egalitarian. Income differences in Australia are almost identical to those in the U.S. The difference between the richest and poorest fifths of the population is greatest in Brazil, where the income of the wealthiest is on the average twenty-seven times that of the poorest; it is the smallest in Japan, where the richest earn only three times as much as the poorest quintile (*Britannica Book of the Year*, 1993). Of course, household income is not the only way to measure economic inequality, but it is a reasonable approximation. According to the calculations of Kevin Philips, a GOP strategist under Nixon, the decade of the 1980s may have resulted in even worse polarizations in wealth than those reflected in the above statistics (Philips 1990).

91   **Farming became the main form of subsistence:** This brief
      sketch is inspired in great part by Karl Wittfogel's (1957) exhaus-
      tive study of the origins of despotism in lands where extensive
      irrigation was possible, e.g., Mesopotamia, Egypt, China, the
      Indus valley. Wittfogel claimed that similar social systems arose
      within ecologies containing a potentially rich source of water
      which then had to be distributed by a complex network of canals
      so as to be usable for farming. Farmers were forced to cooperate
      in a closely knit social network to manage the irrigation networks.
      Technological bureaucracies developed to supervise the social net-
      work, and absolute rulers (e.g., pharaohs, the Chinese emperors)
      emerged at the head of the bureaucracies.

94   **How the feudal system developed in Europe:** The history of
      the stirrup and its effect on European civilization is in White
      (1966). Others have claimed similar effects for the introduction of
      other technologies, such as the water mill (Bloch 1967), the yoke
      harness (Lefebvre des Noettes 1931), the rudder (Lefebvre des
      Noettes 1932), the spinning wheel, and the power loom (Thomp-
      son 1963); and, in modern times, the automobile and television.

95   **Exploitation of women and children:** Some blood-curdling
      accounts of forced labor and prostitution in Asia are recorded in
      the reports by Schmetzer (1991a, b, c, d).

      "Sexual dimorphism": For example, in most monkey species
      such as the patas, geladas, and hamadryas baboons, adult males
      weigh about twice as much as the females (Kummer 1968). Similar
      and even greater ratios prevail among many other mammalian
      species.

96   **Child workers during the Industrial Revolution:** A good
      introduction to the changes in living conditions brought on by
      industrialization is the work of E. P. Thompson (1963). The cita-
      tion is from page 347.

      Child abuse and neglect: For a summary of recent statistics, see
      the Winter 1993 issue of the journal *Daedalus,* and Csikszent-
      mihalyi (1993a). The figures on children in the United States are
      from Konner (1991) and from the *Highlights of Official Aggregate
      Child Neglect and Abuse Reporting* published by the American Hu-
      mane Association (1987). On the state of the world's children, see
      United Nations Children's Fund (UNICEF) (1990).

98   **Extroversion:** The qualities that lead to success in our society (but not necessarily to happiness or satisfaction) are summarized in Bee (1992). Among them extroversion—or the interest and the ability to interact easily with other people—is perhaps the leading trait.

99   **Personality strength:** This trait was described by Noelle-Neumann (1983; see also Weimann 1991). Similar concepts are "hardiness" (Kobasa 1979), "coping" (Lazarus 1966, Antonovsky 1979), "self-efficacy" (Bandura 1977), and "competence" (Sternberg and Kolligian 1990).

101   **Selective marriage practices:** The effects of homogamy—the tendency for people to marry individuals who are similar to them in social and cultural backgrounds—on socio-cultural speciation have been discussed in Csikszentmihalyi (1973).

102   **Inheritance laws in the Soviet Union:** The impact of inheritance laws and other policies on the family in the USSR is dealt with in Coser (1951).

109   **The recent savings-and-loan fiasco:** Examples of bankrupt speculators who profited from the forced sales of assets of the corporations they helped to destroy were reported by Tackett (1991) in the *Chicago Tribune*.

111   **Mimetic parasites:** How fake holy men exploit their naive followers is described in Peters (1991).

112   **Defense spending, United States *vs*. Japan:** The figures come from a report by Evans (1991). The latest figures indicate yearly per capita spending on military protection of $231 in Japan, and $1,222 in the United States. Of the central government expenditures, 6 percent go to the military in Japan, 25 percent in the United States. Only a very few countries, like Quatar, Nicaragua, Israel, Yugoslavia, and the Sultanate of Brunei, spend more of their government resources on defense. (*Britannica Book of the Year,* 1993).

114   **From the novelist Dostoyevsky to the sociologist Pareto:** Dostoyevsky's ideas about the human tendency to prefer illusion to reality is perhaps most vividly expressed in the "Legend of the Grand Inquisitor" contained in the *Brothers Karamazov*. Pareto's ideas on the same subject can be found in the collected volumes of his works (Pareto 1917, 1919).

CHAPTER 5

PAGE
121
"A meme has its own opportunities . . .": The quote about the potential conflict between memes and genes is from Dawkins (1982, 110).

122
How does one select between alleles?: Recently the so-called "rational choice" model of decision making, originally developed in economics, has been widely adopted also by the other social sciences, such as psychology (Tversky and Kahneman 1986) and sociology (Coleman 1990). For a critical review of the rational choice models in the social sciences, see Cook and Levi (1990). Although this is a promising and powerful approach to understanding the mechanism of mimetic selection, there is a danger in assuming that what seems "rational" in terms of present knowledge and conditions will in fact turn out to be the best choice.

124
Weber saw the early stages of capitalist competition: The thesis about the relationship between the orderly work of the early Protestants and their ability to accumulate capital is developed in Weber (1930).

Weapons provide . . . the best-documented history . . . : For an example of how a particular weapon develops, see *The Social History of the Machine Gun* by John Ellis (1986).

126
Samuel Colt: Colt's revolver, which he invented in 1833, was the first firearm to be effective when used while riding horseback. Its invention coincided with the great westward expansion, and the six-shooter became part of the history and folklore of the American West. Ten years after he started producing the weapon that made his name famous, Colt's business nearly failed; it was saved only by a government order, in 1847, for one hundred revolvers to be used in the Mexican War (Carruth 1987).

John Taliaferro Thompson: Even though Thompson had tried to sell his invention to the military and the police, the real niche for the tommy gun became the underworld spawned by Prohibition. Thompson himself was horrified all through his life that his gun had been made famous by gangsters (Helmer 1970).

Memes and Addictions: Although every civilization developed intoxicants based on alcohol or other drugs, the sudden introduction of a previously unknown substance into an old culture usually has disastrous consequences. For instance, brandy, rum, and cane alcohol were Europe's "poisoned gifts" to the civilizations of the Americas (Braudel 1985, 248). See also Tiger (1992).

127   **Tobacco is a good example:** Early settlers in America were amazed to see Indians smoking, but the soon-transplanted tobacco plant quickly became enormously popular in Europe, where for a time it was thought to have curative powers. Its popularity guaranteed its economic importance, and the first successful crop was grown in Virginia in 1612 by John Rolfe. Because of the labor-intensive quality of the product, tobacco-growing soon came to require a large number of slaves; relatively unheralded at the time, this development became an important political and social issue some two hundred years later (Carruth 1987).

128   **Lindbergh's account . . . Beryl Markham's exploits:** The account of his pioneering solo flight across the Atlantic is in Lindbergh (1953). The description of the early safari-exploring flights is in the autobiography of Beryl Markham (1942).

129   **Antoine de Saint-Exupéry:** The autobiographical novel about the first airborne mail routes in South America is by Saint-Exupéry (1931).

130   **153 electronic appliances:** The earlier figure was computed by Buckminster Fuller, the latter by Ward and Dubos (1972).

       Isaac Asimov was probably right: Asimov's views on technology can be found in Asimov and Walker (1990). For more scholarly treatments of this subject see, for example, Karl Wittfogel (1957) or Lewis Mumford (1938).

131   **Development of true literacy:** For a brief history of literacy see the Summer 1990 issue of the journal *Daedalus,* and Csikszentmihalyi (1990b). The origins of writing in China are described by Keightley (1978).

132   **Books experience an intense competition for survival.** According to Annick Smith (1992, 257), during Buffalo Bill Cody's lifetime (from 1846 to 1917), there were 1700 novels written about him in the United States. Not one of them is still in print.

Futurists' manifestos: Futurism is said to have originated with the publication of a manifesto written by the Italian poet Filippo Tommaso Marinetti in the French newspaper *Le Figaro* in 1909. It contained the famous statements: "We will destroy museums, libraries, and fight against moralism, feminism, and all utilitarian cowardice. . . . We will glorify war—the only true hygiene of the world—the beautiful Ideas which kill . . ." The musician Luigi Russolo contributed to later manifestos of the Futurist movement and then published his own *L'arte dei Rumori* (*The Art of Noises*) in 1912.

Colin Martindale: The application of the evolutionary model to understanding changes in the content of poetry, painting, and other art forms is by Martindale (1990). Another psychologist who uses evolutionary models to analyze creative developments is Simonton (1988).

134   **Art follows its own laws:** The various contradictory demands made by the art world on artists are discussed in Getzels and Csikszentmihalyi (1976). The scientists' dependence on the ruling paradigms of the time is described in Brannigan (1981) and Kuhn (1962). For a theory of creativity based on a systems approach that recognizes the mutual dependence of persons, domains, and fields in the production of creative innovations see Csikszentmihalyi (1988a, 1990c).

135   **Television as an addiction:** The literature on the psychological effects of television has grown to enormous proportions, and its conclusions are often contradictory. It would be almost impossible to summarize the various studies and their results. The conclusions I present here are based on the work we have done at our laboratory at the University of Chicago, plus a judicious selection of other researchers' findings; all of them are discussed in the volume *Television and the Quality of Life* (Kubey and Csikszentmihalyi 1990).

137   **Political constitutions:** The earliest work on the evolution of political constitutions was by Caligari and Massimini (1976). See also Massimini, Toscano, and Inghilleri (1986).

Marx gave shape to a recurring utopian idea: Commentaries on Marxism are so numerous that it would be impossible to give a representative selection in such a short space. Of Marx's own writings, some of the best selections are the ones edited by Robert C. Tucker (1972). My first attempt to understand the psychological appeal of Marxism was contained in Csikszentmihalyi (1967).

139   **sumptuary laws:** For the restrictions on lower-class women wearing silk clothes in Connecticut, see Carruth (1989, 21). The dietary restrictions in Hungary are described by Lang (1971, 21). See also Kovi (1985, 19).

141   **We keep stuffing our houses with artifacts:** The way objects in the home are used to enrich the symbolic dimensions of life is described in a monograph based on a study of over three hundred members of typical American families (Csikszentmihalyi and Rochberg-Halton 1981). Additional information on the psychological role of objects is in Rudmin (1991), Csikszentmihalyi (1993b), and Lubar and Kingery (1993).

142   **Long hair:** In 1675, the Massachusetts General Court blamed Indian attacks on "the manifest pride openly appearing amongst us in that long hair, like women's hair, is worn by some men" (Carruth 1987, 21).

CHAPTER 6

PAGE   **virtual ants:** These and other new forms of artificial life are
150   described by Levy (1992).

155   **Seven percent of the energy consumed in the United States:** For this estimate see Kelly (1982, 331).

157   **Complexity is not necessarily the direction:** One of the basic tenets of science—psychology included—is that it deals with what *is,* not with what *ought to be.* In other words, values have no place in scientific investigation. But in my opinion this principle only applies to the description of facts, not to their interpretation. For instance, a cancer biologist should remain completely objective when investigating the behavior of the cells he studies. But once he identifies which are the killer cells and which are the natural protectors of the body, is he not going to take a different attitude toward the two, trying to find ways to eliminate the former, and

strengthen the latter? A similar value-bias is even more inevitable in the human sciences. In other words, I agree with Karl Jaspers's position:

> We call the observation of man's existence "anthropology" and "psychology," while the making of demands upon the innermost nature we call "philosophy." Psychology investigates, makes discoveries, and predicts. Philosophy appeals, projects possibilities, and prepares the way for decision. *But tacitly present in all human psychology is an interest in possibilities and an appeal for further self-development,* just as, in all philosophy, psychology continues to function as a means of expression as well as a condition without which the philosophical appeal would remain thin and insubstantial [italics added] (Jaspers 1969, 127–28).

The Nature of Complexity: Biologists have held for a long time that increasing complexity is the constant feature of evolution (Dobzhansky 1937; Mayr 1942; Waddington 1970). In other words, organisms with more parts (e.g., different cells, organs, etc.), that are more closely communicating with each other, have a tendency to displace less complex organisms as time goes on. In the past few years, complexity has again become a very hot topic because it seems to provide a unified way of understanding events in very different systems—ranging from physics to biology and even economics and other social sciences (Waldrop 1992).

Kauffman (1993, 30) divides systems along a continuum into three types: *ordered, complex,* and *chaotic.* Complex systems that exist "on the boundary between order and chaos" are the most likely to evolve. Ordered (or integrated) systems evolve less readily because they are too rigid and unresponsive to new possibilities. Chaotic (or differentiated) systems evolve slowly because if natural selection finds a better variation, it will not be stable long enough to be transmitted to the next generation. Complex systems are flexible enough to be open to change, yet ordered enough to recognize and stabilize the most adaptive change if and when it occurs.

It is probably more than a coincidence that complex physical systems described by chemists and biologists as existing on the boundary between order and chaos bear a resemblance to the complex psychic state of flow that exists on the boundary between boredom and anxiety. In both cases, the evolution of new traits or new skills proceeds most readily at the interface of order and chaos. That we *enjoy* being on that boundary seems like a gift from Providence; it could be almost interpreted to mean that humans have a vocation for evolution. But it is more likely that all living things—or at least those that will evolve—prefer to dwell on that precarious boundary.

159   **Morality and Evolution:** A brief history of the moral foundations of the evolutionary idea is in Richards (1988). A variety of contemporary perspectives on this issue can be found in Campbell (1975), Alexander (1987), and the following issues of *Zygon: Journal of Religion and Science:* 8 (no. 2); 23 (no. 3); and 23 (no. 4).

160   **Moral systems . . . are entirely relative:** Belief in the relativity of moral systems has become a dogma in much of contemporary social science, and especially in anthropology. The dangers of this position had been clearly foreseen by the sociologist Vilfredo Pareto (1917, 1919). For a contemporary critique of this position see Spiro (1987).

        Eating chicken after a father's death: These and similar culturally idiosyncratic moral beliefs are reported in Shweder, Mahapatra, and Miller (1990). Other treatments of the same topic are in Douglas (1966), Frazer ([1959] 1890), and Rozin and Fallon (1987).

        "Ten Worlds" of Buddhism: It is actually difficult to say what Buddhism teaches, because there are so many varieties of this complex religion, and there is no single dogma common to all believers. The description used here was taken from Ikeda (1988).

161   **Contemporary psychology has not progressed:** That human development consists of a dialectic movement between increasing individuation (i.e., chaos, or differentiation, in our model) and increasing social participation (i.e., order, or integration) is quite clear in the theories of Damon (1983), Erikson (1950), Kohlberg (1984), Loevinger (1976), Levinson (1980), Fowler (1981); see summary by Bee (1992). For instance, the first task of a baby after birth is to differentiate itself from the "oceanic feeling" that at the onset of life seems to envelop the infant. But as soon as the baby

realizes its own individuality, the next stage involves establishing a close and trusting relationship with its mother or caretaker. Such dialectical swings between expressing individuality and freedom on the one hand, and belongingness and dependence on the other, recur several times along the life span.

When the present book was already in print, I became aware of a model for the development of the self by Harvard psychologist Robert Kegan which also describes the growth of the self as alternating between the two opposite poles of integration and differentiation. His study was published under the title *The Evolving Self* (Kegan 1982), a fact of which I had been unaccountably unaware. Unfortunately by that time it was no longer possible to change the title of the present book, a duplication which I regret. It should be noted, however, that Kegan's work deals with the *development* rather than the *evolution* of the self.

164   **Restrictions on marriage:** Among the hundreds of possible examples, one involves the Gusii of West Africa. The anthropologist Robert LeVine (1979, 77–104) writes: "For a typical young man, the timing of his marriage is uncertain; it depends on his family's wealth, his patriarch's willingness to permit him the use of cattle. . . . Wealthy and fortunate young men may be married by age twenty, whereas unfortunates must postpone it until they are able to raise the bridewealth inside the family or through their own efforts—often until thirty or later." So much for the romantic notion that love and procreation in precapitalist societies are free and spontaneous.

169   **The Sage gives free rein . . . :** The excerpt is from *Hsün Tzu* 21:66–67.

171   **If families fail to both support and challenge . . . :** The application of the model of complexity to social systems such as the family requires that we view *differentiation* as the ability of the group to provide freedom and stimulation to its members, and *integration* as the group's ability to provide a feeling of emotional support and belonging. In fact, studies of family dynamics agree that the best family environment is one that here would be called complex, i.e., one that offers both freedom and belongingness. Freedom alone seems to produce children who are competitive but not very happy; emotional support alone results in happier but less achievement-oriented children; when both are lacking, the

children suffer the most (e.g., Rathunde 1989; Rathunde and Csikszentmihalyi 1991).

CHAPTER 7

PAGE **"Oh yes, when I'm working . . ."**: This quotation and the
176 following one ("I try to involve my children . . .") come from the studies of flow with working women reported by Allison and Duncan (1988, 129).

177 **"It's exhilarating to come closer . . ."**: The quotations from the rock climber, surgeon ("The personal rewards . . ."), and chess master ("It is exhilarating . . .") are from *Beyond Boredom and Anxiety,* the earliest book describing the flow experience (Csikszentmihalyi 1975).

"This type of feeling . . .": This and the next quotation from the dance teacher ("I get an immense amount of pleasure . . .") are part of interviews collected by Delle Fave and Massimini (1988, 212).

180 **The mystique of climbing . . . :** The quote is from Csikszentmihalyi (1975, 47–48).

181 **"It is really great . . ."**: This interview with an Italian musician was collected by the Milan research group headed by Professor Massimini and Delle Fave.

181– **An ophthalmological surgeon . . . :** The responses from sur-
82 geons, dancers, and chess masters come from Csikszentmihalyi 1975, especially chapters 5 and 8.

182 **"I knew every single moment . . ."**: The interviews with world champion figure skaters were conducted by the Australian sports psychologist Susan Jackson (1992).

183 **"You are in an ecstatic state . . ."**: The interview with this composer of modern music was reported in Csikszentmihalyi (1975, 44).

"I am generally immersed . . .": The interviews from Bangalore were collected by Massimini and Delle Fave.

184 **Flow provides an escape:** Albert Einstein is supposed to have said that science and the arts are the best forms of escape from

reality that man has devised. In fact, the goal of both the sciences and the arts is to transform reality as we know it and therefore escape its limitations. Of course this kind of escape is very different from the retreat to an even less complex reality that the term usually implies. Einstein's is an escape *forward;* drugs, alcohol, mindless entertainment are *backward* forms of escape, from an evolutionary viewpoint.

185   **Preoccupations that . . . cause entropy in consciousness:** In our studies conducted with the ESM we find that of all the things people think about during the day, the one topic of thought related to the worst moods is the self (e.g., Csikszentmihalyi and Figurski 1982). The reason for this seems to be that generally when a person thinks about him- or herself, the first and often only thoughts that appear in consciousness have to do with things that are going wrong—for instance, about getting old, fat, or losing one's hair, or feeling that one is not successful enough in some aspect of life. Here is a typical response from one of our teenage subjects as she was looking in the bathroom mirror: "A pimple on your face can ruin your entire day; you feel like you are going to crash like an airplane losing a screw from the engine just after takeoff." Of course, those who develop discipline over their consciousness can learn to avoid such feelings of panic at the contemplation of the self.

       "You could get so immersed . . .": The quote is from Robinson (1969, 6).

187   **Jim Macbeth:** The research with long-distance sailors was done by the Australian researcher Macbeth (1988).

188   **People play chess as a substitute . . . :** Some of the psychoanalytic interpretations of why people pursue enjoyable activities such as chess are to be found in Jones (1931) and Fine (1967).

       Those who engage in dangerous sports . . . : The basic work on personality types that need constant excitement was done by Zuckerman (1979). See also Apter (1992).

       The concept of interest: Over a hundred years ago, the psychologist William James (1890) wrote "Millions of items of the outward order are present to my senses which never properly enter into my experience. Why? Because they have no *interest* for me. *My experience is what I agree to attend to.* Only those items which I *notice* shape my mind—without selective interest, experience is an utter chaos." (Vol. 1, 402). See also Dewey (1913); and for contemporary studies on the nature of interest, Renninger et al. (1992) and Schiefele (1991).

189   **How we think causes changes in brain physiology:** The relationship between thinking and physiology has been mentioned earlier in connection with the work of Sperry (1984, 1988) and McClintock (1979, 1987); see also Seligman (1990).

190   **Many jobs . . . consist of repetitive actions:** Studies that have shown the relationship between flow and work are included in the volume *Optimal Experience* (Csikszentmihalyi and Csikszentmihalyi 1988). Modern work settings are discussed in Csikszentmihalyi and LeFevre (1989), while more traditional cultures are treated in Delle Fave and Massimini (1988).

191   **Aristotle was among the first to recognize . . . :** For a contemporary summary of what Aristotle meant by happiness see MacIntyre (1984). For instance, "Human beings, like the members of all other species, have a specific nature; and that nature is such that they have certain aims and goals, such that they move by nature towards a specific *telos*. . . . What then does the good for man turn out to be? Aristotle has cogent arguments against identifying that good with money, with honor or with pleasure. He gives to it the name of *eudaimonia*—as so often there is a difficulty in translation: blessedness, happiness, prosperity. It is the state of being well and doing well in being well, of a man's being well-favored himself and in relation to the divine. . . . The virtues are precisely those qualities the possession of which will enable an individual to achieve *eudaimonia* and the lack of which will frustrate his movement toward that *telos*." (MacIntyre 1984, 148).

"[I]n every action . . .": The citation is from Dante's *De Monarchia* (1317), Book I, Chapter 13, and was translated by this author. Dante, the "Fleeing Ghibelline" who had been banned from Florence because his party had lost out to the opposition, wrote this book in the hope of enticing Henry VII, the Holy Roman Emperor, to invade Italy and bring peace to the constantly quarreling factions of Guelphs and Ghibellines. Thus Dante took it upon himself to start what in terms of modern complexity theory would be called a process of "self-organization," or reduction of entropy in the social system. Because they were several centuries ahead of the times, Dante's efforts failed—but the meme for civic order survived.

192   **The Consequences of Flow:** In terms of the work of contemporary scholars, flow has many similarities with Maslow's concept of self-actualization (1968), White's notion of competence (1959), deCharms' concept of personal causation (1968), Bandura's effectance motivation (1977), Deci and Ryan's autonomy (1985), Amabile's findings on intrinsic motivation (1983), and the influential concept of optimal arousal formulated by Hebb (1955) and further developed by many others (e.g., Apter 1992; Berlyne 1960; Fiske and Maddi 1961). Our contribution differs mainly in that it focuses more on what happens in the ongoing stream of consciousness, and less on the subjective or objective outcomes that the experience might serve.

Paolo Uccello: This is how the Renaissance biographer Giorgio Vasari (1550) concludes his sketch of Uccello: "He left a daughter, who had knowledge of drawing, and a wife, who was wont to say that Paolo would stay in his study all night, seeking to solve the problems of perspective, and that when she called him to come to bed, he would say: 'Oh, what a sweet thing is this perspective!' And in truth, if it was sweet to him, it was not otherwise than dear and useful, thanks to him, to those who exercised themselves therein after his time."

Albert Michelson: This and many other anecdotes about the enjoyment scientists derive from the pursuit of science is reported in Chandrasekhar (1987, 25). Another good example is the fragment he reports from an essay by Poincaré: "The Scientist does not study nature because it is useful to do so. He studies it because he takes pleasure in it; and he takes pleasure in it because it is beautiful. If nature were not beautiful, it would not be worth knowing and life would not be worth living. . . . I mean the intimate beauty which comes from the harmonious order of its parts and which a pure intelligence can grasp." (Chandrasekhar 1987, 59.) For a general discussion of the role of enjoyment in creativity, see Csikszentmihalyi (1988b).

193   **Peak performance:** Two publications comparing peak perform-
      ance and flow are Privette (1983) and Privette and Bundrick
      (1991). An interesting study showing how flow supports peak
      performance in swimming was conducted by the Japanese sport
      psychologist Riho Tonoue (1992).

      Talent development: The results of this longitudinal study have
      been published in a volume entitled *Talented Teenagers* (Csikszent-
      mihalyi, Rathunde, and Whalen 1993). The differences between
      students talented in math and in the arts have been reported in
      Csikszentmihalyi and Schiefele (1992).

194   **Self-esteem:** People's self-esteem is not a constant, but fluctuates
      during the day depending on the environment and one's perform-
      ance. In flow—when both challenges and skills are high—people
      typically report high self-esteem, i.e., they feel satisfied with their
      own performance, feel good about how they are doing, and feel
      that they are living up to their own and others' expectations.
      Moreover, individuals who experience flow more frequently have
      higher overall levels of self-esteem than people who experience
      flow more rarely (Wells 1988; Whalen and Csikszentmihalyi
      1989).

195   **Stress Reduction:** For a beginning analysis of how flow experi-
      ences can moderate stress among business executives, see Donner
      and Csikszentmihalyi (1992).

      Clinical Applications: The use of the Experience Sampling
      Method in psychotherapy is described in the volume edited by
      deVries (1992); an especially relevant chapter is the one by Delle
      Fave and Massimini (1992).

197   **Juvenile delinquency:** The intrinsic rewards of juvenile crime
      are discussed in Csikszentmihalyi and Larson (1978).

199   **The frequency of flow varies greatly:** For ways of measuring
      the frequency of flow with the use of the ESM see Csikszent-
      mihalyi and Csikszentmihalyi (1988) and Csikszentmihalyi, Ra-
      thunde, and Whalen (1993).

CHAPTER 8

PAGE
207

Flow can . . . lead to entropy: For the physicists who loved building the bomb, see Csikszentmihalyi (1985). Crime, especially juvenile delinquent behavior, is often an attempt to overcome boredom in situations that fail to offer meaningful opportunities for action (Csikszentmihalyi and Larson 1978).

209–
12

György Faludy: The biographical sketch included here is based on an interview with the poet conducted at his home in May 1991. Faludy's works include the translation of one thousand four hundred poems, ranging from the Greek Archilokos (7th century B.C.) to the contemporary verses of Garcia Lorca and Paul Celan (Faludy 1988). The collection of poetry from the prison camps, from which the excerpt quoted was taken, was published as *Börtönversek (Prison Verses)* in 1989, after the Communist regime began to fall apart in Hungary.

213

Susie Valdez is a Hispanic woman . . . : The quote from Suzie Valdez is from Colby and Damon (1992, 64).

213–
14

I call him Ben: The case history of Ben is part of the longitudinal study of talented teenagers reported in Csikszentmihalyi, Rathunde, and Whalen (1993). That book reports on various ways to study and measure complexity—as a feature of experiences, of personalities, and of families—and it shows that adolescents who develop personal complexity tend to have a more positive quality of experience, and to be more successful academically.

215

Linus Pauling: Pauling was interviewed on November 20, 1990, by Dr. Kevin Rathunde, then a member of my staff at the University of Chicago, in the context of the study entitled *Creativity in Later Life,* sponsored by the Spencer Foundation.

216

What Is the Self?: This account of its development is an extremely simplified summary of the very complex description offered by Dennett (1991).

217

The Nuer people of East Africa: The Nuer were studied by Evans-Pritchard (1974); for the quotation about the role of the spear in defining the self of Nuer males, see p. 233.

219

Abraham Maslow: Maslow's hierarchy of needs is most extensively presented in *The Farther Reaches of Human Nature* (1971).

Evolving Images of the Ideal Self: The arguments presented in this section have been developed in greater length in a recent article in the journal *Poetics* (Csikszentmihalyi 1992).

221 **Caduevo Indians of Brazil:** The Caduevo Indians and the role of body-painting in general are described in Lévi-Strauss (1967, 176).

222 **Metals as body ornaments:** The ornamental function of metallurgy is described in Renfrew (1986, 144, 146).

224 **In a study of over three hundred . . . :** The study of eighty-two families is the one reported in Csikszentmihalyi and Rochberg-Halton (1981).

225 **The bullroarer that Australian aborigines rattle:** The *churinga* is described in Emile Durkheim's classic book, *The Elementary Forms of Religious Life* (1967, 141).

The *molimo* trumpet: The *molimo* trumpet and its uses are mentioned by the anthropologist Colin Turnbull (1961, 80).

225– **Ceremonial masks:** Francesco Monti (1969, 9–15) developed
26 the argument about the transcendent function of masks.

226 **The sacred objects of the Arunta:** The Arunta of Australia and their use of the *nurturya* is described in Durkheim (1967, 145).

Medieval cathedrals: The reference is to Adams (1905).

227 **The ideal for human perfection:** Greek ideals of selfhood as represented in early sculpture are from Arnold Hauser's magisterial study of the evolution of art (Hauser 1951, 70).

229 **The great cycles of frescoes . . . :** The educational uses of Medieval frescoes on church walls are discussed in Lavin (1990).

229– **Giovanni Dominici:** Dominici's ideas about interior decoration
30 are quoted in Freedberg (1989, 4).

230 **Giulio Mancini:** Mancini's views about how pictures can help in procreating healthy children are detailed in Mancini (1956).

230– **It is probably erroneous . . . :** That African and other pre-
31 literate representations of the human figure in distorted form express a basic existential dread pervasive in such societies is an interpretation discussed in Price (1989). This interpretation is op-

posed to the one advanced by Monti (see note to pp. 225–26); however, both may be true.

231   **Commercial advertising:** The iconography of advertising is discussed, among others, by Goffman (1979) and Jhally (1990).

232   **The moral universe of the TV commercial:** The quote about TV commercials as religious drama is from Esslin (1976, 271). The quotation about advertising as gospel ("an ultimate source . . .") is from Kavanaugh (1981, 15–16).

As Sorokin has attempted to prove . . . : Sorokin's analysis of history in terms of alternating cycles of sensory and ideational cultures is contained in *Social and Cultural Dynamics* (1962); see also Csikszentmihalyi (1991).

233   **The computer as a metaphor of the self:** This idea was developed by Sherry Turkle (1984).

234   **"quantum self":** The quantum self is described in Zohar (1990) and Lancaster (1991).

"The human being is an open possibility . . .": The Karl Jaspers quote is from his *General Psychopathology,* originally published in 1923 (Jaspers 1965, 766).

234–   **The Development of the Self Through the Life Span:** Fur-
37   ther readings on the stages alluded to here are to be found in Damon (1983), Fowler (1981), Kohlberg (1984), Loevinger (1976), and Maslow (1968). Each one of these models of development recognize a dialectic movement between differentiation and integration.

235   **Brahmin male:** The ideal career for the life of traditional Hindu Brahmins is described in Rudolph and Rudolph (1978).

236   **Stricter social controls:** See, for instance, Huxley (1967), Koestler (1960), and Orwell (1949).

240   **Currently, spirituality is at an ebb:** For a psychological view of how contemporary culture has failed to provide spiritual directions, see Massimini and Delle Fave (1991).

241–   **Related to spirituality is the concept of wisdom:** A recent
44   collection of psychological approaches to the subject of wisdom is

to be found in Sternberg (1990). The section here is based on a
chapter in that volume (Csikszentmihalyi and Rathunde, 1990).

242   **"He who considers absolutely . . ."**: Thomas Aquinas, *Summa
       Theologica,* 1,6.

243   **"First among the virtues . . ."**: Plato, *Republic,* 4:428.

       "Wisdom is the supreme part of happiness.": These lines are
       the last ones uttered by the chorus of *Antigone.*

243–   **"The most manifest sign of wisdom . . ."**: Montaigne, *Essays,*
44   1, 25.

245   **Vera Rubin:** Rubin was interviewed for the study, *Creativity in
       Later Life,* by Carol Mockros, a member of my staff, on October
       9, 1992.

246–   Recently I came across a historical reference very reminiscent of
47   Zeke's story. Patrick O'Brian (1993, 19–20) mentions that as re-
       cently as 250 years ago a popular sport at Eton—one of the most
       prestigious boys' schools in England—was to release a ram in the
       middle of the campus. The boys, armed with special clubs, then
       beat the ram to death. O'Brian quotes another historian (Hollis
       1960): ". . . [in 1730] the ram broke loose from the hunt, ran up
       the High Street over Windsor Bridge and through the market with
       the boys in hot pursuit until eventually they caught it and beat it
       to death. . . . Therefore, for the future, as a reform, the ram was
       hamstrung and made to hobble round and round School Yard with
       the boys in pursuit and beating it until it was dead."
           The reason for presenting such gruesome details is that it is
       important not to forget how thin is the veneer of civilization
       spread over even the best of us. Complacency may easily lead to
       disillusion and despair. The atrocities now being perpetrated in
       Bosnia, in Somalia, in India, in the Middle East—all seats of an-
       cient cultures—are unfortunately not the exception but the rule.
       Only by actively resisting the entropy of violence is it possible to
       keep it at bay.

247   **Jerome Bettis:** From an interview with Joseph Tybor published
       in the *Chicago Tribune,* 11 September 1992.

CHAPTER 9

PAGE   **Social and cultural systems:** My view of how social systems
253   operate is heavily dependent on what used to be called the "struc-
       tural-functional" school in sociology and anthropology, especially
       as it has been defined by Talcott Parsons (1951). The basic premise
       of this approach is that each social system—whether as simple as a
       family or as complex as a nation-state—must take care of certain
       basic *functions* in order to survive. In order to take care of these
       functions, the social system must develop *structures*—e.g., institu-
       tions and roles—that will do these jobs. For example, all social
       systems must solve the problem of *adaptation,* i.e., of extracting
       calories from the environment for their own use. This function
       dictates the necessity of productive technologies like hunting or
       farming, forms of exchanging goods, and so on.

       In the past two decades, structural-functionalism in sociology
       and anthropology has been attacked for downplaying conflict and
       change in social systems, and all but abandoned in favor of sym-
       bolic interactionist, rational choice, and lately post-structuralist
       views of how societies operate. The main objection against the
       Parsonian model of society—a mistaken one, in my view—has
       been that it was too static, too rigid, and too prescriptive. Perhaps
       stressing the evolutionary context of social systems will avoid this
       problem.

254   **Johann Huizinga:** In *Homo Ludens* (Huizinga [1939] 1970).

254–   That programming and working with computers can engender
55   deep flow experiences was recognized a long time ago (Turkle
       1984). Since then the flow theory has inspired the design of dif-
       ferent kinds of "seductive software," and has been used to make
       the learning of computer interaction easier (Davis et al. 1989;
       Ghani 1990; Malone 1987).

256   **Stefan Linder:** The analysis of the hidden costs of leisure was
       conducted by the Swedish economist Steven Linder (1970). See
       also Scitovsky (1976) for a compelling analysis of the irrationality
       of consumer behavior.

258   **". . . how Confucianism began . . .":** The section on the
       origins of Confucianism is largely based on the very interesting
       work by Robert Eno (1990). See also Creel (1960, 13).

258– **Tseng Tien:** This quotation is from Confucius, *Analects,*
59   11.24.

259   **". . . [Confucius's] students were a cut above . . .":** Frederick
      Mote (1971, 41).

260   **"By the beginning of the seventh century . . .":** Hitti
      (1970, 25).

262– **the Society of Jesus:** For brief analyses of how the Jesuit order
63   produced flow experiences, see Isabella Csikszentmihalyi (1986,
      1988) and Toscano (1986).

263– The history of how the Protestant Ethic developed is told in
65   Weber (1930); especially relevant are pp. 71, 112, and 117.

267   **When John Locke developed those doctrines . . . :** The
      argument that Locke's individualistic philosophy has caused exces-
      sive differentiation in the American polity follows the diagnosis in
      the work of Robert Bellah and his co-authors, *The Good Society*
      (1991), which has greatly influenced the writing of this section. See
      also Murray (1988) for applications of flow theory to issues of
      governance.

      John Adams: Quoted by Bellah (1991, 180) referring to Howe
      (1966, 185).

270   **. . . species increase their competitive edge . . . :** Donald
      Campbell's elaboration of the idea of evolutionary epistemology
      can be found in Campbell (1976). A similar idea is expressed in
      Popper's (1963) notion of social engineering.

271– **. . . real democracy existed only once . . . :** The political
72   philosophy of the visionary scholar Hannah Arendt is best ex-
      pressed in her *The Human Condition* (Arendt 1958).

272   **. . . most citizens ignore politics . . . :** See Didion (1989, 99).

272– **Educating for the Good Society:** Some of the ideas in this
76   section were developed in Csikszentmihalyi (1993a).

273– **Utopian thinkers from Plato to Huxley . . . :** What Plato
74   thought about education can be found in the *Symposium* and in
      Phaedrus. An influential contemporary restatement of Plato's edu-
      cational ideas is in the book by a late colleague, Alan Bloom

(Bloom 1987). Huxley's educational ideas are expressed in *Island* (Huxley 1967).

274   **Gregory Bateson:** For Gregory Bateson's ideas concerning education, see Bateson (1972).

CHAPTER 10

PAGE   . . . **grateful that the "good old days" are past:** I am thinking
279   in particular of the deadpan accounts of the mechanical, soulless life in the big cities written in the first third of this century by the sociologists of the "Chicago school." For the account of lower-class existence in big cities, see Cressey (1932); for the equally sterile life of the rich, see Zorbaugh (1929). A thorough review of the work of the early urban sociologists is in Burgess (1926).

280–   **". . . the long, solitary task of perfecting himself.":** Robert-
81   son Davies's comment was quoted in the *Chicago Tribune Magazine* of 4 October 1992.

282   **Arnold Toynbee, the British historian . . . :** Arnold Toynbee ([1936] 1954) is another social scientist who, like Parsons or Sorokin, has fallen out of favor because his vision was too broad to satisfy the current vogue for specialization. Yet his Study of History is a masterpiece that will be read long after most contemporary monographs are forgotten.

283–   . . . **the Key School in Indianapolis . . . :** The Key School has
85   been written up extensively by the media; for a report on one facet of its operations, see Whalen and Csikszentmihalyi (1990). There are surely hundreds, perhaps even thousands, of such reform-oriented schools around the country, and my impression is that most of them make a positive contribution. It is amazing to see that so many different pedagogical approaches, often at odds with each other, succeed in instilling children with a sense of intellectual curiosity and discipline. Apparently what counts is not so much the method used, but the teachers' enthusiasm and concern for each student as an individual.

286   **every social system must attend to four major tasks:** Here, as earlier, I am relying on Talcott Parsons' General Action System model (Parsons 1951). The four functions are: *adaptation* (which generates economic and productive institutions), *goal-attainment*

(which leads to political and legal institutions), *integration* (making statuses and social roles necessary), and *pattern-maintenance* (the need that makes cultural and value systems necessary). According to the model, any human group must find ways to take care of these four functions by enlisting individuals to fill out appropriate roles, or it will soon cease to exist.

291   **. . . afraid of personal death:** The fear of death being the ultimate threat to the self, it is the most powerful cause of psychic entropy. Hence one of the main tasks of every culture is to invent credible explanations for what will happen to the individual after his or her demise. Some cultures succeed in leveraging socially desirable outcomes through the fear of death: the Greek hero could gain immortality through his worthy deeds, otherwise he would be forgotten; Christians could go to heaven if they behaved; the Hindu could be liberated from physical life and its illusions by controlling his desires; the Muslim who died fighting to defend his faith would earn entrance to Paradise. Thus the fear of death becomes a mechanism for social control: sometimes aiding complexity, yet often encouraging a form of collective neurosis (Brown 1959) that hinders evolutionary progress.

But at their deepest center, most religions and philosophies recognize that a person cannot reach inner harmony if he or she spends too much time worrying about death. The general consensus is not to repress death's existence, but rather to integrate the knowledge of the finitude of personal consciousness into one's life so that it will enrich and deepen each experience. This is what the existentialists mean by the concept of "Being towards Death" (Heidegger 1962) and what Castaneda's Yaqui mentor meant when he suggested letting death be one's counselor (Castaneda 1971). This is the reason why monks used to take turns at night in the monasteries shaking each other awake with the words: "Brother, remember you have to die!" *Memento mori* can of course easily degenerate into meaningless cant or neurotic obsession. But its original intent was to focus attention on what really mattered in life by contrasting it with its end, thus making each moment count.

What does the evolutionary perspective add to such ancient ways of making the inevitability of death work—either for social or for individual ends? If it is true that each of us is part of the universal energy pulsing through the vast emptiness of space, if each person's consciousness is due to the momentary combination of matter (and spirit?) flowing through the cosmos—like the image created by a kaleidoscope that will break up and recombine in endless beautiful combinations—then we need not fear death as the end of existence. Those religions that have increased complexity in this world have already said as much: we were made of dust, and to dust we shall return; but our essence shall survive in the dimension where the First Mover is revealed.

What that dimension is, no religion can tell—and certainly none of our sciences, despite their intimate acquaintance with what is supposed to have happened during each billionth of a second after the moment of creation. If there is one central task for human evolution to accomplish, it might be this: To come ever closer to getting a glimpse of the universal order, and of our part in it. The task is to understand in what sense what Carlyle said might be true: "Nothing that was worthy in the past departs; no truth or goodness realized by man ever dies, or can die."

To figure out how this is true must involve a process of gradual revelations, of endless discoveries evolving through the millennia; an unfolding task in which what we now call science and what we call religion will blend, and then grow into hitherto undreamed of powers of understanding.

REFERENCES

Adams, H. [1905] 1959. *Mont Saint-Michel and Chartres*. Garden City, N.Y.: Doubleday Anchor.

Aeschbacher, U. 1992. Der Krieger—oder: Das unheimliche Liebäugeln mit der Faschismus. *Intra, Psychologie und Gesellschaft* 15:42–45.

Alain [Emile Chartier, pseud.]. 1989. *Alain on Happiness*. Evanston, Ill.: Northwestern University Press.

Alexander, R. D. 1985. A biological interpretation of moral systems. *Zygon: Journal of Religion and Science* 20:3–20.

———. 1987. *The biology of moral systems*. New York: Aldine de Guyter.

Allison, M. T., and M. C. Duncan. 1988. Women, work, and flow. In *Optimal experience: Psychological studies of flow in consciousness*, ed. M. Csikszentmihalyi and I. S. Csikszentmihalyi, 118–37. New York: Cambridge University Press.

Amabile, T. M. 1983. *The social psychology of creativity*. New York: Springer-Verlag.

American Humane Assoc. 1987. *Highlights of Official Aggregate Child Neglect and Abuse Reporting*. Washington, D.C.

Anderson, A. R., ed. 1964. *Minds and machines*. Englewood Cliffs, N.J.: Prentice-Hall.

Anderson, M. 1986. Varieties of animal companionship. *Central Issues in Anthropology* 6 (no. 2): 1–11.

Andreasen, N. C. 1987. Creativity and mental illness: Prevalence rates in writers and their first-degree relatives. *American Journal of Psychiatry* 144 (no. 10): 1288–92.

Antonovsky, A. 1979. *Health, stress, and coping*. San Francisco: Jossey Bass.

Apter, M. J. 1992. *The dangerous edge: The psychology of excitement*. New York: The Free Press.

Arendt, H. 1956. *The human condition*. Chicago: University of Chicago Press.

Argyle, M. 1987. *The psychology of happiness*. London: Methuen.

Aries, P., and G. Duby, eds. 1987. *A history of private life*. Cambridge, Mass.: Belknap Press.

Asimov, I., and F. Walker. 1990. *The march of the millennia*. New York: Walker.

Bandura, A. 1977. Self-efficacy: Toward a unifying theory of behavioral change. *Psychological Review* 84:191–215.

Bateson, G. 1972. *Steps to an ecology of the mind*. New York: Ballantine.

Bee, H. L. 1992. *The journey of adulthood*. New York: Macmillan.

Bellah, R. N., R. Madsen, W. M. Sullivan, A. Swidler, and S. M. Tipton. 1991. *The good society*. New York: Alfred Knopf.

Benedict, R. 1934. *Patterns of culture*. Boston: Houghton-Mifflin.

Berger, P. L., and T. Luckmann. 1967. *The social construction of reality*. Garden City, N.Y.: Anchor Books.

Berlyne, D. E. 1960. *Conflict, arousal, and curiosity*. New York: McGraw Hill.

Bexton, W. H., W. Heron, T. H. Scott. 1954. Effects of decreased variation in the sensory environment. *Canadian Journal of Psychology* 8:70–76.

Bloch, M. 1967. *Land and work in medieval Europe*. Berkeley: University of California Press.

Bloom, A. 1987. *The closing of the American mind*. New York: Simon & Schuster.

Bly, R. 1990. *Iron John*. New York: Addison-Wesley.

Boyer, L. B. 1955. Christmas neurosis. *Journal of the American Psychoanalytic Association* 3:467–88.

Bradburn, N. 1969. *The structure of psychological well-being*. Chicago: Aldine.

Brannigan, A. 1981. *The social basis of scientific discoveries*. New York: Cambridge University Press.

Braudel, F. 1985. *The structures of everyday life*. Vol. 1. New York: Harper & Row.

Britannica Book of the Year. 1993. Chicago: The Encyclopaedia Britannica Press, 546–755.

Brown, N. O. 1959. *Life against death*. Middletown, Conn.: Wesleyan University Press.

Bruner, J. S., A. Jolly, and K. Sylva. 1976. *Play—Its role in development and evolution*. New York: Basic Books.

Burgess, E. W., ed. 1926. *The urban community*. Chicago: University of Chicago Press.

Burhoe, R. W. 1982. Pleasure and reason as adaptations to nature's requirements. *Zygon* 17 (no. 2): 113–31.

Cabanac, M. 1971. Physiological role of pleasure. *Science* 173:1103–7.

Caligari, P., and F. Massimini. 1976. *Introduzione alla teoria dei valori umani*. Milan: Instituto Editoriale Internazionale.

Carlyle, T. 1838. *Critical and Miscellaneous Essays: Sir Walter Scott*. Edinburgh.

Campbell, A. P., P. E. Converse, and W. L. Rodgers. 1976. *The quality of American life*. New York: Russell Sage.

Campbell, D. T. 1975. On the conflicts between biological and social evolution and between psychology and moral tradition. *American Psychologist* 30:1103–26.

————. 1976. Evolutionary epistemology. In *The library of living philosophers*, ed. D. A. Schlipp, 413–63. LaSalle, Ill.: Open Court.

Carruth, G. 1987. *What happened when: A chronology of life and events in America*. New York: Harper & Row.

Castaneda, C. 1971. *A separate reality*. New York: Simon & Schuster.

Cattell, J. P. 1955. The holiday syndrome. *Psychoanalytic Review* 42:39–43.

Chandrasekhar, S. 1987. *Truth and beauty: Aesthetics and motivations in science*. Chicago: University of Chicago Press.

Cohn, N. 1957. *The pursuit of millennium*. London.

Colby, A., and W. Damon. 1992. *Some do care*. New York: The Free Press.

Coleman, J. 1990. *Foundations of social theory*. Cambridge, Mass.: Belknap Press.

Cook, K. S., and M. Levi. 1990. *The limits of rationality*. Chicago: University of Chicago Press.

Coppinger, R., and C. S. Smith. 1983. The domestication of evolution. *Environmental Conservation* 10 (no. 4): 283–92.

Coser, L. A. 1951. Some aspects of Soviet family policy. *The American Journal of Sociology* 54 (no. 5): 424–54.

Creel, H. G. 1960. *Confucius and the Chinese way*. New York: Harper Torchbooks.

Cressey, P. G. 1932. *The taxi-dance hall: A sociological study in commercialized recreation and city life*. Chicago: University of Chicago Press.

Csikszentmihalyi, I. 1986. Il flusso di coscienza in un contesto storico: Il caso dei gesuiti. In *L'esperienza quotidiana,* ed. F. Massimini and P. Inghilleri, 181–96. Milan: Franco Angeli.

————. 1988. Flow in a historical context: The case of the Jesuits. In *Optimal experience: Psychological studies of flow in consciousness,* ed. M. Csikszentmihalyi and I. S. Csikszentmihalyi, 232–48. New York: Cambridge University Press.

Csikszentmihalyi, M. 1967. Marx: A socio-psychological evaluation. *Modern Age* 11 (no. 3): 273–82.

————. 1973. Socio-cultural speciation and human aggression. *Zygon* 8 (no. 2): 96–112.

————. 1975. *Beyond boredom and anxiety*. San Francisco: Jossey-Bass.

————. 1978. Attention and the wholistic approach to behavior. In *The stream of consciousness*, ed. K. S. Pope and J. L. Singer, 335–58. New York: Plenum.

————. 1981. Leisure and socialization. *Social Forces* 60:332–40.

————. 1985. Reflections on enjoyment. *Perspectives in Biology and Medicine* 28 (no. 4): 469–97.

————. 1988a. Society, culture, and person: A systems view of creativity. In *The nature of creativity: Contemporary psychological perspectives*, ed. R. J. Sternberg, 325–39. New York: Cambridge University Press.

————. 1988b. Motivation and creativity: Towards a synthesis of structural and energistic approaches to cognition. *New Ideas in Psychology* 6 (no. 2): 159–76.

————. 1988c. Solving a problem is not finding a new one: A response to Herbert Simon. *New Ideas in Psychology* 6 (no. 2): 183–86.

. 1990a. *Flow: The psychology of optimal experience*. New York: Harper & Row.

————. 1990b. Literacy and intrinsic motivation. *Daedalus* 119 (no. 2): 115–40.

————. 1990c. The domain of creativity. In *Theories of creativity*, ed. R. Albert and M. Runco, 190–214. Newbury Park, Calif.: Russel Sage.

————. 1991. Consciousness for the twenty-first century. *Zygon* 26 (no. 1): 7–25.

————. 1992. Imagining the self: An evolutionary excursion. *Poetics* 21:153–67.

————. 1993a. Contexts of optimal growth in childhood. *Daedalus* 122 (no. 1): 31–56.

————. 1993b. Why we need things. In *History from things: Essays on material culture*, ed. S. Lubar and W. D. Kingery, 20–29. Washington, D.C.: Smithsonian Press.

Csikszentmihalyi, M., and I. S. Csikszentmihalyi, eds. 1988. *Optimal experience: Studies of flow in consciousness*. New York: Cambridge University Press.

————. 1993. Family influences on the development of talent. Ciba Foundation symposium on The Origins and Development of High Ability. London, U.K.

Csikszentmihalyi, M., and T. Figurski. 1982. The experience of self-awareness in everyday life. *Journal of Personality* 50 (no. 1): 14–26.

Csikszentmihalyi, M., and R. Larson. 1978. Intrinsic rewards in school crime. *Crime and Delinquency* 24:322–35.

———. (1984). *Being adolescent: Conflict and growth in the teenage years*. New York: Basic Books.

Csikszentmihalyi, M., R. Larson, and S. Prescott. 1977. The ecology of adolescent activities and experiences. *Journal of Youth and Adolescence* 6:281–94.

Csikszentmihalyi, M., and J. LeFevre. 1989. Optimal experience in work and leisure. *Journal of Personality and Social Psychology* 56 (no. 5): 815–22.

Csikszentmihalyi, M., and F. Massimini. 1985. On the psychological selection of bio-cultural information. *New Ideas in Psychology* 3 (no. 2): 115–38.

Csikszentmihalyi, M., and K. Rathunde. 1990. The psychology of wisdom: An evolutionary interpretation. In *Wisdom: Its nature, origins, and development*, ed. R. J. Sternberg, 25–51. New York: Cambridge University Press.

Csikszentmihalyi, M., K. Rathunde, and S. Whalen. 1993. *Talented teenagers: A longitudinal study of their development*. New York: Cambridge University Press.

Csikszentmihalyi, M., and R. Robinson. 1990. *The art of seeing*. Malibu, Calif.: J. P. Getty Press.

Csikszentmihalyi, M., and E. Rochberg-Halton. 1981. *The meaning of things: Domestic symbols and the self*. New York: Cambridge University Press.

Csikszentmihalyi, M., and U. Schiefele. 1992. Arts education, human development, and the quality of experience. In *Arts in Education: The 91st yearbook of the Society for the Study of Education*, ed. G. Reimer and R. A. Smith, 169–91. Chicago: University of Chicago Press.

Damon, W. 1983. *Social and personality development*. New York: W. W. Norton.

Davis, F. D., R. P. Bagozzi, and P. R. Warshaw. 1989. Usefulness versus fun as determinants of intentions to use computers in the workplace. *Working paper*. Ann Arbor, Mich.: University of Michigan Press.

Dawkins, R. 1976. *The selfish gene*. Oxford: Oxford University Press.

———. 1982. *The extended phenotype*. Oxford: Oxford University Press.

deCharms, R. 1968. *Personal causation: The internal affective determinants of behavior*. New York: Academic Press.

Deci, E. L., and R. M. Ryan. 1985. *Intrinsic motivation and self-determination in human behavior*. New York: Plenum Press.

Delle Fave, A., and F. Massimini. 1988. Modernization and the changing contexts of flow in work and leisure. In *Optimal experience: Studies of flow in consciousness,* ed. M. Csikszentmihalyi and I. S. Csikszentmihalyi, 193–213. New York: Cambridge University Press.

————. 1992. The ESM and the measurement of clinical change: A case of anxiety disorder. In *The experience of psychopathology,* ed. M. deVries, 280–89. Cambridge: Cambridge University Press.

Dennett, D. C. 1991. *Consciousness explained.* Boston: Little, Brown.

deVries, M., ed. 1992. *The experience of psychopathology: Investigating mental disorders in their natural settings.* Cambridge: Cambridge University Press.

Dewey, J. 1913. *Interest and effort in education.* Cambridge: The Riverside Press.

Diamond, J. 1992. *The third chimpanzee.* New York: HarperCollins.

Didion, J. 1989. Letter from Los Angeles. *The New Yorker* (24 April): 88–99.

Dobzhansky, T. 1937. *Genetics and the origin of species.* New York: Columbia University Press.

Donaldson, M. 1993. *Human minds: An exploration.* New York: Viking.

Donner, E., and M. Csikszentmihalyi. 1992. Transforming stress to flow. *Executive Excellence* 9 (no. 2): 16–18.

Douglas, M. 1966. *Purity and danger.* London: Routledge and Kegan Paul.

Dozier, R. W., Jr. 1992. *Codes of evolution.* New York: Crown Publishers.

Dreyfus, H. 1979. *What computers can't do: The limits of artificial intelligence.* 2d ed. New York: Harper & Row.

Dubs, H. H. 1928. *The works of Hsüntze.* London.

Durkheim, E. [1912] 1967. *The elementary forms of religious life.* New York: The Free Press.

Edelman, G. M. 1993. *Bright air, brilliant fire: On the matter of the mind.* New York: Basic Books.

Ellis, J. 1986. *The social history of the machine gun.* Baltimore, Md.: The Johns Hopkins University Press.

Eno, R. 1990. *The Confucian creation of heaven.* Albany, N.Y.: State University of New York Press.

Erikson, E. H. 1950. *Childhood and society.* New York: W. W. Norton.

Esslin, M. 1976. Aristotle and the advertisers: The television commercial considered as a form of drama. In *Television: The critical view,* ed. N. Newcomb. New York: Oxford University Press.

Evans, D. 1991. The war that Japan is winning. *Chicago Tribune,* 6 December.

Evans-Pritchard, E. E. [1956] 1974. *Nuer religion.* New York: Oxford University Press.

Faludy, G. 1988. *Test és lélek*. Budapest: Magyar Világ Kiadó.

————. 1989. *Bortonversek 1950–53*. Budapest: Magyar Világ Kiadó.

Faÿ, B. 1966. *Louis XVI, ou la fin d'un monde*. Paris: Librairie Académique Perrin.

Fél, E., and T. Hoffer. 1969. *Proper peasants: Traditional life in a Hungarian village*. Viking Fund Publication no. 46. Chicago: Wenner-Gren Foundation.

Ferenczi, S. 1950. Sunday neuroses. In *Further contributions to the theory and technique of psychoanalysis*, ed. S. Ferenczi, 174–77. London: Hogarth Press.

Fine, R. 1956. Chess and chess masters. *Psychoanalysis* 3:7–77.

Fingarette, H. 1979. The problem of the self in the *Analects*. *Philosophy East and West* 29 (no. 2): 129–40.

Fisher, S. 1970. *Body experience in fantasy and behavior*. New York: Appleton-Century-Crofts.

Fiske, D. W., and S. R. Maddi, eds. 1961. *Functions of varied experience*. Homewood, Ill.: Dorsey Press.

Fowler, J. W. 1981. *Stages of faith*. New York: Harper & Row.

Frazer, J. G. [1890] 1959. *The golden bough: A study in magic and religion*.

Freedberg, D. 1989. *The power of images: Studies in the history and theory of response*. Chicago: University of Chicago Press.

Gardner, H. 1983. *Frames of mind*. New York: Basic Books.

————. 1993. *Creating minds*. New York: Basic Books.

Geiger, K. 1968. *The family in Soviet Russia*. Cambridge, Mass.: Harvard University Press.

Getzels, J. W., and M. Csikszentmihalyi. 1976. *The creative vision: A longitudinal study of problem finding in art*. New York: Wiley Interscience.

Ghani, J. A. 1990. Flow in human–computer interactions: Test of a model. *Unpub. Mscrpt*. San Francisco: National Academy of Management Meeting.

Gilligan, C. 1982. *In a different voice*. Cambridge, Mass.: Harvard University Press.

Gilligan, C., J. V. Ward, and J. M. Taylor. 1988. *Mapping the moral domain: A contribution of women's thinking to psychological theory and education*. Cambridge, Mass.: Harvard University Press.

Goertzel, V., and M. G. Goertzel. 1962. *Cradles of eminence*. Boston: Little, Brown.

Goffman, E. 1979. *Gender advertisements*. New York: Harper & Row.

Granet, M. 1934. *La pensée chinoise*. Paris: F. Alcan.

Grinstein, A. 1955. Vacations—a psychoanalytic study. *International Journal of Psychoanalysis* 36:177–86.

Group for the Advancement of Psychiatry. (1958, August). *The psychiatrist's interest in leisure-time activities.* (Report #39.) New York: Author.

Hauser, A. 1951. *The social history of art.* New York: Alfred A. Knopf.

Hebb, D. O. 1955. Drive and the CNS. *Psychological Review* (July): 243–52.

Heidegger, M. 1962. *Being and time.* New York: Harper & Row.

Helmer, W. J. 1970. *The gun that made the twenties roar.* New York: Macmillan.

Hitti, P. K. 1970. *The Arabs: A short history.* Chicago: Gateway.

Hofstadter, D. R., and D. C. Dennett. 1981. *The mind's I: Fantasies and reflections on self and soul.* New York: Basic Books.

Hollis, C. 1960. *Eton, a history.* London.

Howe, J. R., Jr. 1966. *The changing political thought of John Adams.* Princeton, N.J.: Princeton University Press.

Hubbard, W. 1677. *Narrative of the trouble with the Indians in New England.* Quoted in G. Carruth (1989) *What Happened When* (p. 20). New York: Harper & Row.

Huizinga, J. [1939] 1970. *Homo ludens: A study of the play element in culture.* New York: Harper & Row.

———. 1954. *The waning of the Middle Ages.* Garden City, N.Y.: Doubleday.

Hulme, W. 1977. Human potential in the Lutheran Church. *Dialog* 16: 266.

Huxley, A. 1967. *Island.* New York: Bantam Books.

Ikeda, D. 1988. *Unlocking the mysteries of life and death: Buddhism in the contemporary world.* London: Macdonald.

Ivanhoe, P. J. 1991. A happy symmetry: Xunzi's [Hsün-tzu's] ethical thought. *Journal of the American Academy of Religion* 59 (no. 2): 309–22.

Jackson, S. 1992. Athletes in flow: A qualitative investigation of flow states in elite figure skaters. *Journal of Applied Sports Psychology* 4 (no. 2): 161–80.

James, W. 1890. *Principles of psychology.* Vol. 1. New York: Henry Holt.

Jaspers, K. [1923] 1963. *General psychopathology.* Chicago: University of Chicago Press.

———. 1969. *Nietzsche.* Chicago: Henry Regnery.

Jaynes, J. 1977. *The origin of consciousness in the breakdown of the bicameral mind.* Boston: Houghton Mifflin.

Jhally, S. 1990. *The codes of advertising: Fetishism and the political economy of meaning in the consumer society*. New York: Routledge.

Johnson, C., and R. Larson. 1982. Bulimia: An analysis of moods and behavior. *Psychosomatic Medicine* 44:341–51.

Jones, E. 1931. The problem of Paul Morphy. *International Journal of Psychoanalysis* 12:1–23.

Kauffman, S. A. 1993. *The origins of order: Self-organization and selection in evolution*. New York: Oxford University Press.

Kavanaugh, J. 1981. *Following Christ in a consumer society*. New York: Orbis.

Kaye, K. 1977. Toward the origin of dialogue. In *Studies in mother-infant interaction*, ed. H. R. Schaffer. New York: Academic Press.

Keen, S. 1982. Self-love and the cosmic connection. In *The holographic paradigm*, ed. K. Wilber, 117. Boulder, Colo.: Shambala.

Kegan, R. 1982. *The evolving self*. Cambridge, Mass.: Harvard University Press.

Keightley, D. N. 1978. *The sources of Shang history: The oracle-bone inscriptions of bronze-age China*. Berkeley: University of California Press.

Kelly, J. 1982. *Leisure*. Englewood Cliffs, N.J.: Prentice-Hall.

Klausner, S. Z. 1965. *The quest for self-control*. New York: The Free Press.

Kobasa, S. C. 1979. Stressful life events, personality, and health: An inquiry into hardiness. *Journal of Personality and Social Psychology* 37 (no. 1): 1–11.

Koestler, A. 1960. *The lotus and robot*. London: Hutchinson.

Kohlberg, L. 1984. *Essays on moral development*. Vol. 2, *The psychology of moral development*. San Francisco: Harper & Row.

Konner, M. 1990. Human nature and culture: Biology and the residue of uniqueness. In *The Boundaries of Humanity*, ed. J. J. Sheehan and M. Sosna, 103–24. Berkeley: University of California Press.

———. 1991. *Childhood*. Boston: Little, Brown.

Kovi, P. 1985. *Transylvanian cuisine*. New York: Crown Publishers.

Kubey, R., and M. Csikszentmihalyi. 1990. *Television and the quality of life: How viewing shapes everyday experience*. Hillsdale, N.J.: Lawrence Erlbaum.

Kuhn, T. S. 1962. *The structure of scientific revolutions*. Chicago: University of Chicago Press.

Kummer, H. 1968. *Social organization of hamadryas baboons*. Chicago: University of Chicago Press.

Lancaster, B. 1991. *Mind, brain and human potential: The quest for an under-standing of self*. Rockport, Mass.: Element.

Lang, G. 1971. *The cuisine of Hungary*. New York: Atheneum.

Lanternari, V. 1965. *The religions of the oppressed: A study of modern messianic cults*. New York: Mentor Books.

Latourette, K.S. [1946] 1970. *A short history of the Far East*. New York: Macmillan.

———. 1959. *The Chinese: Their history and culture*. New York: Macmillan.

Lau, D. C. 1953. Theories of human nature in Mencius and Shyntzy. *Bulletin of the School of Oriental and African Studies* 15:541–65.

Lavin, M. A. 1990. *The place of narrative*. Chicago: University of Chicago Press.

Lazarus, R. S. 1966. *Psychological stress and the coping process*. New York: McGraw-Hill.

Lazarus, R. S., and S. Folkman. 1984. *Stress, appraisal, and coping*. New York: Springer.

Lefebvre des Noettes, M. 1931. *L'atteluge et le cheval de selle à travers les ages*. Paris: Presse Universitaire de France.

———. 1932. Le gouvernail: Contribution à l'histoire de l'esclavage. *Memoires de la Societé des Antiquaires de France* 78:712–45.

Lepper, M. R., and D. Greene, eds. *The hidden costs of reward: New perspectives on the psychology of human motivation*. Hillsdale, N.J.: Lawrence Erlbaum.

LeVine, R. A. 1979. Adulthood among the Gusii. In *Themes of work and love in adulthood*, ed. N. Smelser and E. Erikson, 77–104. Cambridge, Mass.: Harvard University Press.

LeVine, R. A., and D. T. Campbell. 1972. *Ethnocentrism: Theories of conflict, ethnic attitudes, and group behavior*. New York: Wiley.

Levinson, D. J. 1980. Toward a conception of the adult life course. In *Themes of work and love in adulthood*, ed. N. Smelser and E. Erikson, 265–90. Cambridge, Mass.: Harvard University Press.

Lévi-Strauss, C. 1967. *Tristes tropiques*. New York: Atheneum.

Levy, S. 1992. *Artificial life: The quest for a new creation*. New York: Pantheon.

Lindbergh, C. 1953. *The spirit of St. Louis*. New York: Scribner.

Linder, S. 1970. *The harried leisure class*. New York: Columbia University Press.

Loevinger, J. 1976. *Ego development*. San Francisco: Jossey-Bass.

Lubar, S., and W. D. Kingery, eds. 1993. *History from things: Essays on material culture*. Washington, D.C.: Smithsonian Institution Press.

Macbeth, J. 1988. Ocean cruising. In *Optimal experience: Psychological studies of flow in consciousness*, ed. M. Csikszentmihalyi and I. S. Csikszentmihalyi, 214–31. New York: Cambridge University Press.

MacIntyre, A. 1984. *After virtue: A study in moral therapy*. Notre Dame, Ind.: University of Notre Dame Press.

Malone, T. W., and M. R. Lepper. 1987. Making learning fun: A taxonomy of intrinsic motivation for learning. In *Aptitude, Learning, and Instruction*, ed. R. E. Snow and M. J. Farr. Hillsdale, N.J.: Lawrence Erlbaum.

Mancini, G. [1613] 1956. *Considerazioni sulla pittura*, ed. A. Marucchi. Rome.

Mandler, G. 1975. *Mind and body: Psychology of emotion and stress*. New York: W. W. Norton.

Markham, B. [1942] 1983. *West with the night*. San Francisco: North Point Press.

Martin, J. 1981. Relative deprivation: A theory of distributive injustice for an era of shrinking resources. *Research in Organizational Behavior* 3:53–107.

Martindale, C. 1990. *The clockwork muse: The predictability of artistic change*. New York: Basic Books.

Maslow, A. 1968. *Toward a psychology of being*. New York: Van Nostrand.

———. 1971. *The farther reaches of human nature*. New York: Viking.

Massimini, F., and A. Delle Fave. 1991. Religion and cultural evolution. *Zygon: Journal of Religion and Science* 16 (no. 1): 27–48.

Massimini, F., M. Toscano, and P. Inghilleri. 1986. La selezione culturale umana. In *L'esperienza quotidiana: Teoria e metodo d'analisi*, ed. F. Massimini and P. Inghilleri, 19–64. Milan: Franco Angeli.

Mayr, E. 1982. *The growth of biological thought*. Cambridge, Mass.: Belknap Press.

McClintock, M. K. 1979. Innate behavior is not innate: A biosocial perspective on parenting. *Signs* 4 (no. 4): 703–10.

———. 1987. A functional approach to the behavioral endocrinology of rodents. In *Psychobiology of Reproduction*, ed. D. Crews, 176–203. Englewood Cliffs, N.J.: Prentice-Hall.

Merleau-Ponty, M. 1962. *Phenomenology of perception*. New York: Humanities.

Michalos, A. C. 1985. Multiple discrepancy theory (MDT). *Social Indicators Research* 16:347–413.

Miller, J. B. 1976. *Toward a new psychology of women*. Boston: Beacon Press.

Miller, G. A. 1983. Informavors. In *The study of information*, ed. F. Machlup and U. Mansfield. New York: Wiley.

Monod, J. 1971. *Chance and necessity*. New York: Random House.

Monti, F. 1969. *African masks*. London: Paul Hamlyn.

Moore, R., and D. Gilette. 1990. *King, warrior, magician, lover: Rediscovering the archetypes of the mature masculine*. New York: Harper & Row.

Mote, F. 1971. *Intellectual foundations of China*. New York: Alfred A. Knopf.

Mumford, L. 1938. *The culture of cities*. New York: Harcourt-Brace.

Munro, D. 1988. *Images of human nature: A Sung portrait*. Princeton, N.J.: Princeton University Press.

Murray, C. 1988. *In pursuit of happiness and good government*. New York: Simon & Schuster.

Myers, D. G. 1992. *The pursuit of happiness*. New York: William Morrow & Co.

Neisser, U. 1976. *Cognition and reality: Principles and implications of cognitive psychology*. San Francisco: Freeman.

Nietzsche, F. [1883–1885] 1930. *Also Sprach Zarathustra*. Leipzig: Krönen.

Noelle-Neumann, E. 1983. *Spiegel-Dokumentation: Personlichkeitsstarke*. Hamburg: Spiegel-Verlag.

O'Brian, P. 1993. *Joseph Banks: A life*. Boston: David Godine.

Orwell, G. 1949. *Nineteen eighty-four*. London: Secker & Warburg.

Pareto, V. 1917. *Traite de sociologie generale*. Vol. 1. Paris.

———. 1919. *Traite de sociologie generale*. Vol. 2. Paris.

Parsons, T. 1951. *The social system*. Glencoe, Ill.: The Free Press.

Peters, T. 1991. *The cosmic self*. San Francisco: HarperCollins.

Philips, K. P. 1990. *The politics of rich and poor: Wealth and the American electorate in the Reagan aftermath*. New York: Random House.

Piaget, J. 1951. *Play, dreams and imitation in childhood*. New York: W. W. Norton.

———. 1971. *Biology and knowledge*. Chicago: University of Chicago Press.

Polanyi, K. 1957. *The great transformation*. Boston: Beacon Press.

Popper, K. [1945] 1963. *The open society and its enemies*. New York: Harper & Row.

Price, S. 1989. *Primitive art in civilized places*. Chicago: University of Chicago Press.

Prigogine, I., and I. Stengers. 1984. *Order out of chaos*. New York: Bantam.

Privette, G. 1983. Peak experience, peak performance, and flow: A comparative analysis of positive human experiences. *Journal of Personality and Social Psychology* 45 (no. 6): 1361–68.

Privette, G., and C. M. Bundrick. 1991. Peak experience, peak performance, and flow: Personal descriptions and theoretical constructs. *Journal of Social Behavior and Personality* 6 (no. 5): 169–88.

Radakrishnan, S. 1956. *East and west*. New York.

Rathunde, K. 1989. The context of optimal experience: An exploratory model of the family. *New Ideas in Psychology* 7:91–97.

Rathunde, K., and M. Csikszentmihalyi. 1991. Adolescent happiness and family interaction. In *Parent-child relations throughout life,* ed. K. Pillemer and K. McCartney, 143–62. Hillsdale, N.J.: Lawrence Erlbaum.

Renfrew, C. 1986. Varna and the emergence of wealth in prehistoric Europe. In *The social life of things,* ed. A. Appadurai, 141–68. New York: Cambridge University Press.

Renninger, K. A., S. Hidi, and A. Krapp. 1992. *The role of interest in learning and development*. Hillsdale, N.J.: Lawrence Erlbaum.

Richards, R. J. 1988. The moral foundations of the idea of evolutionary progress: Darwin, Spencer, and the neo-Darwinians. In *Evolutionary progress,* ed. M. H. Nitecki, 129–48. Chicago: University of Chicago Press.

Robinson, D. 1969. The climber as a visionary. *Ascent* 9:4–10.

Robinson, J. P. 1977. *How Americans use time*. New York: Praeger.

Rosenblith, J., and J. Sims-Knight. *In the beginning: Development in the first two years of life*. Monterey, Calif.: Brooks/Cole.

Rozin, P., and A. E. Fallon. 1987. A perspective on disgust. *Psychological Review* 94:23–41.

Rudmin, F. W. 1991. *To have possessions: A handbook on ownership and property*. A special issue of the *Journal of Social Behavior and Personality* 6 (no. 6).

Rudolph, S., and L. Rudolph. 1978. Rajput adulthood: Reflections on the Amar Singh diary. In *Adulthood,* ed. E. Erikson, 149–72. New York: W. W. Norton.

Russell, B. 1991. *La Conquista della Felicità*. (Originally: *The Conquest of Happiness*. London: Allen & Unwin, 1930). Milano: Editori Associati.

Sachs, O. 1993. Making up the mind. *The New York Review of Books* (8 April): 42–48.

Sahlins, M. D. 1972. *Stone-age economics*. Chicago: Aldine Press.

Saint-Exupéry, A. [1931] 1966. *Vol de Nuit*. London: Heineman.

Sartre, J. P. 1956. *Being and nothingness*. New York: Philosophical Library.

Schiefele, U. 1991. Interest, learning, and motivation. *Educational Psychologist* 26 (nos. 3 and 4): 299–323.

———. 1991a. Slavery alive and well in Asia. *Chicago Tribune*, 17 November.

———. 1991b. Children modern–day serfs in Asia's merciless sweatshops. *Chicago Tribune*, 18 November.

———. 1991c. Girls from Manila awaken to nightmare in Japan. *Chicago Tribune*, 20 November.

———. 1991d. China's slavers willing to murder to cover tracks. *Chicago Tribune*, 21 November.

Scitovsky, T. 1976. *The joyless economy*. New York: Random House.

Seligman, M. E. P. 1975. *Helplessness: On depression, development, and death*. San Francisco: Freeman.

———. 1990. *Learned optimism*. New York: Alfred A. Knopf.

Shweder, R. A., M. Mahapatra, and J. G. Miller. 1990. Culture and moral development. In *Cultural psychology: Essays on comparative human development*, ed. J. W. Stigler, R. A. Shweder, and G. Herdt, 130–204. New York: Cambridge University Press.

Simon, H. A. 1988. Creativity and motivation: A response to Csikszentmihalyi. *New Ideas in Psychology* 6 (no. 2): 177–81.

Simonton, D. K. 1988. *Scientific genius: A psychology of science*. New York: Cambridge University Press.

Smith, A. 1992. Better than myth. In *The last best place*, ed. W. Kittredge and A. Smith. Seattle: University of Washington Press.

Sorokin, P. 1962. *Social and cultural dynamics*. New York: Bedminster.

Sperry, R. W. 1984. Consciousness, personal identity, and the divided brain. *Neuropsychologia* 22:661–73.

———. 1988. Psychology's mentalist paradigm and the religion/science tension. *American Psychologist* 43:607–13.

Spiro, M. E. 1987. *Culture and human nature: Theoretical papers of Melford E. Spiro*. Chicago: University of Chicago Press.

Sternberg, R. J. 1990. *Wisdom: Its nature, origins, and development*. New York: Cambridge University Press.

Sternberg, R. J., and J. Kolligian, Jr. 1990. *Competence considered*. New Haven, Conn.: Yale University Press.

Strack, F., M. Argyle, and N. Schwartz, eds. 1990. *The social psychology of subjective well-being*. New York: Pergamon.

Szalai, A., ed. 1965. *The use of time: Daily activities of urban and suburban populations in twelve countries*. Paris: Mouton.

Tackett, M. 1991. Big-time debtor guides $500 million RTC deal. *Chicago Tribune,* 7 November.

Thompson, E. P. 1963. *The making of the English working class*. New York: Viking.

Toscano, M. 1986. Scuola e vita quotidiana: Un caso di selezione culturale. In *L'esperienza quotidiana,* ed. F. Massimini and P. Inghilleri, 305–18. Milan: Franco Angeli.

Tiger, L. 1992. *The pursuit of pleasure*. Boston: Little, Brown.

Tolman, E. C. 1948. Cognitive maps in rats and men. *Psychological Review* 55:189–208.

Tonoue, R. 1992. *Assessing sport-related mental states using Experience Sampling Method*. Unpublished manuscript, Fukuoka University, Fukuoka, Japan.

Toynbee, A. J. [1936] 1954. *A study of history*. 10 Vols. Oxford: Oxford University Press.

Tucker, R. C., ed. 1972. *The Marx-Engels reader*. New York: W. W. Norton.

Turkle, S. 1984. *The second self: Computers and the human spirit*. New York: Simon & Schuster.

Turnbull, C. M. 1961. *The forest people*. Garden City, N.Y.: Doubleday.

Tversky, A., and D. Kahneman. 1986. Rational choice and the framing of decisions. *Journal of Business* 59 (no. 4): 251–78.

Tybor, J. 1992. Interview with Jerome Bettis. *Chicago Tribune,* 11 September.

UNICEF. 1990. *The State of the World's Children 1990*. New York: Oxford University Press.

Vasari, G. [1550] 1959. *Lives of the most eminent painters, sculptors, and architects*. New York: The Modern Library.

Waddington, C. H. 1966. *Principles of development and differentiation*. New York: Macmillan.

———. 1970. The theory of evolution today. In *Beyond reductionism,* ed. A. Koestler and J. R. Smythies. New York: Macmillan.

Waldrop, M. M. 1992. *Complexity: The emerging science at the edge of order and chaos*. New York: Simon & Schuster.

Wapner, S., and S. Werner, eds. *The body precept*. New York: Random House.

Ward, B., and R. Dubos. 1972. *Only one earth: The care and maintenance of a small planet*. New York: W. W. Norton.

Warner, W. L. 1958. *A black civilization*. New York: Harper & Brothers.

350   REFERENCES

Weber, M. [1930] 1958. *The Protestant ethic and the spirit of capitalism.* London: Allen & Unwin.

Weimann, V. G. 1991. The influentials: Back to the concept of opinion leaders? *Public Opinion Quarterly* 55:267–79.

Wells, A. 1988. Self-esteem and optimal experience. In *Optimal experience: Psychological studies of flow in consciousness,* ed. M. Csikszentmihalyi and I. S. Csikszentmihalyi, 327–41. New York: Cambridge University Press.

Whalen, S., and M. Csikszentmihalyi. 1989. A comparison of the self-image of talented teenagers with a normal adolescent population. *Journal of Youth and Adolescence* 18 (no. 2): 131–46.

———. 1991. *Putting flow theory into educational practice.* Unpublished manuscript. Chicago: The University of Chicago.

Wheeler, J. A., and W. H. Zurek, eds. 1983. *Quantum theory and measurement.* Princeton, N.J.: Princeton University Press.

White, L., Jr. 1966. *Medieval technology and social change.* New York: Oxford University Press.

White, R. W. 1959. Motivation reconsidered: The concept of competence. *Psychological Review* 66:297–333.

Wittfogel, K. 1957. *Oriental despotism.* New Haven, Conn.: Yale University Press.

Zohar, D. 1990. *The quantum self: Human nature and consciousness defined by the new physics.* New York: Morrow.

Zorbaugh, H. 1923. *The Gold Coast and the slum.* Chicago: University of Chicago Press.

Zuckerman, M. 1964. Perceptual isolation as a stress situation: A review. *Archives of General Psychiatry* 11:225–76.

———. 1979. *Sensation seeking.* Hillsdale, N.J.: Lawrence Erlbaum.

INDEX